THE SOLAR SYSTEM

ASTEROIDS, METEORITES, AND COMETS

REVISED EDITION

Linda T. Elkins-Tanton

Facts On File
An imprint of Infobase Publishing

To my son Turner Bohlen:
May you find many things in your life as wondrous and
beautiful as a passing comet on its travels around the Sun.

Asteroids, Meteorites, and Comets, Revised Edition

Copyright © 2010, 2006 by Linda T. Elkins-Tanton

Facts On File, Inc.
An imprint of Infobase Publishing
132 West 31st Street
New York NY 10001

Library of Congress Cataloging-in-Publication Data
Elkins-Tanton, Linda T.
    Asteroids, meteorites, and comets / Linda T. Elkins-Tanton—Rev. ed.
        p. cm.—(The solar system)
    Includes bibliographical references and index.
    ISBN 978-0-8160-7696-3
1. Asteroids. 2. Meteorites. 3. Comets. I. Title.
    QB651.E45 2011
    523.5—dc22   2009035380

Facts On File books are available at special discounts when purchased in bulk quantities for businesses, associations, institutions, or sales promotions. Please call our Special Sales Department in New York at (212) 967-8800 or (800) 322-8755.

You can find Facts On File on the World Wide Web at http://www.factsonfile.com

Text design and composition by Annie O'Donnell
Illustrations by Dale Williams
Photo research by Elizabeth Oakes
Cover printed by Bang Printing, Brainerd, Minn.
Book printed and bound by Bang Printing, Brainerd, Minn.
Date printed: August 2010

Printed in the United States of America

10 9 8 7 6 5 4 3 2 1

This book is printed on acid-free paper.

Contents

Foreword

While I was growing up, I got my thrills from simple things—one was the beauty of nature. I spent hours looking at mountains, the sky, lakes, et cetera, and always seeing something different. Another pleasure came from figuring out how things work and why things *are* the way they *are*. I remember constantly looking up things from why airplanes fly to why it rains to why there are seasons. Finally was the thrill of discovery. The excitement of finding or learning about something new—like when I found the Andromeda galaxy for the first time in a telescope—was a feeling that could not be beat.

Linda Elkins-Tanton's multivolume set of books about the solar system captures all of these attributes. Far beyond a laundry list of facts about the planets, the Solar System is a set that provides elegant descriptions of natural objects that celebrate their beauty, explains with extraordinary clarity the diverse processes that shaped them, and deftly conveys the thrill of space exploration. Most people, at one time or another, have come across astronomical images and marveled at complex and remarkable features that seemingly defy explanation. But as the philosopher Aristotle recognized, "Nature does nothing uselessly," and each discovery represents an opportunity to expand human understanding of natural worlds. To great effect, these books often read like a detective story, in which the 4.5-billion year history of the solar system is reconstructed by integrating simple concepts of chemistry, physics, geology, meteorology, oceanography, and even biology with computer simulations, laboratory analyses, and the data from the myriad of space missions.

Starting at the beginning, you will learn why it is pretty well understood that the solar system started as a vast, tenuous ball of gas and dust that flattened to a disk with most of the mass—the future Sun—at the center. Much less certain is the transition from a dusty disk to the configuration with the planets, moons, asteroids, and comets that we see today. An ironic contrast is the extraordinary detail in which we under- stand some phenomena, like how rapidly the planets formed, and how depressingly uncertain we are about others, like how bright the early Sun was.

Once the planets were in place, the story diverges into a multitude of fascinating subplots. The oldest planetary sur- faces preserve the record of their violent bombardment his- tory. Once dismissed as improbable events, we now know that the importance of planetary impacts cannot be overstated. One of the largest of these collisions, by a Mars-sized body into the Earth, was probably responsible for the formation of the Earth's Moon, and others may have contributed to extinc- tion of species on Earth. The author masterfully explains in unifying context the many other planetary processes, such as volcanism, faulting, the release of water and other volatile elements from the interiors of the planets to form atmospheres and oceans, and the mixing of gases in the giant planets to drive their dynamic cloud patterns.

Of equal interest is the process of discovery that brought our understanding of the solar system to where it is today. While robotic explorers justifiably make headlines, much of our current knowledge has come from individuals who spent seemingly endless hours in the cold and dark observing the night skies or in labs performing painstakingly careful anal- yses on miniscule grains from space. Here, these stories of perseverance and skill receive the attention they so richly deserve.

Some of the most enjoyable aspects of these books are the numerous occasions in which simple but confounding ques- tions are explained in such a straightforward manner that you literally feel like you knew it all along. How do you know what is inside a planetary body if you cannot see there? What makes solar system objects spherical as opposed to irregular in shape? What causes the complex, changing patterns at the top of Jupiter's atmosphere? How do we know what Saturn's rings are made of?

When it comes right down to it, all of us are inherently explorers. The urge to understand our place on Earth and the extraordinary worlds beyond is an attribute that makes us uniquely human. The discoveries so lucidly explained in these volumes are perhaps most remarkable in the sense that they represent only the tip of the iceberg of what yet remains to be discovered.

—Maria T. Zuber, Ph.D.
E. A. Griswold Professor of Geophysics
Head of the Department of Earth,
Atmospheric and Planetary Sciences
Massachusetts Institute of Technology
Cambridge, Massachusetts

Preface

On August 24, 2006, the International Astronomical Union (IAU) changed the face of the solar system by dictating that Pluto is no longer a planet. Though this announcement raised a small uproar in the public, it heralded a new era of how scientists perceive the universe. Our understanding of the solar system has changed so fundamentally that the original definition of *planet* requires profound revisions.

While it seems logical to determine the ranking of celestial bodies by size (planets largest, then moons, and finally asteroids), in reality that has little to do with the process. For example, Saturn's moon Titan is larger than the planet Mercury, and Charon, Pluto's moon, is almost as big as Pluto itself. Instead, scientists have created specific criteria to determine how an object is classed. However, as telescopes increase their range and computers process images with greater clarity, new information continually challenges the current understanding of the solar system.

As more distant bodies are discovered, better theories for their quantity and mass, their origins, and their relation to the rest of the solar system have been propounded. In 2005, a body bigger than Pluto was found and precipitated the argument: Was it the 10th planet or was, in fact, Pluto not even a planet itself? Because we have come to know that Pluto and its moon, Charon, orbit in a vast cloud of like objects, calling it a planet no longer made sense. And so, a new class of objects was born: the dwarf planets.

Every day, new data streams back to Earth from satellites and space missions. Early in 2004, scientists proved that standing liquid water once existed on Mars, just a month after a mission visited a comet and discovered that the material in its nucleus is as strong as some *rocks* and not the loose pile of ice and dust expected. The MESSENGER mission to Mercury, launched in 2004, has thus far completed three flybys and will enter Mercury orbit at 2011. The mission has already proven that Mercury's core is still molten, raising fundamental questions about processes of planetary evolution, and it has sent back to Earth intriguing information about the composition of Mercury's crust. Now the New Horizons mission is on its way to make the first visit to Pluto and the Kuiper belt. Information arrives from space observations and Earth-based experiments, and scientists attempt to explain what they see, producing a stream of new hypotheses about the formation and evolution of the solar system and all its parts.

The graph below shows the number of moons each planet has; large planets have more than small planets, and every year scientists discover new bodies orbiting the gas giant planets. Many bodies of substantial size orbit in the asteroid belt, or the Kuiper belt, and many sizable asteroids cross the orbits of planets as they make their way around the Sun. Some planets' moons are unstable and will in the near future (geologically speaking) make new ring systems as they crash into their hosts. Many moons, like Neptune's giant Triton, orbit their planets backward (clockwise when viewed from the

The mass of the planet appears to control the number of moons it has; the large outer planets have more moons than the smaller, inner planets.

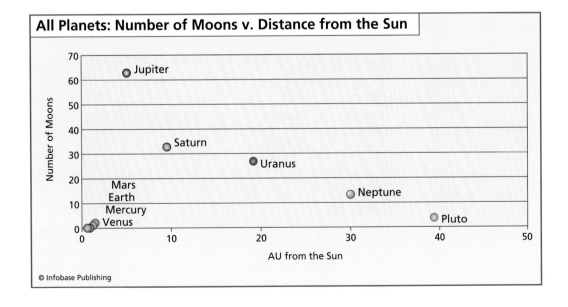

All Planets: Number of Moons v. Distance from the Sun

© Infobase Publishing

North Pole, the opposite way that the planets orbit the Sun). Triton also has the coldest surface temperature of any moon or planet, including Pluto, which is much farther from the Sun. The solar system is made of bodies in a continuum of sizes and ages, and every rule of thumb has an exception.

Perhaps more important, the solar system is not a static place. It continues to evolve—note the drastic climate changes we are experiencing on Earth as just one example—and our ability to observe it continues to evolve, as well. Just five planets visible to the naked eye were known to ancient peoples: Mercury, Venus, Mars, Jupiter, and Saturn. The Romans gave these planets the names they are still known by today. Mercury was named after their god Mercury, the fleet-footed messenger of the gods, because the planet Mercury seems especially swift when viewed from Earth. Venus was named for the beautiful goddess Venus, brighter than anything in the sky except the Sun and Moon. The planet Mars appears red even from Earth and so was named after Mars, the god of war. Jupiter is named for the king of the gods, the biggest and most powerful of all, and Saturn was named for Jupiter's father. The ancient Chinese and the ancient Jews recognized the planets as well, and the Maya (250–900 C.E., Mexico and environs) and Aztec (~1100–1700 C.E., Mexico and environs) knew Venus by the name Quetzalcoatl, after their god of good and light, who eventually also became their god of war.

Science is often driven forward by the development of new technology, allowing researchers to make measurements that were previously impossible. The dawn of the new age in astronomy and study of the solar system occurred in 1608, when Hans Lippenshey, a Dutch eyeglass-maker, attached a lens to each end of a hollow tube and thus created the first telescope. Galileo Galilei, born in Pisa, Italy, in 1564, made his first telescope in 1609 from Lippenshey's model. Galileo soon discovered that Venus has phases like the Moon does and that Saturn appeared to have "handles." These were the edges of Saturn's rings, though the telescope was not strong enough to resolve the rings correctly. In 1610, Galileo discovered four of Jupiter's moons, which are still called the Galilean satellites. These four moons were the proof that not every heavenly body orbited the Earth as Ptolemy, a Greek philosopher, had asserted around 140 C.E. Galileo's discovery was the beginning of the end of the strongly held belief that the Earth is the center of the solar system, as well as a beautiful example of a case where improved technology drove science forward.

The concept of the Earth-centered solar system is long gone, as is the notion that the heavenly spheres are unchanging and perfect. Looking down on the solar system from above the Sun's north pole, the planets orbiting the Sun can be seen to be orbiting counterclockwise, in the manner of the original *protoplanetary disk* of material from which they formed. (This is called *prograde* rotation.) This simple statement, though, is almost the end of generalities about the solar system. Some planets and dwarf planets spin backward compared to the Earth, other planets are tipped over, and others orbit outside the *ecliptic* plane by substantial angles, Pluto in particular (see the following figure on *obliquity* and orbital *inclination*). Some planets and moons are still hot enough to be volcanic, and some produce *silicate* lava (for example, the Earth and Jupiter's moon Io), while others have exotic lavas made of molten ices (for example, Neptune's moon Triton).

Today, we look outside our solar system and find planets orbiting other stars, more than 400 to date. Now our search for signs of life goes beyond Mars and Enceladus and Titan and reaches to other star systems. Most of the science presented in this set comes from the startlingly rapid developments of the last 100 years, brought about by technological development.

The rapid advances of planetary and heliospheric science and the astonishing plethora of images sent back by missions motivate the revised editions of the Solar System set. The multivolume set explores the vast and enigmatic Sun at the center of the solar system and moves out through the planets, dwarf planets, and minor bodies of the solar system, examining each and comparing them from the point of view of a planetary scientist. Space missions that produced critical data for the understanding of solar system bodies are introduced in each volume, and their data and images shown and discussed. The revised editions of *The Sun, Mercury, and Venus, The Earth and the Moon,* and *Mars* place emphasis on the areas of unknowns and

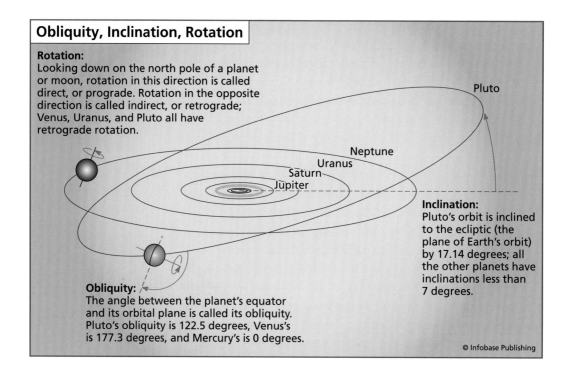

Obliquity, Inclination, Rotation

Rotation:
Looking down on the north pole of a planet or moon, rotation in this direction is called direct, or prograde. Rotation in the opposite direction is called indirect, or retrograde; Venus, Uranus, and Pluto all have retrograde rotation.

Pluto

Neptune
Uranus
Saturn
Jupiter

Inclination:
Pluto's orbit is inclined to the ecliptic (the plane of Earth's orbit) by 17.14 degrees; all the other planets have inclinations less than 7 degrees.

Obliquity:
The angle between the planet's equator and its orbital plane is called its obliquity. Pluto's obliquity is 122.5 degrees, Venus's is 177.3 degrees, and Mercury's is 0 degrees.

© Infobase Publishing

Obliquity, orbital inclination, and rotational direction are three physical measurements used to describe a rotating, orbiting body.

the results of new space missions. The important fact that the solar system consists of a continuum of sizes and types of bodies is stressed in the revised edition of *Asteroids, Meteorites, and Comets.* This book discusses the roles of these small bodies as recorders of the formation of the solar system, as well as their threat as *impactors* of planets. In the revised edition of *Jupiter and Saturn,* the two largest planets are described and compared. In the revised edition of *Uranus, Neptune, Pluto, and the Outer Solar System,* Pluto is presented in its rightful, though complex, place as the second-largest known of a extensive population of icy bodies that reach far out toward the closest stars, in effect linking the solar system to the galaxy itself.

This set hopes to change the familiar and archaic litany *Mercury, Venus, Earth, Mars, Jupiter, Saturn, Uranus, Neptune, Pluto* into a thorough understanding of the many sizes and types of bodies that orbit the Sun. Even a cursory study of each planet shows its uniqueness along with the great areas of knowledge that are unknown. These titles seek to make the familiar strange again.

Acknowledgments

Foremost, profound thanks to the following organizations for the great science and adventure they provide for humankind and, on a more prosaic note, for allowing the use of their images for these books: the National Aeronautics and Space Administration (NASA) and the National Oceanic and Atmospheric Administration (NOAA), in conjunction with the Jet Propulsion Laboratory (JPL) and Malin Space Science Systems (MSSS). A large number of missions and their teams have provided invaluable data and images, including the *Solar and Heliospheric Observer (SOHO), Mars Global Surveyor (MGS), Mars Odyssey,* the *Mars Exploration Rovers (MERs), Galileo, Stardust, Near-Earth Asteroid Rendezvous (NEAR),* and *Cassini.* Special thanks to Steele Hill, SOHO Media Specialist at NASA, who prepared a number of images from the SOHO mission, to the astronauts who took the photos found at Astronaut Photography of the Earth, and to the providers of the National Space Science Data Center, Great Images in NASA, and the NASA/JPL Planetary Photojournal, all available on the Web (addresses given in the reference section).

Many thanks also to Frank K. Darmstadt, executive editor; to Jodie Rhodes, literary agent; and to E. Marc Parmentier at Brown University for his generous support.

Introduction

Asteroids, Meteorites, and Comets, Revised Edition, discusses the solar system bodies that are not one of the eight planets or their moons. This field is moving so quickly that it has affected the whole of planetary science: The great numbers and significant sizes of the bodies being found in the distant Kuiper belt have forced a redefinition of what a planet is, effectively demoting Pluto, and are changing the theories of solar system formation, as well as inspiring a new generation of space missions to the outer solar system. This revised edition will cover the exciting new science concerning the massive collection of smaller bodies orbiting the Sun, including asteroids in the main asteroid belt as well as elsewhere throughout the solar system, comets both from the Kuiper belt and from the much-more-distant Oort cloud, and the interplanetary dust left in their wakes.

Because for so many centuries mankind could only differentiate the largest of the planets from the background of stars, a culture has developed that thinks of the solar system as a Sun orbited by nine (now eight, with Pluto's demotion) planets. Increasingly, as observers' abilities to see smaller and smaller bodies in the solar system improves because of better instrumentation, and as scientists continue trying to catalog the number of large asteroidal bodies that might someday collide with Earth, the solar system is viewed as a collection of objects with a whole continuum of sizes. The Sun is orbited by material that ranges in size from grains of interplanetary dust to the giant Jupiter, and the planets in their turn are orbited by moons from less than a kilometer in radius to the mammoth Ganymede with a radius of 1,645 miles (2,631 km).

All Orbits: Asteroid Belt, Kuiper Belt, Oort Cloud

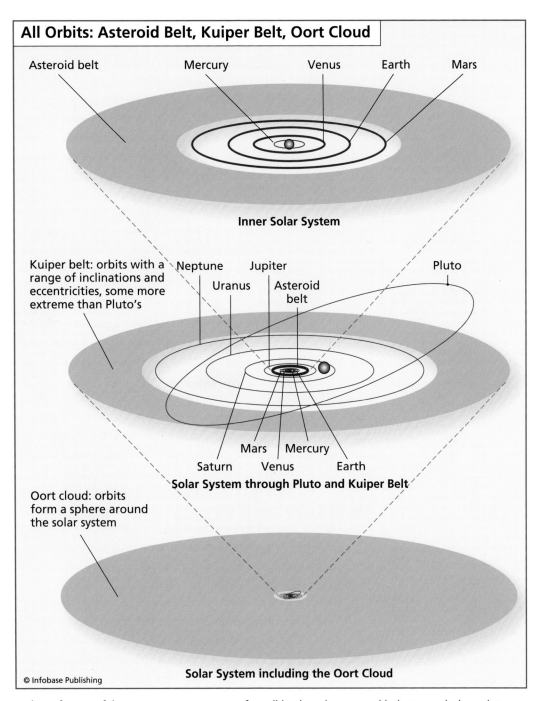

Asteroid belt   Mercury   Venus   Earth   Mars

Inner Solar System

Kuiper belt: orbits with a range of inclinations and eccentricities, some more extreme than Pluto's

Neptune   Jupiter   Pluto

Uranus   Asteroid belt

Mars   Mercury

Saturn   Venus   Earth

Solar System through Pluto and Kuiper Belt

Oort cloud: orbits form a sphere around the solar system

Solar System including the Oort Cloud

© Infobase Publishing

Orbits of some of the major concentrations of small bodies: the asteroid belt, Kuiper belt, and Oort cloud. All the orbits are far closer to circular than shown in this oblique view, which was chosen to show the inclination of Pluto's orbit to the ecliptic.

The new data and images from the astonishingly successful Deep Impact and Stardust missions are one reason for adding the great asset of full-color photos to this edition. The feats of these missions—sending an impactor into a comet to discover the physical and chemical characteristics of its crust and interior and capturing particles from a comet's tail and returning them safely to Earth—have changed scientists' views on solar system formation and the nature of comets. *Stardust* brought us images of tiny particles that made up our solar system, the Antarctic Meteorite Search brings back hundreds or even thousands of meteorites from Antarctica every year, and continuing surveys of the skies discover new asteroids, comets, and Kuiper belt and Oort cloud objects. All of these small bodies inspire new knowledge of the solar system formation and also offer spectacular images that we have used for this volume.

Both the small size of some of these objects and the extreme distance of others prevented their discovery for centuries, but their inventory grows almost daily as new sightings are made. In the 19th century when asteroids were first discovered, the continuum of sizes in the solar system was not understood. Scientists and the populace widely believed that stable planetary orbits precluded the possibility of swarms of smaller orbiting objects, and, when Ceres and the other early asteroids were discovered, they were at first classified as planets. When scientists realized with a shock that these first large asteroids were just a part of a huge population they were demoted from planet status. Asteroids now are commonly known as minor planets. In chapter 1 the discoveries of the asteroids are described, along with the long centuries of argument over the nature of meteorites and impact craters.

The process of discovering and understanding these small bodies is an important part of their story. The centuries of disbelief that rocks (meteorites) could fall from the sky prevented their accurate description as well as any understanding of the process of meteorite impacts. Understanding the immense damage possible from a large meteorite impact is new to the latter part of the 20th century. The current state of understanding of impacts is discussed in chapter 2. Most of Earth's impact

craters are heavily weathered and therefore difficult to
study, while fresher impact
craters are found on the Moon
and to a lesser extent on Mars.
The fresh craters on these and
other bodies (such as Saturn's
moon Dione, shown in the
photo at right) form a great
natural laboratory for studying the processes and effects of
impacts. Because large impacts
are the only natural disaster
known that can cause global
extinctions, the possibility of
future impacts on Earth is a
significant concern.

Saturn's moon Dione shows many impact craters in this mosaic image of Voyager 1 photographs. The largest crater is about 60 miles (100 km) in diameter and shows a central peak. (NASA/JPL/ Voyager 1)

Meteorites fall to Earth at
an astonishing rate, thousands
per year, with a combined weight of at least several tons per
year. Few are found, because at first glance meteorites look
much like Earth rocks. Over time, though, enough meteorites have been collected so that their compositions have been
grouped into classes. At the same time, discoveries of asteroids
have accelerated, and some information about their compositions has been obtained by remote sensing as well as by a few
space missions. In chapter 3, the orbits, sizes, and compositions of asteroids are discussed, along with the correlations
scientists have been able to make between meteorite classes
and asteroids. Meteorites are now known to be small fragments of asteroids that have fallen into Earth's gravity field.

Though the majority of asteroids orbit in the main asteroid
belt between Mars and Jupiter, scientists have found a number of additional populations elsewhere in the solar system.
A number of astronomers and planetary scientists dedicate
their time to finding and cataloging asteroids that might in
future strike the Earth. Other astronomers are focusing on
the outer solar system, building the database on the Kuiper
belt. In early 2004, one such search found a still more distant

object: the first body within the Oort cloud, what had until then been a theoretical population of icy bodies orbiting from 70 to 30,000 times as far from the Sun as is the Earth. The new farthest-known object in the solar system has been named Sedna, after an Inuit goddess.

These distant populations of icy bodies are thought to be the sources of comets. The distinctive bright tail of a comet consists of gases that are boiled from their frozen state by the heat of the Sun as the comet travels the part of its orbit closest to the Sun. Comets are the subject of chapter 4, which covers what is known about these enigmatic bodies, including hypotheses about where they originate in the solar system, how long they last, and what happens when their orbiting ends.

The study of the smaller bodies in the solar system is among the most active of planetary sciences. Their study has only been possible as increasingly good instrumentation provides new information. Information from recent space missions to asteroids and comets has shown the basic similarities between the two kinds of bodies, in particular the unexpected rocky strength of a cometary body and the ability of some asteroids to develop cometary tails during parts of their orbits. Beyond their great importance as possible Earth impactors, all the small bodies provide information about the early formation processes of the solar system, since they have gone through little later processing. This volume describes a continually changing body of information about the primordial matter that the solar system formed from, the great quantity of small bodies that orbit among and threaten the larger planets, from inner-solar-system asteroids to the most remote icy bodies at the outer edges of the solar system, partway to the nearest stars.

Definitions and Discoveries of Small Solar System Bodies

While there are now clear definitions for the terms *asteroid, meteorite,* and *impact crater,* these definitions have been hard won through centuries of scientific investigation. For millennia, meteorites have been recognized as unusual rocks, but asteroids were entirely unknown until the early 17th century, and impact craters have only been recognized as such for a century or less. Fundamental beliefs about the stability of the universe and the safety of Earth stood in the way of this science more, perhaps, than other disciplines. For centuries, the deeply held beliefs that all objects orbited in their own paths, never wavering nor departing, made the idea that meteorites might fall to Earth from space impossible. The idea that catastrophically large impacts might occur on the Earth, threatening life itself, was completely unthinkable.

WHAT ARE ASTEROIDS, COMETS, METEORITES, AND METEORS?

Asteroids and comets are bodies that orbit the Sun, just as the planets do. While there is a continuum of sizes of objects in the solar system, from the Sun to a grain of interplanetary dust (see figure on page 3), until the early 19th century and the development of telescopes, observers were unable to detect any but the largest planets. Planets, therefore, dominate the image of the solar system. The great abundance of smaller bodies is still being discovered and now is categorized under the name "minor planets."

Comets are icy bodies in highly elliptical orbits around the Sun. Asteroids are, by definition, rocky bodies less than 621 miles (1,000 km) in diameter that orbit the Sun. Although comets appear from Earth to be bright objects, the comet Halley, for example, absorbs 96 percent of the light that strikes it, making it one of the darkest bodies in the solar system. In contrast to comets, asteroids were not thought to shed gas and therefore lack the beautiful streaming tails of comets. Recently, though, some asteroids have been found that give off a comet-like coma (the head of a comet consisting of a cloud of gas and dust) so the delineation between comets and asteroids is not as clear as had previously been presented. Some asteroids may have begun as comets and since lost all their ices and gases. Two asteroids that have gassy comas only at their orbital *perihelia* (their closest approach to the Sun) are 2060 Chiron and 4015 Wilson-Harrington.

A member of the Centaur family of asteroids, 2060 Chiron orbits between Saturn and Neptune. Its unstable orbit suggests it was once a Kuiper belt object that received some sort of gravitational perturbation from a larger body that threw it into its current orbit. It has a hazy, luminous cloud around it, indicating that it is degassing or shedding ices. Chiron is therefore one of the enigmatic objects that lies somewhere between the definition of an asteroid and that of a comet.

To add to the confusion between designations, until recently all asteroids were thought to orbit in a direct sense (see figure on page 4), in the same direction around the Sun as the major planets (it has been known for a long time that some comets orbit in a *retrograde* sense). In 1999 for the first time, two objects found to have retrograde orbits failed to show any icy content or gassy tails, even when examined closely and at length. These objects are named 1999 LD_{31} and 1999 LE_{31} and were discovered only four nights apart and have orbital inclinations of 160° and 152°, respectively, so not only do they orbit in a retrograde sense, but their orbits lie far out of the ecliptic plane.

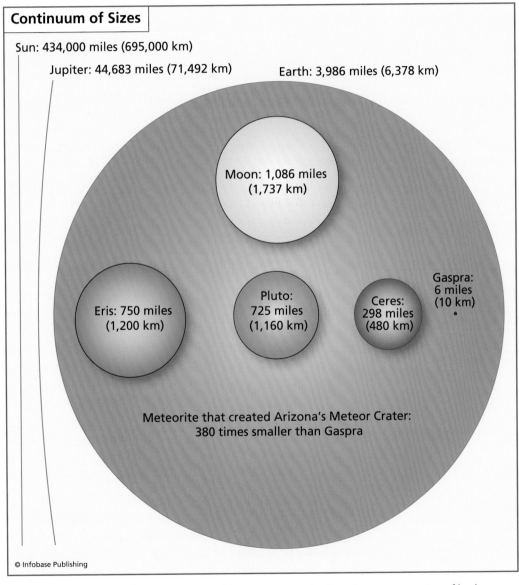

Continuum of Sizes

Sun: 434,000 miles (695,000 km)

Jupiter: 44,683 miles (71,492 km)

Earth: 3,986 miles (6,378 km)

Moon: 1,086 miles (1,737 km)

Gaspra: 6 miles (10 km)

Eris: 750 miles (1,200 km)

Pluto: 725 miles (1,160 km)

Ceres: 298 miles (480 km)

Meteorite that created Arizona's Meteor Crater: 380 times smaller than Gaspra

© Infobase Publishing

Rather than a family of planets interspersed by some asteroids, the solar system consists of bodies over a continuum of sizes—from the Sun, with a radius of 434,000 miles (695,000 km), to interplanetary dust, about 10 trillion times smaller.

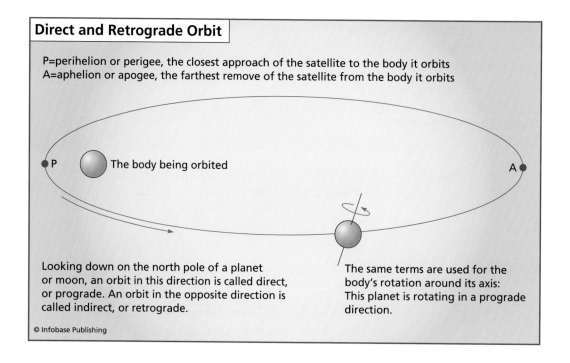

Direct and Retrograde Orbit

P=perihelion or perigee, the closest approach of the satellite to the body it orbits
A=aphelion or apogee, the farthest remove of the satellite from the body it orbits

P   The body being orbited   A

Looking down on the north pole of a planet
or moon, an orbit in this direction is called direct,
or prograde. An orbit in the opposite direction is
called indirect, or retrograde.

The same terms are used for the
body's rotation around its axis:
This planet is rotating in a prograde
direction.

© Infobase Publishing

All planets and most asteroids orbit the Sun directly, although some comets and asteroids orbit in a retrograde sense.

The line between comets and asteroids thus continues to blur. Some asteroids have gassy tails, some orbit in a retrograde sense, and some have orbits outside the ecliptic plane, all attributes previously reserved for comets. In general, though, bodies considered to be asteroid-like are thought to have formed in the denser, hotter parts of the inner solar system where the *terrestrial planets* formed. The bodies considered more cometlike acquired their *volatiles* (*elements* and molecules that evaporate or liquefy at relatively low temperatures, such as water and carbon dioxide) toward the outer solar system, in the region of the gas giant planets. It makes sense, then, that all these bodies would have a range of volatile contents. Comets and asteroids are all remnant *planetesimals* (material that failed to be incorporated into a planet early in solar system formation) and thus are probably formed from the same materials as the planets that formed near them.

Meteorites are rocky bodies that have fallen to Earth. Before they fell, they were considered meteoroids if they were between four-thousandths of an inch (100 μm) and about four inches (10 cm) and considered asteroids if they were larger.

Meteorites are related to asteroids: The only idea scientists have for the process that creates meteorites is the collision and breakup of asteroids. Recently it has been shown that large, irregularly shaped asteroids, such as 6 Hebe, 4 Vesta,

DEFINITIONS OF SOLAR SYSTEM OBJECTS

Name	Definition
asteroid	a rocky body with a diameter of less than 620 miles (1,000 km) and a total size that is larger than about four inches (10 cm) that orbits the Sun
bolide	any object striking another object, used when its specific type is unknown
comet	an icy body in a highly elliptical orbit around the Sun (though the distinction between comets and asteroids is not always clear)
dwarf planet	an object in orbit around the Sun that is massive enough to have its own gravity pull itself into a round (or nearly round) shape, but has not cleared the neighborhood of its orbit
fireball	a visual phenomenon on Earth: objects larger than dust that make streaks of light as they enter the Earth's atmosphere
meteor	a visual phenomenon on Earth: grains of dust that make streaks of light as they enter the Earth's atmosphere
meteorite	a rocky body that has fallen to Earth
meteoroid	a rocky body with a diameter between about four-thousandths of an inch (100 µm) and four inches (10 cm) that orbits the Sun
minor planet	all naturally occurring objects orbiting the Sun that are not planets; informal
moon	a naturally occurring body orbiting a planet or other larger body (Earth's Moon is capitalized while others are not)
object or body	any naturally occurring macroscopic thing orbiting the Sun; used particularly when its specific type (e.g., asteroid, comet) is unknown
planet	in this solar system anything that orbits the Sun has a round (or nearly round) shape and is the only significant object in its orbit. Mercury, Venus, Earth, Mars, Jupiter, Saturn, Uranus, and Neptune only; extrasolar planets are being discovered now in other distant solar systems.
small solar system body	all objects orbiting the Sun except planets, dwarf planets, and moons

and 8 Flora, are associated with swarms of small asteroids and meteoroids, totaling in the tens of millions. It is thought that these swarms are the source of the meteorites that collide with Earth.

The term *meteor* is only applicable to a visual phenomenon on Earth (see boxed definitions on page 5). Meteors are grains of dust that make streaks of light as they enter the Earth's atmosphere. Bodies larger than dust that enter the atmosphere can also glow brightly, and these are usually referred to as fireballs. Some fireballs have glowed so brightly that they illuminated 400,000 square miles (150,000 km²) of land surface on

DISCOVERING PLANETS: THE TITIUS–BODE LAW

Johann Daniel Titius noticed in the mid-18th century that if the planets are numbered beginning with Mercury = 0, Venus = 3, and doubling thereafter, so Earth = 6, Mars = 12, and so on, and then four is added to each of the planets' numbers and each is divided by 10, a series is created that very closely approximates the planets' distances from the Sun in astronomical units, or AU. (AU is defined as the distance from the Earth to the Sun; see GLOSSARY.) The final series he came up with is 0.4, 0.7, 1.0, 1.6, 2.8, 5.2, 10. In the following table, the planets are listed with their distances from the Sun and the Titius-Bode rule prediction. Remember that these calculations are in AUs: Mercury is 0.4 AU on average away from the Sun, and the Earth is 1 AU away.

The original formulation by Titius, published by Bode, stated mathematically, was

$$a = \frac{(n + 4)}{10},$$

where a is the average distance of the planet from the Sun in AU and $n = 0, 3, 6, 12, 24, 48. \ldots$

Though now the rule is often written, with the same results, as

$$r = 0.4 + 0.3 \, (2^n).$$

where r is the orbital radius of the plan, and n is the number of the planet.

the Earth (about the size of Kentucky). The word *bolide* is used for a falling object of any variety, but especially for those that create large fireballs.

DISCOVERING THE ASTEROIDS

In the 1760s, Johann Daniel Titius, a Prussian astronomer at the University of Wittenberg, began thinking about the distances of the planets from the Sun. Why are the inner planets closer together than the outer planets? In 1766, he calculated the average distance that each planet lies from the

This series actually predicted where Uranus was eventually found, though, sadly, it completely fails for Neptune. There is no physical basis for the formation of this rule, and there are still no good theories for why the rule works so well for the planets up through Uranus.

TITIUS-BODE RULE PREDICTIONS		
Planet	**Average AU from the Sun**	**Titius-Bode rule prediction**
Mercury	0.387	0.4
Venus	0.723	0.7
Earth	1.0	1.0
Mars	1.524	1.6
asteroid belt	2.77	2.8
Jupiter	5.203	5.2
Saturn	9.539	10.0
Uranus	19.18	19.6
Neptune	30.06	38.8

Sun, and he noted that each planet is about 1.5 times farther out than the previous planet. This rule was published and made famous in 1772 (without attribution to Titius) by Johann Elert Bode, a German astronomer and director of the Berlin Observatory, in his popular book *Anleitung zur Kenntnis des gestirnten Himmels* (Instruction for the knowledge of the starry heavens). Bode did so much to publicize the law, in fact, that it is often known simply as Bode's Law. Both scientists noticed that the rule predicts a planet should exist between Mars and Jupiter, though no planet was known to be there. There began a significant effort to find this missing planet, leading to the discovery of the main asteroid belt.

In 1800, a Hungarian baron named Franz Xavier von Zach, astronomer to the duke of Gotha and director of the Seeberg Observatory, sponsored a special search for the suspected missing planet. The initial group of six astronomers met for a conference in Lilienthal, Germany. Additional astronomers were invited to join until the illustrious group totaled 24:

* Johann Elert Bode in Berlin, director of the Berlin Observatory, founder of the journal Berliner Astronomische Jahrbüche, who named Uranus after William Herschel discovered the new planet
* Thomas Bugge in Copenhagen, a Danish professor of mathematics and astronomy and director of the Copenhagen Observatory
* Johann Carl Burckhardt in Paris, who was born in Leipzig but became a naturalized Frenchman and succeeded Joseph-Jérôme Le Français de Lalande as director of the Paris Observatory
* Johann Tobias Bürg in Vienna, a professor at the University of Vienna and assistant at the Vienna Observatory who was commended by the French Academy for his computations concerning the Moon
* Ferdinand Adolf von Ende in Celle
* Johann Gildemeister in Bremen
* Karl Ludwig Harding in Lilienthal, a professional astronomer who discovered three comets

* William Herschel in Slough, an amateur astronomer who made immense contributions to the field, including the discovery of Uranus, the first new planet discovery since prehistoric times
* Johann Sigismund Gottfried Huth in Frankfurt
* Georg Simon Klügel in Halle, a mathematician most famous for discoveries in trigonometry and for his dictionary of mathematics
* J. A. Koch in Danzig (Gdansk), an astronomer who discovered the fifth known variable star
* Nevil Maskelyne in Greenwich, director of the Royal Observatory
* Pierre-François-André Mechain in Paris, a close collaborator with Messier on surveys of deep space and comet searches
* Daniel Melanderhielm in Stockholm, professor of astronomy in Uppsala
* Charles Messier in Paris, the astronomer of the French navy, one of the most prominent figures in the history of astronomy, creator of the Messier catalog of nebulas, and discoverer of 20 comets
* Heinrich Wilhelm Mattäus Olbers in Bremen, who was principally a physician but excelled as an astronomer in his spare time and developed one of the first functional techniques for calculating the orbit of a comet; he is famous for asking "Why is the sky dark at night?"
* Barnaba Oriani in Milan, director of the Brera Observatory
* Giuseppi Piazzi in Palermo, professor at the University of Palermo who went on to find the first asteroid without having received his invitation to join the society
* Johann Hieronymus Schroeter in Lilienthal, an administrator and lawyer whose astronomical papers and findings along with those of von Ende and Harding were lost when Lilienthal was burned by Napoleonic forces in 1813
* Friedrich Theodor Schubert in St. Petersburg, a professor of mathematics and astronomy

* Jöns Svanberg in Uppsala
* Jacques-Joseph Thulis in Marseille, director of both the academy and the observatory in Marseille
* Julius Friedrich Wurm, professor at Blauebeuren, Germany
* Franz Xavier von Zach, founder of the society, director of the Gotha Observatory

They divided the sky into 24 zones along the zodiac (recall that the constellations of the zodiac lie on the arc across the sky that the planets appear to travel, when seen from Earth, so any new, unidentified planet would be expected to travel the same path) and assigned each of the zones to an astronomer. They named themselves the Vereinigte Astronomische Gesellschaft, commonly called the Lilienthal Society. They came to be known more widely by the charming name Celestial Police (Himmel Polizei) because they were charged to "arrest" the missing planet. Their search was made possible by the advances in telescopes that had been made since the invention of the device in 1608.

On January 1, 1801, Giuseppi Piazzi, a Sicilian monk making his nightly observations from a telescope atop the royal palace in Palermo, sighted the first orbiting asteroid known to humans. He saw a faint object that was not listed on the star maps. At first he thought it was a comet, since comets were the only type of orbiting object that humans had ever seen, aside from the planets. As he continued to observe it, he saw that it did not look or move like a comet, and he began to suspect, as he wrote, that it "might be something better."

Gioacchino Giuseppi Maria Ubaldo Nicolò Piazzi had been born to a noble family and, while he had joined an order of monks, he also held the chairs of mathematics and astronomy at the respected University of Palermo. In the years before 1801, Piazzi had traveled throughout Europe visiting other scholars and then oversaw the building of one of the world's most advanced telescopes at the palace in Palermo. Piazzi's name is on the list of the Celestial Police although they neglected to formally invite him, and at the time of his discovery he was ignorant of his inclusion. Piazzi was notified of his invitation indirectly through another member, Oriani, in May 1801, after the dwarf planet Ceres had been discovered.

During his detailed observations of this new body, he fell sick and had to give up observations for a time. When he recovered, he went eagerly to resume his study of this strange new object, but he could not find it, as it had moved too near the Sun in its orbit. Piazzi notified the scientific community of his observations, but no one could find the celestial body. Not even the famous astronomer William Herschel could find it. At last the astonishingly brilliant mathematician Carl Friedrich Gauss, only 24 at the time, took Piazzi's observations and calculated where in the sky the body should now be found, based on the current knowledge of orbital dynamics. He passed his calculations to von Zach, the founder of the Celestial Police, who immediately found the body exactly where Gauss said it should be.

At first this body was thought to be the missing planet between Mars and Jupiter, but soon it was realized that the body was just too small. Piazzi named the tiny object Ceres (actually, he named the asteroid Ceres Ferdinandea, after King Ferdinand of Sicily, but this addendum was later challenged and dropped). The discovery of Ceres fueled the energy of the Celestial Police. In 1802, Olbers found a second tiny object and named it Pallas, and in 1804, Harding found a third, Juno. Olbers discovered Vesta in 1807, and that was the final discovery of a small body by the Celestial Police. Bode was troubled by these findings, as were other members of the scientific community, because the tiny size and number of these bodies seemed to disrupt the natural harmonious order of the planets. Would the maker of the universe have left a gap in the order of the planets, the community wondered? Briefly the idea arose that a planet had existed and was shattered, but a universe subject to such immense and capricious forces of nature was horrifying to those men of the Enlightenment.

Within a month of the discovery of Pallas, scientists began to realize that a new class of solar system objects had been discovered. Herschel suggested naming these small bodies asteroids, which means "starlike," because the movement of a bright orbiting asteroid seen through a telescope was reminiscent of the tracks of stars across the night sky as the Earth turns. (There was also a small movement to call them "planetkins.") In 1815, the Celestial Police finally stopped hunting for the missing planet, having concluded that only a collection of small bodies took up those orbits between Mars and Jupiter.

Following the discovery of Vesta in 1807, no further asteroids were discovered until 1845. By 1857, about 50 asteroids had been discovered, including Juno (diameter about 150 miles, or 240 km), Astraea (74 miles, or 119 km), Hebe (115 miles, or 185 km), Iris (127 miles, or 203 km), Flora (84 miles, or 135 km), and Metis (115 miles, or 184 km). By 1900, 463 asteroids were known. Initially each asteroid was also assigned a symbol (much as the planets have symbols), but this system quickly became cumbersome as the numbers of discovered asteroids multiplied. Several of these symbols are shown in the figure on page 13.

By about 1850, a system of temporary numbers, called "provisional designations," had been developed for assignment to each new possible asteroid discovery. It was thought at the time that there would be no more than 26 new discoveries per half-month, and so each half-month of the year is assigned a letter: The first half of January is called A, the second half B, the first half of February C, and so on. Within each half-month, new discoveries are given letter designations as well, with the first asteroid of each half-month called A. For example, the first asteroid discovered in the second half of February of the year 2004 has the provisional designation 2004 DA (the D is for the second half of February, and the A means the first asteroid of that month).

Unfortunately, this system quickly became too constraining, as the rate of asteroid discoveries accelerated. By the 1890s, photographic film could be used to search for asteroids: If a camera's shutter is left open for some period of time, an asteroid moves fast enough to appear as a streak, while stars in the background are more stable. If more than 26 new asteroids are discovered in a half-month, then the next asteroid gets the designation A_1, and the next B_1, and so on through the next alphabet (although the letters I and Z are not used, because they resemble the numbers 1 and

2), until it is used up and a third alphabet begins, with designation A_2, and so on. The last asteroid discovered in one especially productive half-month was designated 1998 SL_{165}, meaning the namers had gone halfway through their 166th alphabet! This represents more than 4,000 objects discovered in that half-month.

Symbol Collection

Symbols for Asteroids or Dwarf Planets

Ceres

Pallas

Juno

Vesta

Iris

Flora

Metis

Pluto

Symbols for Planets

Mercury

Venus

Earth

Mars

Jupiter

Saturn

Uranus

Neptune

Sun

Moon

© Infobase Publishing

Many solar system objects have simple symbols, including the Sun, the planets, and some asteroids.

To be issued a final number and have its provisional designation taken away, a new asteroid's orbit must be determined closely, and it also must be confirmed that it is not a new sighting of a previously known object. The new asteroid must be observed at *opposition* (see figure below) four times to make it an official part of the permanent record. In the year 2000, 40,607 minor planets were confirmed and numbered—that year was the high point. However, 36,459 of the discoveries in 2001 were numbered, 26,703 of those in 2002, 15,356 from 2003, and fewer than 1,000 from 2008. The history of minor planet discoveries by year is shown in the figure on page 15. By September 2009, there were 219,018 confirmed and num-

Opposition and conjunction are the two cases when the Earth, the Sun, and the body in question form a line in space.

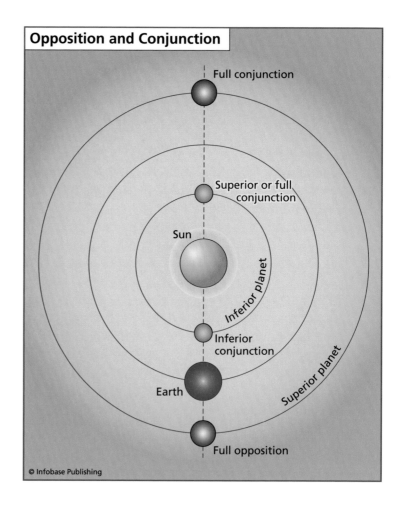

Opposition and Conjunction

Full conjunction

Superior or full conjunction

Sun

Inferior planet

Inferior conjunction

Earth

Superior planet

Full opposition

© Infobase Publishing

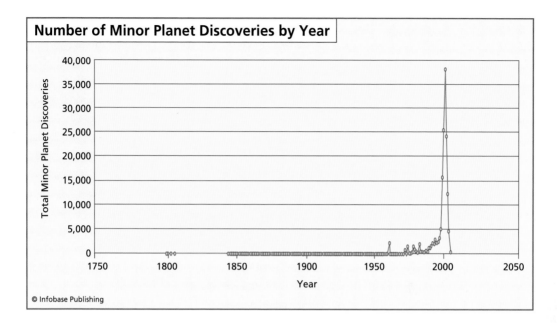

Number of Minor Planet Discoveries by Year

© Infobase Publishing

bered minor planets in total, 161,322 unnumbered objects with fairly well-determined orbits, and 79,931 unnumbered objects with poorly known orbits. There are thought to be millions of asteroids in the solar system, so searchers have a long way to go.

Final asteroid numbers go in order of confirmation. Thus, Ceres is number 1 and is formally notated 1 Ceres. At the time of this writing, more than 180,000 minor planets have been numbered and had their orbits characterized. Most still have names (about 60 percent at this time) in addition to numbers.

The discoverer of an asteroid has a decade to suggest a name for his or her object once it has its permanent number. (See the sidebar "Tom Burbine: Meteorites, Asteroids, and Remote Sensing.") The name must be approved by the 11-member "Small Bodies Names Committee." About the first 400 asteroids were named after figures from classical mythology, but since that time many other categories of names have been used. Asteroids have been named after famous or accomplished people of all stripes, family members, committees, plants, and even machines. Asteroids with special numbers often get special names, as in 1000 Piazzi (the discoverer of the first asteroid),

The number of minor planet discoveries by year peaked in the year 2000 as interest and technology converged on the problem; further discoveries are more difficult because of small size, dimness, and distance from the Earth. (Data from the IAU, Minor Planet Center)

2000 William Herschel, 3000 Leonardo da Vinci, 4000 Hipparchus, 5000 IAU (the International Astronomical Union), 6000 United Nations, 7000 Marie and Pierre Curie, 8000 Isaac Newton, and 9000 Hal (named for the computer, Hal 9000, in the movie *2001: A Space Odyssey*). The asteroid 6765 Fibonacci is named because 6765 is a number in the Fibonacci sequence, a mathematical sequence discovered and investigated by Leonardo Pisano, a 13th-century mathematician whose nickname was Fibonacci (meaning "little son of Bonaccio," his father's name). A few of the 85,000 numbered asteroids are listed in the table on page 17, including 78433 Gertrudolf, one of the highest-numbered asteroids to have a name.

THE LONG DEBATE OVER THE NATURE OF METEORITES

The discovery of asteroids was immensely exciting to the scientific community, and scientists immediately began creating theories of their formation. Immediately they understood that these were small, rocky bodies orbiting the Sun; there was no controversy about their characteristics, only about their creation. After all, their discovery was easily explained by improvements in telescopes and the diligence of scientists in mapping the heavens, and the paths of asteroids in their orbits around the Sun could be tracked. The possibility that these small bodies could have any interaction with the Earth, however, was long disbelieved and then hotly debated, before the current view of the solar system was developed. Despite the fact that each year the Earth collects about 300,000 meteorites as it orbits around the Sun, for many centuries Western scientists were unwilling to believe that meteorites could fall from space.

Meteorites have been noticed and collected by humans for thousands of years. Records of meteorite falls in Crete exist from as long ago as 1478 B.C.E., and China and Greece record events from 650 B.C.E. In Nogata, Japan, the Suga Jinja Shinto shrine keeps an apple-size meteorite that fell to Earth in 861 C.E. The Greeks and Romans also enshrined meteorites, which

SIGNIFICANT ASTEROIDS

Number	Name	Diameter (miles [km])	Discoverer, Location	Date
1	Ceres (now classified as a dwarf planet)	577 × 596 (930 × 960)	G. Piazzi, Palermo	1801
2	Pallas	354 × 326 × 300 (570 × 525 × 482)	H. W. Olbers, Bremen	1802
3	Juno	150 (240)	K. Harding, Lilienthal	1804
4	Vesta	326 (525)	H. W. Olbers, Bremen	1807
5	Astraea	74 (119)	K. L. Hencke, Driesen	1845
6	Hebe	114 (185)	K. L. Hencke, Driesen	1847
7	Iris	126 (203)	J. R. Hind, London	1847
8	Flora	84 (135)	J. R. Hind, London	1847
9	Metis	114 (184)	A. Graham, Markree	1848
10	Hygiea	279 (450)	A. de Gasparis, Naples	1849
15	Eunomia	169 (272)	A. de Gasparis, Naples	1851
243	Ida	36 × 14 (58 × 23)	J. Palisa, Vienna	1884
433	Eros	21 × 8 × 8 (33 × 13 × 13)	G. Witt, Berlin	1898
951	Gaspra	12 × 7 × 7.5 (19 × 12 × 11)	G. N. Neujmin, Simeis	1916

(continues)

SIGNIFICANT ASTEROIDS (continued)

Number	Name	Diameter (miles [km])	Discoverer, Location	Date
1566	Icarus	0.9 (1.4)	W. Baade, Palomar	1949
1862	Apollo	1 (1.6)	K. Reinmuth, Heidelberg	1932
2062	Aten	0.6 (0.9)	E. F. Helin, Palomar	1976
2060	Chiron	111 (180)	C. T. Kowal, Palomar	1977
3554	Amun	1.6 (2.5)	C. S. and E. M. Shoemaker, Palomar	1986r
78433	Gertrudolf	(?)	S. F. Honig, Palomar	2002

they called *lapis betilis,* from a Hebrew word, *betyls,* meaning "home of God." All these stories indicate recognition that the meteorites are special stones, and some indicate that they fell onto the surface of the Earth. Despite these glimmerings of understanding, any furtherance of the science in the West was delayed by centuries of misunderstanding and confusion. In 77 C.E., Pliny the Elder made a catalog of the enshrined meteorites in Rome, but he also listed (as having fallen from the sky) bricks, wool, and milk! As Harry McSween wrote in *Meteorites and Their Parent Bodies,* this uncritical assortment of fact and fantasy about objects falling from the sky delayed acceptance of the reality of meteorites for centuries.

The Greek philosopher Aristotle (384–322 B.C.E.) stated that it was patently impossible for stones to fall from the sky, as there was no matter up there to fall, apart from the planets themselves. Instead, he proposed a different solution:

(continues on page 22)

TOM BURBINE: METEORITES, ASTEROIDS, AND REMOTE SENSING

When Tom Burbine was a child, he read comic books about interstellar adventures. Unlike most, he did not see any reason that the great stories about life on other planets, meteorites, and exotic materials like kryptonite had to end when he closed the book; he went in search of these topics in real life. Burbine studied physics at college, but it did not capture his interest. In his senior year, the school newspaper featured an article on a faculty member who did research on asteroids, and Burbine went to see him. Had this professor, Mike Gaffey, not been as friendly and supportive as he was, Tom might never have gotten involved in the field.

The research Burbine began with Professor Gaffey launched the studies on asteroids, meteorites, and their links that he has pursued ever since. In this first project, he examined light curves from asteroids. These are plots of how the sunlight intensity reflecting off an asteroid and being measured in a telescope on Earth changes with time. The light intensity is thought to be controlled by the area of the asteroid facing the Earth. If the asteroid is shaped like a football, then when the asteroid has a pointed end facing the Earth, it has the least possible area facing the Earth and reflecting light toward the Earth. If the asteroid has its side toward Earth, then it would reflect its maximum amount of light. (See the figure on page 20.) The question was, can the light curve be matched with a shape model for the asteroid?

Unfortunately, asteroids also have differences in their surface compositions that change how much light is reflected. (This is called *albedo*. For example, ice has a higher albedo than a lawn does.) If the asteroid has a shiny end, it might reflect as much light as its broad side. Therefore, there is no unique solution for shape that can be derived from a light curve.

Following his master's degree, Burbine interned at the Minor Planet Center at the Harvard-Smithsonian Center for Astrophysics. The Minor Planet Center is responsible for keeping orbital data and observations for all minor planets, comets, and moons. Burbine's position was not a scientific internship—he was limited to data entry and helping with mailings—but he was there every day, seeing the activities, listening to the science, and above all meeting people. He became friends with Brian Marsden, the director of the center. There are many advantages to having friends in the scientific field—years later Marsden named an asteroid after Burbine: 5159 Burbine.

(continues)

(continued)

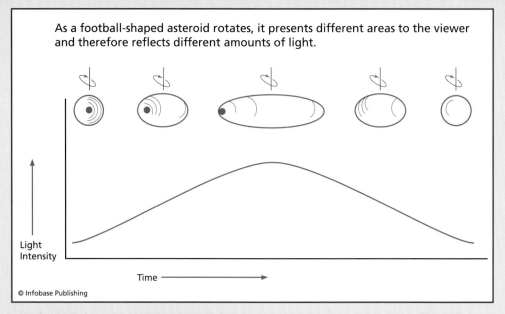

As a football-shaped asteroid rotates, it presents different areas to the viewer and therefore reflects different amounts of light.

Light Intensity

Time

© Infobase Publishing

As a football-shaped asteroid rotates, its face appears to change area and therefore reflects different amounts of light to the Earth.

Subsequently, Burbine suggested names for several asteroids, with some success. He proposed naming an asteroid after George Takei, who played Mr. Sulu on the original *Star Trek* television series, which had to be approved by the Committee on Small Body Nomenclature of the International Astronomical Union. Only about 10,000 asteroids have been named after specific people, out of about 400,000 such bodies currently known to exist. When this asteroid name was approved, the story was picked up by the Associated Press, then by CNN, and Burbine was interviewed several times. Eventually he even received a call from Takei himself.

After the Minor Planet Center, Burbine continued his tour of important space science centers by working on mirrors for the Chandra X-Ray Observatory mission. *Chandra*, which launched in 1999, follows an elliptical orbit about one-third of the distance between the Earth and the Moon, and it observes X-ray emissions from deep space. *Chandra* required exceptionally smooth mirrors for the careful observing it was meant to do, and Burbine helped calibrate these mirrors at the Brookhaven

National Laboratory. Eventually, Burbine entered a Ph.D. program at MIT. While studying, he continued to work on spectra from asteroids, working to match asteroid compositions with known meteorite compositions. He found that the smaller asteroids were easier to match with meteorites than the larger asteroids, perhaps because larger asteroids have more altered surfaces due to space weathering and so do not display clear mineral signatures. Earlier attempts to match asteroid spectra with meteorites from Earth were exceptionally frustrating, as none appeared to match. Gradually, scientists came to the conclusion that surfaces long exposed in space change over time.

After his Ph.D. work was completed, he returned to work on another mission, NEAR Shoemaker, to visit the asteroid Eros in 2001. The space probe actually touched down on the asteroid and took measurements of its composition. Burbine worked on matching the compositional data from the asteroid with the library of meteorites on Earth and found that Eros is a space-weathered ordinary chondrite, the most common kind of chondritic meteorite.

Burbine is presently at Mount Holyoke College, where he teaches subjects in astronomy and planetary science. His students have the opportunity to observe Mars, Saturn, and to see recent lunar eclipses. He is also starting a program to use small telescopes to measure asteroid light curves. This is something an amateur astronomer can do with a small, 6- or 8-inch (15.2- or 20.3-cm) telescope. This time, undergraduates at Mount Holyoke will be collecting them, rather than Burbine himself, demonstrating the full circle of mentoring and research.

His research has now branched out to a variety of related subjects, including trying to match the compositions of Earth and Mars to combinations of meteorite compositions. Neither planet can be made with just one or two of the known meteorite compositions, though they are thought to represent materials from the early solar system that accreted together to make the planets. Though enstatite chondrites match the oxygen isotopes of the Earth, matching the magnesium to silicon ratio the Earth appears to have is not easy, using the library of meteorites from Earth falls. Thus, the combination of materials that made the Earth remains unknown.

And still, after all these years, he continues to work on light curves and spectra from asteroids. He has hundreds of spectra that he is trying to match to meteorites, and he is working on smaller and smaller space objects, including near-Earth asteroids.

(continued from page 18)

Meteorites are the tops of volcanoes that have been blown off at the site of some distant eruption, falling to Earth from a clear sky. This explanation was largely rejected at the time but came to be increasingly widely accepted, especially when Ptolemy (87–150 B.C.E.) hypothesized that the solar system consisted of a series of spheres nested inside each other, each bearing a planet and thus allowing their constant spinning motion. Since the spheres were solid, nothing could fall between one sphere and another, and so all meteorites had to originate on Earth.

Still, the fascination with meteorites never flagged. In 1492, a 280-pound (127-kg) meteorite fell to Earth in the town of Ensisheim, France (at that time part of Germany). The Holy Roman Emperor Maximilian happened to be traveling nearby and ordered that the meteorite be preserved in the church in Ensisheim as an omen of divine protection. Sir Isaac Newton, on the other hand, disbelieved that there could be small, rocky bodies in space. He stated "to make way for the regular and lasting motions of the planets and comets, it is necessary to empty the heavens of all matter." Though in the end he was proved incorrect, at least Newton had a scientific conjecture of why meteorites could not have fallen from space.

The general view of the 17th and 18th centuries was that God had put all things in the solar system in their rightful places and thus none should fall catastrophically into the others. Ernst Florens Friedrich Chladni, a German scientist whose primary field of study was not astronomy nor geology but acoustics, disagreed with popular opinion and published in 1794 what might be the seminal book on meteorites, *On the Origin of the Pallas Iron and Others Similar to It, and on Some Associated Natural Phenomena*. In this book, Chladni argued that meteorites fall from the sky and are extraterrestrial in origin. He stated that they are small bodies traveling through space that are attracted by Earth's gravity to fall through the atmosphere, and that fireballs are meteorites heated to incandescence (glowing from heat) by air friction. In these assertions, scientists now find that he was completely right, but he was about a century ahead of his time in his thinking and received mainly ridicule when he published his carefully thought-out book.

A few years later, however, a fall occurred in England that could not be ignored. As Ursula Marvin writes in her paper, "Ernst Florens Friedrich Chladni (1756–1827) and the Origins of Modern Meteorite Research," a 56-pound (25-kg) stone fell at Wold Cottage, England, at 3:30 P.M. on Sunday, December 13, 1795. Several people were startled by a whizzing sound and a series of explosions, and one laborer in particular was startled when the black stone broke through the clouds and struck the ground just 30 feet (9.1 m) from where he stood. The impact showered him with earth, and when he ran up to investigate he saw that the stone had penetrated 12 inches of soil and an additional half-foot of the underlying limestone bedrock.

The landowner, an eccentric writer, took full advantage of this unusual occurrence, displaying the stone in London and erecting a monument where it fell. The publicity meant that the stone came to the attention of researchers, and a sample finally came to the young chemist Edward C. Howard and his colleague Jacques-Louis, comte de Bournon (who fled to England following the French Revolution). The two began the first chemical analysis of meteorites. They analyzed a number of fallen stones with the state-of-the-art techniques of the time, which were actually quite good at determining compositions.

Howard and de Bournon published a paper describing the four main components of the stones: "curious globules," martial pyrites, grains of malleable iron, and fine-grained earthy matrix. These were painstakingly separated and analyzed. The chemists correctly determined that the "martial pyrites" were unlike any known sulfide—in fact they were troilite (FeS), a hallmark of meteorites and rare on Earth. The abundance of nickel ($\sim$ 10 percent) in the malleable iron absolutely differentiated these rocks from anything yet found on Earth. This iron component is now thought to most closely resemble the Earth's core.

The paper went on to describe in great detail the compositions of the meteorites. These were the first meteorites to be taken apart, grain by grain, and compared to known terrestrial rocks, and a portion of scientists began to think carefully about whether meteorites might in fact come from space. Pierre-Simon Laplace, famous as a mathematician, suggested the rocks might actually be volcanic in origin, but from volcanoes on the Moon rather than the Earth. Then, in 1803 the town of L'Aigle in France received an amazing meteorite shower that totaled about 3,000 stones following three loud explosive bangs. The whizzing sounds that accompanied the stones' falls and the thunderlike booming that continued for some minutes frightened the townspeople and created a large, irrefutable group of witnesses. People who immediately went to look at the stones found them warm to the touch and smelling of sulfur.

Within a decade, most Europeans believed in an extraterrestrial origin for meteorites, but North American scientists lagged behind them in this belief by almost a century. In 1807, a meteorite fell in Weston, Connecticut, and two Yale professors wrote that they had determined that the bolide had fallen from space. There is a persistent story that Thomas Jefferson read their report and retorted: "I would find it easier to believe that two Yankee professors would lie, than that stones should fall from the sky." There appears to be no record of this comment, however, and Ursula Marvin of the Harvard-Smithsonian Center for Astrophysics reports that the closest remark recorded from Jefferson on the subject is as follows:

> We certainly are not to deny what we cannot account for. . . . it may be very difficult to explain how the stone you possess came into the position in which it was found. But is it easier to explain how it got into the clouds from whence it is supposed to have fallen?
>
> The actual fact, however, is the thing to be established.

Jefferson may not have believed the hypothesis wholeheartedly, but in the best scientific tradition what he wanted was for the truth to be proven in a clear way.

In 1908, the largest meteorite event in modern history occurred over Tunguska, Siberia, though at the time it was not known what caused the immensely bright flash and magnitude 8 earthquake. What was later determined to be the airburst explosion of a bolide about 200 feet (60 m) in diameter lit up night skies like daylight as far away as London. Seven hundred square miles (1,800 km²) of Siberian woodland were either flattened or burned, though because of the extreme remoteness of the area, only two people are thought to have been killed. In 1908, Russian politics were in a state of flux, and it was not until 1927 that anyone traveled to the area to try to determine what had happened. Even then, the flattened and burned woodland made a startling spectacle, but the cause remained undetermined for decades, until impact theory caught up with the evidence.

In the late 20th century, many more bolide falls were described, partly because there were more people watching and partly because their cause was understood and so their occurrence could be more clearly described without as much fear or superstition. At about 4:00 A.M. on December 5, 1999, a brilliant bolide was seen across parts of the southeastern United States. The light from this bolide was so bright that it was seen by hundreds of witnesses covering most of Alabama and parts of Georgia, Tennessee, and Florida. It is estimated that the light was bright enough to disturb people within about 200 miles (300 km) of the bolide flight path. Hundreds of calls went in to local and state police, fire departments, and emergency management agencies. The light was described as briefly being as bright as midday sunshine and in fact was bright enough to cast clear moving shadows that were recorded by regular security cameras throughout the flight path. These films were then used to reconstruct the path of the bolide, based on the movement of the shadows. The areas closest to the end of the flight path experienced ground shaking and rumbling sounds, and several simultaneous ground fires sprang up in a forest of young pines near Harpersville, Alabama. Despite all this apparent energy and the size of the bolide, no debris—in fact, no surface disturbance—was found by any of the many subsequent investigators. Either some small craters remain unfound, or the bolide disintegrated in a thorough way, though no final explosion was witnessed.

The technique of finding meteorite falls from photographs of the fiery flight from different angles is currently being used in a concerted way in Europe. Starting in the 1960s in what was then Czechoslovakia, a series of cameras were set up to take photos of the whole sky each evening. This network now consists of 25 stations spaced about 60 miles (100 km) apart from each other, within Germany, the Czech Republic, Slovakia, Austria, Switzerland, and Luxembourg. These cameras are collectively called the European Fireball Network. By using fisheye lenses or convex mirrors, each night the cameras take a single exposure image of the sky that lasts all night. In these images, stars create curved lines because of the spinning of the Earth during the night, and bolide falls appear as bright streaks, generally at an angle to the star tracks.

On April 6, 2002, a large meteorite fell over Austria and southern Germany, creating a bright fireball and a sonic boom that rattled windows and shook the ground. Its fall was recorded by the European Fireball Network, and by analyzing the fireball track on images from various stations the direction and angle of its descent was calculated. The fireball stage began at a height of 53 miles (85 km) and ended at a height of 10 miles (16 km). Because the fireball still existed at the relatively low altitude of 10 miles (16 km height), it was thought that the meteorite itself must have survived the fall, and so a search was begun. A first piece, weighing 3.8 pounds (1.7 kg), was found after three months, and a second piece, weighing 3.5 pounds (1.6 kg), was found more than a year after the fall.

While meteorites are traveling in space, their surfaces are bombarded by cosmic rays. The amount of damage to *minerals* in the meteorite can be measured, and thus the length of time that the meteorite has been exposed to cosmic rays can be calculated. In the case of these two pieces, it was found that their exposure age was 48 million years. This means that prior to 48 million years ago, the pieces were shielded from cosmic rays by being a part of a larger *parent body,* and that 48 million years ago, some event broke up the parent body into smaller pieces, including these two meteorites. The likely breakup event is a collision with another asteroid body. For 48 million years, this meteorite orbited the Sun, before it was swept up by the passing Earth and plummeted into Germany.

Every year several dozen large bolides enter Earth's atmosphere. These bodies usually explode in the upper atmosphere, and those few that fall farther are generally unseen. The U.S. Defense Support Program's satellite network detects airbursts in the upper atmosphere, which are much more common than one might expect: Each year a dozen explosions with the equivalent energy of 10,000–20,000 tons of explosives occur in the upper atmosphere. In 1963, an airburst explosion equivalent to 500,000 tons of explosives occurred over South Africa and was mistaken for a nuclear test by South Africa. Airbursts observed by people are frequently reported as UFOs.

THE SLOW HISTORY OF RECOGNIZING IMPACT CRATERS

Galileo discovered the wide extent of lunar cratering in 1610, when he was the first to look at the Moon through a telescope. The largest of the round lunar basins have always been clearly visible to the eye, but the extent of smaller cratering cannot be seen without a telescope. The image on page 28 from *Galileo* in 1992 shows a number of the larger basins with good clarity. The North Polar region is near the top part of the photomosaic. Mare Imbrium is the dark area on the left, Mare Serenitatis is at center, and Mare Crisium is the circular dark area to the right. Bright crater rim and ray deposits are from Copernicus, an impact crater about 60 miles (95 km) in diameter.

When scientists first described craters on the Moon they were all assumed to be of volcanic origin. Even John Herschel, son of the discoverer of Uranus, wrote in 1869 that the lunar features offer "in its highest perfection, the true volcanic character." Herschel even reported seeing volcanic eruptions on the Moon, an unlikely scenario, since the most recent proven lunar eruptions (from dating of returned samples) are more than 3 billion years old. Even the youngest estimated flows (from visual relationships of flows with craters and other flows) are no younger than 1 billion years old. As early as 1655, Robert Hooke, perhaps the greatest experimental

This mosaic of Galileo images shows the lunar basins. The North Polar region is near the top part of the mosaic, which also shows Mare Imbrium, the dark area on the left; Mare Serenitatis, at center; and Mare Crisium, the circular dark area to the right. Bright crater rim and ray deposits are from Copernicus, an impact crater 60 miles (100 km) in diameter. (NASA/JPL/Galileo)

scientist of the 17th century, wrote that the craters and basins may have been formed by bursting bubbles breaching the lunar surface from a boiling interior. Hooke considered but rejected an impact theory because he could not imagine where the impacting bodies could have come from. Though he was wrong, Hooke was oddly on the right track: In the last few decades, it has been discovered that the solid rock of a planet flows like a liquid under the great pressures of impact and may assume liquidlike forms. The central peak of a complex crater is an example, such as the peak seen here in the beautiful lunar crater Copernicus. Copernicus, about 60 miles (96 km) in diameter, is a large young crater visible northwest of the center of the Moon's Earth-facing side. Though at about 1 billion years old it is not as bright and fresh as other craters, Copernicus has many bright *ejecta* rays surrounding it. The image of Copernicus shown on page 29 was taken by the Lunar Orbiter 2 mission.

The giant Mare Orientale as well as an average cratered surface on the Moon are shown in the images on page 30. The small craters may be imagined as burst bubbles, though they are now known to have nothing to do with bubbles. However, the immense Orientale cannot be mistaken for a bursting bubble. These images show the importance of high-resolution telescopes and space missions in determining causation. (See the sidebar "Who Decides Which Space Missions Get Launched?") In the left image of this pair from the Galileo mission craft, Orientale is centered on the Moon. Its complex rings can be seen, but its center contains only a small pool of mare *basalt*. The outermost of the complex rings is the Cordillera Mountain scarp, almost 560 miles (900 km) in diameter. By contrast, the older Oceanus Procellarum covers the upper right of the Moon in this image, with the Mare Imbrium above it and the small Mare Humorum beneath. In the right image, Imbrium lies on the extreme left limb of the Moon.

In the image on page 35 from the Apollo 12 mission, the Herschel crater, 25 miles (40 km) in diameter, is at the center of the frame. Herschel lies at 5.7°S and 2.1°W in the lunar highlands. To the right is the 102-mile- (164-km-) diameter crater Ptolomaeus.

Herschel's floor is well defined and covered with rubble, showing a clear central peak and terraced walls. Ptolomaeus's floor, on the other hand, is relatively smooth and flat, despite

Copernicus crater is relatively young, as shown by its bright ejecta rays not yet dimmed by the action of solar wind and disturbances from other impacts. (NASA/JPL/ USGS/Lunar Orbiter 2)

These two views of Mare Orientale, taken by the Galileo spacecraft, also show large regions of dark mare basalt. (NASA/JPL/Galileo)

the fact that it is a larger crater. The flatness of Ptolomaeus's floor is due to basalt filling, much as the large mare basins are filled. Ptolomaeus's basalt filling is pocked with small impacts that are thought to have been caused by material excavated by Herschel (these are called Herschel's "secondaries").

The first suggestion that craters may be formed by impact came in 1824 when Franz von Paula Gruithuisen, a professor of astronomy at Munich, hypothesized on meteorite impacts. The scientific community, however, discounted his idea, probably because he was known for extravagant hypotheses based on irreproducible data. (He claimed, for example, that there was advanced life on the Moon based on his "observations" of roads, cities, and temples.) Not until 1892 was the impact theory revived, when Grove Karl Gilbert, an American geologist, suggested that a giant impact had created the Mare Imbrium on the Moon. Gilbert himself then went to Meteor Crater in Arizona and declared it to be volcanic in origin!

Argument over Meteor Crater was so lengthy and confusing that the feature itself was entirely omitted from state maps prior to 1912. Meteor Crater, also called Barringer Crater, after the man who bought the rights to the land around the crater,

(continues on page 35)

WHO DECIDES WHICH SPACE MISSIONS GET LAUNCHED?

When the National Aeronautics and Space Administration (NASA) needs to make high-level decisions, for example, about what kinds of space missions should be done, guidance comes largely from the following sources: the president of the United States, top NASA administrators, and science advisory groups. Space research can be a presidential priority, as it was under Presidents Johnson and Kennedy during the Apollo era, and as President George Bush made it with his directive about lunar exploration and settlement. In 2004, President Bush announced a new Vision for Space Exploration, saying, in part:

> [The Vision for Space Exploration] is a sustainable and affordable long-term human and robotic program to explore space. We will explore space to improve our lives and lift our national spirit. Space exploration is also likely to produce scientific discoveries in fields from biology to physics, and to advance aerospace and a host of other industries. This will help create more highly skilled jobs, inspire students and teachers in math and science, and ensure that we continue to benefit from space technology, which has already brought us important improvements in areas as diverse as hurricane forecasting, satellite communications, and medical devices.

Under the guidance of the presidential directive, a number of advisory groups make recommendations to NASA. Perhaps the most important and influential science advisory groups are those from the National Academies of Sciences and Engineering, in which membership is a high honor given to accomplished scientists by their peers already in the academy. The National Academies advise government on policy decisions and serve as oversight committees on government affairs. Other important science advisory groups are open to any interested scientists and focus on specific mission goals: the Venus Exploration Advisory Group (VEXAG), the Lunar Exploration Advisory Group (LEXAG), the Mars Exploration Advisory Group (MEPAG), and the Outer Planets Exploration Advisory Group (OPAG).

NASA's Science Mission Directorate, currently under the leadership of Ed Weiler, takes ideas and recommendations and fashions NASA policy from them. NASA's road map for space exploration includes answering the following science research objectives:

(continues)

(continued)

1. How did the Sun's family of planets and minor bodies originate?
2. How did the solar system evolve to its current diverse state?
3. What are the characteristics of the solar system that led to the origin of life?
4. How did life begin and evolve on Earth and has it evolved elsewhere in the solar system?
5. What are the hazards and resources in the solar system environment that will affect the extension of human presence in space?

The road map calls for a series of small (Discovery Program, meant to launch one mission every 12 to 24 months), medium (New Frontiers Program, meant to launch one mission about every 36 months), and large (flagship) class missions, supported by a balanced program of research and analysis and creative education and public outreach. These are supplemented by the ongoing Explorers Program, which has run a long series of missions set at under $180 million.

In the past, NASA announced plans to explore a certain planet or region of space and solicited independent bids and competitions for spacecraft, operations, and science investigations. These missions were very large in scope, carrying many instruments, involving large groups of people, taking many years to get organized and launched, and often costing billions of dollars.

The current movement to smaller missions led by scientists is a significant departure from that earlier management style. Proposals for New Frontiers, Explorers, and Discovery missions are solicited by the publication of NASA's Announcements of Opportunity, in which NASA issues detailed guidelines for mission proposals. Each mission proposal is led by a principal investigator (PI), typically a scientist at a university or research institution.

The PI selects team members from industry, small businesses, government laboratories, and universities to develop the scientific objectives and instrument payload. The team brings together the skills and expertise needed to carry out a mission from concept development through data analysis. The PI is responsible for the overall success of the project by assuring that cost, schedule, and performance objectives are met.

Once a PI decides to propose a mission and has a target in mind, he or she needs to find two key partners: one who can build the mission and one who can manage and operate it. These can be the same organization, but more often they are separate. The partner to build the mission is usually a defense contractor or other corporation with experience in this area, such as Lockheed-Martin, Ball Aerospace, or AeroAstro. The management and operations partner is often a NASA center, such as the Jet Propulsion Laboratory (at the California Institute of Technology) or the Goddard-Applied Physics Laboratory (at Johns Hopkins University). The PI also invites a number of scientists to be on the science team for the mission, and together they decide which measurements they want to make and then work with the engineers to determine how these measurements might be made.

Even the proposal phase of a mission is immensely time-consuming and expensive. It involves multiple trips to meet with the team, many telephone conferences, and a considerable amount of data analysis, budgeting, and even building instruments, testing, and proving feasibility. For example, to prove to the scientists who assess the multiple proposals fighting for selection that an instrument will work on Venus, it may be necessary to find a lab somewhere in the world where the instrument can be placed in a chamber to make measurements under Venus surface conditions, at 855°F (457°C) and about 100 times Earth's atmospheric pressure. The resulting proposal is usually hundreds of pages long. It is likely to be rejected, as there are more proposals by far than available mission budgets, and no scientists are paid to write proposals.

The Discovery Program has existed for some years now and has developed the following 11 missions to date:

1. Near Earth Asteroid Rendezvous, or NEAR, launched in 1996;
2. Mars Pathfinder, launched in 1996;
3. Lunar Prospector, launched in 1998;
4. Stardust, launched in 1999;
5. Genesis, launched in 2001;
6. Comet Nucleus Tour, or CONTOUR, launched in 2001;
7. MESSENGER, launched in 2004;
8. Deep Impact, launched in 2005;
9. Dawn, launched in 2007;
10. KEPLER, launched in 2009; and
11. GRAIL, selected in 2007 and scheduled to launch in 2011.

Five additional missions (ASPERA-3, M3, EPOXI, Stardust-NExT, and Strofio) have been named Discovery Missions of Opportunity. In some cases, these are extended missions using healthy spacecraft that have completed their original mission. EPOXI, for

(continues)

(continued)

example, is a new mission using the *Deep Impact* spacecraft, which is still functioning out in space. Other Missions of Opportunity involve adding experiments to spacecraft being launched for existing missions.

The Space Studies Board, a committee within the National Academies, first issued reports recommending that the New Frontiers Program be established and then which planetary targets should be considered when choosing missions for the New Frontiers Program. In their first recommendation, the Space Studies Board listed Venus, Jupiter, the south polar region of the Moon, and outer solar system objects as desired targets for exploration. New Frontiers' first mission launched was New Horizons, the mission for outer solar system research that left Earth in 2006. In 2011, the mission Juno is expected to launch, with the aim of conducting in-depth observations and measurements of Jupiter.

The New Frontiers Program seeks to contain total mission cost and development time and to improve performance through the use of validated new technologies, efficient management, and control of design, development, and operations costs while maintaining a strong commitment to flight safety. The cost for the entire mission must be less than $750 million. In their most recent recommendation in spring 2008, the targets have been broadened so greatly that any high-quality science-driven mission may be considered. The call for proposals has been made, and the process of selection for the next New Frontiers mission will begin in 2009.

There is a lot of emphasis right now at NASA on who gets to be a PI; no longer can any scientist interested in a mission manage to cobble together a team and send in a proposal. In the Discovery and New Frontiers Programs, the PIs have a huge role, far larger than existed in older missions. The PI–led missions have tended to have cost overruns, so NASA is more concerned about having someone experienced. Prospective PIs are now required to go to a PI summer school run by NASA and to qualify through an online survey.

Most important, however, the space sciences community is small, and team members and PIs are likely to be known by anyone else in the community. Publishing scientific papers, attending conferences, and participating in advisory councils all create name recognition if not personal friendships. For anyone interested in space science, showing up and getting to know the community is the most important first step, along with conducting interesting science and publishing it. This process can begin in college or even in high school—interested high school students can get summer jobs in science labs at universities and in small numbers each year they do attend scientific conferences, hitting the ground running.

(continued from page 30)
is a clean, round crater three-quarters of a mile (1.2 km) in diameter, 560 feet (170 m) deep, and with a rim of rock blocks 150 feet (45 m) high around its edge. Meteor Crater lies in the middle of a great flat plain in Arizona. When first found by Europeans, the crater had about 30 tons (27,000 kg) of iron meteorite pieces scattered over a diameter of about six miles (10 km). The image on page 36 of Meteor Crater was taken by an astronaut on the *International Space Station* on February 11, 2004. The crater looks much as a lunar crater might appear through a tele-

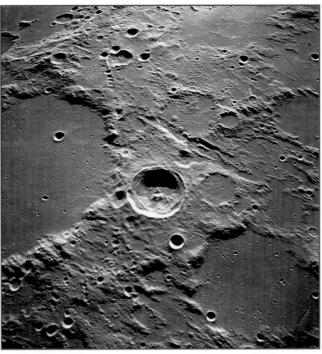

scope. The prominent canyon meandering across the scene is Canyon Diablo, which drains northward toward the Little Colorado River and eventually to the Grand Canyon. Interstate 40 highway crosses and nearly parallels the northern edge of the scene.

The lunar crater Herschel is bare of lava, while its neighbor Ptolomaeus has a smooth lava filling. (NASA/NSSDC/ Apollo 12)

In 1891, Gilbert, then the chief geologist for the U.S. Geological Survey (USGS), set out to determine how the crater was formed. Gilbert reasoned that if an iron meteorite had created the crater, as possibly implied by the pieces of iron meteorite scattered around the site, the impactor would have had to be nearly as big as the crater itself. The impactor itself, therefore, should be detectable beneath the bottom of the crater. Since Gilbert could not detect a large mass of iron under the crater using any current technique, he concluded that the crater had to have been formed by a giant steam explosion (his only alternative hypothesis), despite the complete lack of any other evidence of steam activity in the area. At the time Gilbert was making his investigations, though, no scientist had suggested that a giant impact could cause

Canyon Diablo and Meteor Crater (Earth Sciences and Image Analysis Laboratory, NASA Johnson Space Center, eol.jsc.nasa. gov, image number ISS08-E-15268)

an explosion that would both create a crater and destroy the impactor.

Daniel Moreau Barringer, a successful mining engineer, heard about the crater 10 years later. When he learned that small pieces of meteoritic iron were mixed with the ejected rocks of the crater rim and scattered around the surrounding desert floor, Barringer concluded that the crater had resulted from a meteorite impact. The fact that the iron pieces were intermixed with the ejected rock meant that the two events, the crater and the meteorite impact, had happened at the same time. Like Gilbert, Barringer also assumed that the main body of the iron meteorite must still exist intact and buried in the vicinity of the crater. He imagined it represented an immense mining opportunity. Without ever having seen the crater, Barringer formed the Standard Iron Company and began securing mining patents.

Barringer and his colleagues drilled and searched the crater for 27 years, spending more than $600,000 ($10 million in today's money). They found nothing. In the process, though, Barringer was able to put together enough evidence to help convince the scientific community that the crater had been formed by an impact. He found large quantities of silica in a high-pressure crystal form that cannot be formed at the surface of the Earth without an impact. He also documented that the layers of rocks in the ejecta rim of the crater were in the inverse order from their occurrence in the surrounding desert plain. They had been folded back by the blast that produced the crater and so were upside-down where they lay in the crater rim. He and his geologists carefully mapped the land surrounding the crater and demonstrated that there was no other volcanic activity in the area. In 1906 and again in 1909, he presented his arguments for the impact origin of the crater to the Academy of Natural Sciences in Philadelphia. Meteor Crater is now thought to have been created by an iron meteorite about 160 feet (50 m) in diameter falling at about seven miles per second (11 km/sec).

Though impact craters can be clearly seen on other planets and meteorites can be seen falling to Earth, the connection between meteorites and impact craters was hard for scientists to make. The problem was one of scale: Only truly giant meteorites can make craters, and humankind had never witnessed such an event. Small meteorites of the size that fall to Earth every year do not make dramatic craters. Small meteorites simply fall onto the surface of the ground and stay there looking like normal rock. Larger meteorites may bury themselves in the earth to about the depth of their own diameter. There is really no resemblance between these relatively slow meteorite falls and the giant, cosmic-speed falls that cause crater formation. Small meteorites are slowed by air friction to the point that they make almost no impression on the Earth when they fall, while giant meteorites are not appreciably slowed by the atmosphere.

Not until the 1920s were theories developed showing that a large impact would create an explosion (the ideas of high temperatures and shock waves were not associated with impacts until then), and it was not until the 1960s that any scientist stood up and strongly stated that craters on the Moon were of impact origin. At the late date of 1967, Sir Patrick Moore, astronomer and later host of the BBC series *The Sky at Night*, and Dr. Peter Cattermole, a lecturer at the University of Wales, wrote about the impact theory in their book *The Craters of the Moon: An Observational Approach*. In complete opposition to the impact theory of crater formation, they wrote, "the present writers are in the strongest possible disagreement with such a view."

Even the early lunar missions failed to clear up the controversy, and it was not until the Apollo missions and later that impact became accepted as the way all craters are made on the Moon. It took even longer for craters on Earth to be believed as impact generated.

Impact craters on Earth were attributed to "cryptovolcanic" activity for centuries, meaning that the crater was believed to be created by a volcanic eruption, but the volcanism itself was undetectable, or "cryptic." Round depressions called craters can be formed by volcanic explosions (for example, Crater Lake in the American Cascade Mountain Range). Volcanic craters are clearly associated with volcanic activity and almost always form at the top of a raised volcano, while impact craters may have central peaks, raised and inverted rims, and high-pressure minerals and are not associated with volcanic activity except when exceptionally large. The recognition of impact craters on Earth was delayed by the very different appearance of the Moon and even Mars, on which many ancient craters are preserved. *Plate tectonics* and the erosive action of water on the Earth create a young, fresh surface, wiping away or disguising impact craters.

In 1980, Luis and Walter Alvarez, Frank Asaro, and Helen Michel published a paper in the journal *Science* titled "Extraterrestrial Cause for the Cretaceous-Tertiary Extinction," claiming that a meteorite impact caused the Cretaceous-Tertiary extinction. As a result, their hypotheses were widely criticized and disbelieved in the scientific community. A series of angry arguments raged for about a decade. In the paper, the scientists suggest that the dense plume from the impact, combined with the soot from global forest fires, filled the atmosphere and blocked sunlight, creating an artificial winter that killed

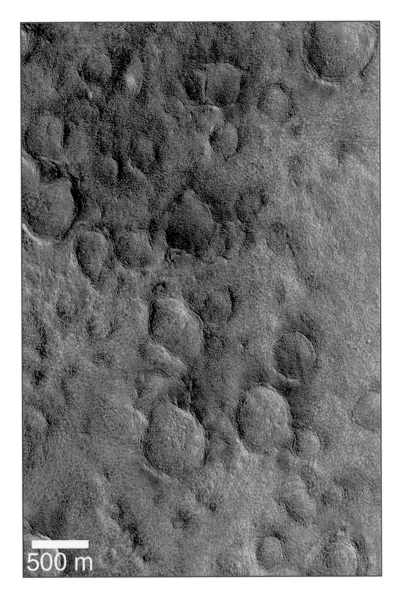

500 m

The Mars Orbital Laser Altimeter *first showed that the apparently smooth northern plains actually consist of a smooth younger surface that lies draped over a heavily cratered surface. The extent of buried craters, here shown in the Utopia region, shows that the northern lowlands have crust of almost the same age as the southern highlands. (NASA/JPL/ Malin Space Science Systems)*

vegetation. The death of vegetation eventually killed the animals that ate the vegetation, and so on up the food chain, worldwide. The rock record at that exact point in time, 65 million years ago, is highly enriched in iridium, an element common in meteorites but rare on Earth. The layer also contains soot from huge forest fires and tiny glassy spheres solidified from the molten ejecta of the impact crater. Finally, evidence from the chemistry of the rocks at that geologic boundary was compiled from many places around the globe, and at last the crater was found, partly on land but mostly in the shallow sea off the Yucatán Peninsula. This crater, named Chicxulub, is 180 miles (300 km) in diameter. Twenty years after the original scientific paper, the meteorite theory for the extinction of the dinosaurs is largely accepted.

Searching for evidence of meteorite impacts on Earth is far harder than, for example, searching for impacts on the Moon or Mars. On Earth, craters have been erased by plate tectonics and by the fast process of erosion by water and vegetation. On Mars, by contrast, some craters have been buried by dust and then later revealed by erosion, as shown in this image. Wind erosion has created ridges and revealed the location of formerly buried meteor craters in the image on page 39, which encompasses about 1.9 square miles (3 km²) only about 100 miles from the original Viking landing site. Sediments have draped over the craters, softening their outlines until they were difficult to see in low-resolution images.

About 20 million years ago, a large bolide impact struck near this site in Devon Islands, in Canada's Arctic, ejecting material that fell to create these hills. Few hills on Earth are produced by impacts, though almost all the hills on the Moon were created in this way. (NASA/JPL/ASU)

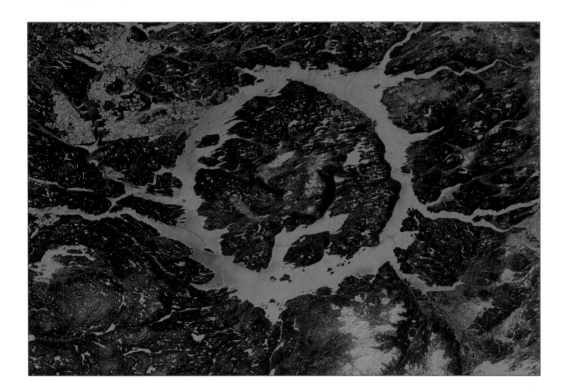

On Earth, erosion generally acts against the ability to recognize craters. The Manicouagan crater in eastern Canada, shown in the image above, is an excellent example of an ancient crater partly erased by erosion until it consists of nothing but a circular lake. This image of the crater was taken by an astronaut from the space shuttle *Endeavour* and shows the reservoir now filling the crater frozen in winter.

There are about 170 known terrestrial craters, ranging in age from a few thousand to 2 billion years old and in size up to several hundred kilometers in diameter. Newly verified impact sites are presented at scientific conferences every year. The largest known craters are listed in the table on page 43. Not all can be seen at the surface of the Earth; Chicxulub, for example, is best detected by anomalies in the gravity field.

The Aorounga crater in the Sahara of northern Chad is an unusually clear example of a terrestrial impact. The concentric ring structure left of center is the Aorounga impact crater with a diameter of about 10.5 miles (17 km). Aorounga may

The Manicouagan impact crater in eastern Canada has been so eroded over time that only a circular depression, filled here with frozen water, remains. (Earth Sciences and Image Analysis Laboratory, NASA Johnson Space Center, eol.jsc.nasa.gov, image number ISS06-E-47702)

The Aorounga impact structure in northern Chad is several hundreds of millions of years old. (NASA/JPL/NIMA)

have formed as part of a multiple impact event. A proposed second crater, similar in size to the main structure, appears as a circular trough surrounding a central peak in the center of the image. A third structure, also about the same size, is seen as a dark, partial circular trough with a possible central structure in the right center of the image. This proposed crater chain could have formed when a 0.5–1 mile- (1–2 km-) diameter object broke apart before impact.

A good example of how hard it can be to confirm a circular feature as an impact crater on Earth is the five-mile (8-km) feature known as the Iturralde Structure. Possibly proof of the Earth's most recent large impact event, the Iturralde Structure is a recording of an impact that might have occurred between 11,000 and 30,000 years ago. Iturralde is in an isolated part of the Bolivian Amazon. Although the structure was identified on satellite photographs in the mid-1980s, its location is so remote that it has only been visited by scientific investigators twice, most recently by a team from NASA's Goddard Space Flight Center in September 2002. The feature is a closed depression only about 66 feet (20 m) in depth. Its rim cuts into the heavily vegetated soft sediments of this part of Bolivia. Thick

SELECTED TERRESTRIAL IMPACT CRATERS

Crater name	State/Province	Country	Diameter (miles [km])	Approximate age (millions of years)
Vredefort		South Africa	190 (300)	2020
Sudbury	Ontario	Canada	150 (250)	1850
Chicxulub	Yucatán	Mexico	110 (180)	65
Manicouagan	Québec	Canada	60 (100)	214
Popigai		Russia	60 (100)	35
Acraman	South Australia	Australia	55 (90)	450
Chesapeake Bay	Virginia	U.S.	53 (85)	35
Puchezh-Katunki		Russia	50 (80)	175
Morokweng		South Africa	44 (70)	145
Kara		Russia	40 (65)	73
Beaverhead	Montana	U.S.	38 (60)	625
Tookoonooka	Queensland	Australia	34 (55)	130
Charlevoix	Québec	Canada	34 (54)	360
Kara-Kul		Tajikistan	33 (52)	within 5 Myr of present
Siljan		Sweden	33 (52)	368
Montagnais	Nova Scotia	Canada	28 (45)	50

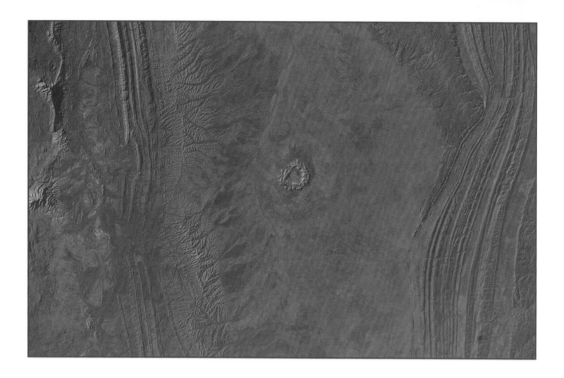

Gosses Bluff impact crater in Australia was created by an impactor probably about 0.6 miles (1 km) in diameter about 142 million years ago. (Earth Sciences and Image Analysis Laboratory, NASA Johnson Space Center, eol.jsc.nasa.gov, image number ISS07-E-5697)

vegetation makes its identification doubly difficult, since there are little hard rocks to preserve shock features.

Gosses Bluff, an impact crater sandwiched between the Macdonnell Ranges to the north and the James Range to the south in Australia's Northern Territory, shown in the image above, is about 100 miles (160 km) west of Alice Springs. Australia makes a great natural laboratory for impact structure study, since it is so dry that many craters have been preserved on its surface. Gosses Bluff is one of the most studied craters. The isolated circular feature within the crater consists of a central ring of hills about 2.8 miles (4.5 km) in diameter. The grayish feature surrounding the inner ring probably marks the original boundary of the outer rim.

Not all perfectly round features with concentric terraces are impact craters. This prominent circular feature, known as the Richat Structure, is in the Sahara of Mauritania. Richat has a diameter of 30 miles (50 km) and was understandably initially mistaken for a possible impact crater. It is now known to be an eroded circular dome of layered *sedimentary rocks*.

This view, generated from a *Landsat* satellite image, exaggerates vertical expression by a factor of six to make the structure more apparent. The height of the mesa ridge in the center of the view is about 935 feet (285 m).

Researchers are working on a method for determining when hypervelocity impacts occurred even when their craters are hard to find. By measuring the concentration of elements in deep-sea sediments that are commonly found in meteorites but not in Earth sediments, the traces of ancient meteorite strikes can be found. Iridium, nickel, and *isotopes* of osmium are promising tracers for meteorite impact. Unfortunately, deep-sea sediment cores cannot go back in time more than about 200 million years, which is the age of the oldest oceanic *crust*. (Older oceanic crust has already been subducted under a continent and recycled into the *mantle*.) Other researchers are applying the technique to lake sediments.

Why is it important to know when meteorites struck the Earth in the past? By correlating the ages of the likely meteorite strikes with the ages of other global catastrophes, such as extinctions, investigators can better understand the role of meteorite impacts on the development of life on Earth. A more

The round Richat Structure in Mauritania is formed by a pattern of eroded sedimentary rock, not by an impact crater. (NASA/ JPL/NIMA)

complete record of recent impacts also helps us predict the likelihood of future impacts. Humankind is just beginning to understand the effects of giant impacts as we have never witnessed a giant impact on Earth.

About 25 years ago, a geologist suggested that in 1178 five men in Canterbury, England, actually witnessed the formation of one of the Moon's youngest craters, now named Giordano Bruno. They testified to having seen a "flaming torch" spring from the face of the Moon, "spewing out . . . fire, hot coals and sparks." Their testimony was recorded in a medieval chronicle in Canterbury. Recently Paul Withers at the University of Arizona made a convincing argument that they could not have witnessed the formation of Giordano Bruno: The size of Giordano Bruno, 10 times as wide as Meteor Crater on Earth, would require an impacting meteorite 0.5–3 miles (1–5 km) in diameter and would have launched 10 million tons of rock from the Moon into the Earth's atmosphere. This ejecta would have produced a blindingly bright weeklong meteor storm on Earth, with more than 50,000 meteors per hour. No historical accounts of such an event are found in any known record. Withers suggests that the Canterbury men witnessed a large meteor entering the Earth's atmosphere from directly in front of the Moon from their point of view.

With this compelling story disproved, there is no record of any human witnessing any giant impact on a terrestrial planet. People living today have, however, seen a giant impact on a gas giant planet. In 1994, the comet Shoemaker-Levy struck Jupiter, and the *Galileo* space probe took images. The fragments of Shoemaker-Levy were large enough that even though they struck the far side of Jupiter, they blew incandescent vapor plumes thousands of kilometers high and were plainly visible using telescopes on Earth. Studying these impacts has helped us understand giant impacts in general, but their effects on Earth are still poorly understood.

Processes and Effects of Impacts on Planets

While the smallest meteorites simply fall to Earth like a tossed stone, larger bodies can create the most catastrophic natural disasters possible in the universe. Bodies that are large enough to retain their orbital speed (cosmic speed) while falling through the atmosphere push before themselves massive shock waves that blow impact craters into the surface of the planet and literally vaporize the body itself along with some of the impacted surface. Now that some of the physics of this astonishing process have been explained, humankind is aware of and vigilant about asteroids near enough to threaten Earth.

THE PROCESS OF SMALL METEORITE FALLS

Between sea level and about 63 miles (100 km) above the Earth, the air is dense enough to create significant friction with a falling bolide. Air friction both ablates and decelerates the bolide. Only cosmic-speed bodies glow and appear as fireballs; bodies that have been slowed to their terminal velocities no longer glow. (See the sidebar "Terminal Velocity" on page 48.) Thus, bright, visible meteorites or comets are either in the process of slowing to their terminal velocities, or they are so large that they will never slow to their terminal velocity. While falling at supersonic speeds (about 1,115 feet per second, or 340 m/sec), the bolide will also create sonic booms, whistles, and rumbles. Small bolides are broken apart and slowed to their

TERMINAL VELOCITY

It was brilliant Galileo who discovered that all objects fall to Earth with the same acceleration, which is denoted g (32 feet per second squared, or 9.8 m/sec^2). Other planets, with other masses, have gravitational accelerations different from Earth's, but every object on a given planet falls with the same acceleration, no matter its size or density. When an object falls through a fluid, however, or even through the air, it experiences a drag, or slowing force, because of friction between the moving object and the molecules of air or fluid. For a dense object falling a small distance, this drag is negligible, and the object has an acceleration very close to g. (Density is important only because drag affects an object's surface; a less dense object with the same mass will have a larger surface area than will a denser object.) Drag increases with velocity. Think of trying to wave your arm underwater: If you wave it slowly, it is easy, but if you try to wave it fast, you feel the strong force holding your arm back. If almost any object falls a very long way, then its velocity will increase according to the acceleration of gravity, and its drag will also increase until the force is no longer negligible. Eventually, the force will balance the acceleration of gravity, and the object will stop accelerating. It will fall thereafter at a constant velocity, the fastest velocity it can obtain under the influence of gravity and against the influence of drag. This final constant velocity is known as *terminal velocity*.

It can be shown through math called dimensional analysis that drag force F_{drag} in a low-density environment, like air, is expressed as

$$F_{drag} = \rho_a v^2 r^3,$$

where ρ_a is the density of air, v is the velocity of the falling object, and r is the radius of the object, if it is approximated as a sphere. The force of gravity can be calculated by using the familiar expression for force,

$$F = ma = mg,$$

terminal velocity of a few hundred meters per second, nothing compared to their original speed. Depending on the size and shape of the bolide, it may be slowed to its terminal velocity as high as 25 miles (40 km) above the Earth, or it may never slow

with the generic acceleration *a* replaced with *g*, the acceleration of gravity, with which this problem is concerned. The mass *(m)* of the object can also be approximated as ρr^3, where ρ is the density of the falling object, and r^3 is the important part (the only part that varies) of the volume of the sphere that is falling: $(4/3)\pi r^3$. $F = ma$ thus becomes, for gravitational acceleration,

$$F_{gravity} = \rho r^3 g.$$

So how is terminal velocity found from drag force and gravitational force? The terminal velocity is the velocity attained when the two perfectly balance each other, that is, when they are equal. Set drag force equal to gravitational force:

$$\rho_a v^2 r^2 = \rho r^3 g,$$

and solve for velocity, obtaining for terminal velocity $v_{terminal}$

$$v_{terminal} = \left(\frac{\rho}{\rho a} rg\right)^{\frac{1}{2}}$$

Using this simple relation, it can be calculated that a mouse's terminal velocity is only about 50 feet per second (15 m/sec), which is why small animals can sometimes survive falls from heights that people cannot. A person's terminal velocity is about 230 feet per second (70 m/sec), and the terminal velocity of a meteorite with a 60-foot (20-m) radius is about 3,000 feet per second (900 m/sec). That high terminal velocity for large, dense objects like big meteorites explains the huge destructive force of their impacts: Their speed and mass get converted to energy when they strike the Earth, making an explosion and a lot of heat.

to terminal velocity. Bolides larger than about 500 feet (150 m) in diameter, depending on their strength and composition, survive passage through the Earth's atmosphere more or less intact and at or close to their original velocity. Those that continue at cosmic speed are called hypervelocity impactors. They are the impactors that create craters and will be discussed in the following section.

Most fireballs occur after midnight, since meteorites fall onto the Earth most commonly on the side of the Earth that is moving forward in its orbit, and that is the morning side of midnight. Meteorites can fall to the Earth, however, from any angle and at any time of day. Meteors may be orbiting the Sun in the same way the Earth is, called prograde rotation, though others orbit the Sun in the opposite direction, called retrograde. If the Earth and the meteorite are orbiting the Sun in the same direction and the Earth sweeps the meteorite up with its leading face, then the Earth was moving faster than the meteorite and the meteorite strikes the surface with a lower relative velocity. If the meteorite has a retrograde orbit it strikes the Earth with a much greater relative velocity, like two trains crashing head-on, rather than one speeding train catching up to and bumping into another train traveling in the same direction. Based on an analysis of relative velocities and directions of strike, the speed of meteorites with respect to the Sun is thought to be six to 25 miles per second (10–40 km/sec), and the speed of comets is thought to be higher, at 25–44 miles per second (40–70 km/sec). The Earth itself travels through space at about 19 miles per second (30 km/sec).

Meteorites between the size of a grain of sand and about four inches (10 cm) in diameter create a bright light trail and usually burn up in the atmosphere. Meteorites between about four inches (10 cm) and three feet (1 m) may survive the burning of entry to land on the Earth's surface. Meteorites larger than a meter or two usually detonate in the upper atmosphere, releasing energy equivalent to several thousand tons of TNT, though they may make it to the surface. Meteorites even larger than that have enough mass to reach the Earth's surface, where they impact with devastating consequences.

Meteorites large enough to fall all the way to Earth but too small to make a hypervelocity impact lose an estimated 30–60 percent of their mass as they pass through the atmosphere, mainly from melting from the heat of friction with the air. Many meteorites break into smaller pieces while they fall. The fragments of a fracturing meteorite fall in a characteristic pattern called a strewn field, shaped like an oval, with the largest pieces traveling farther downrange.

Sometimes the meteorite stays oriented in the same direction throughout its fall, and the process of melting shapes it into a cone, with a thick layer of glass on its back. This glass is the result of melting a crystalline silica-rich meteorite into a liquid that cools to a glass if it is cooled fast enough. This glass is a solid without crystalline ordering, technically a very thick liquid similar to window glass. Other meteorites develop small, smooth depressions, called regmaglypts, over their surfaces. These may be formed from selective melting of parts of the meteorite during flight, or they may be caused by air turbulence; their formation is not well understood. All falling meteorites form a fusion crust of some thickness, created by melt or partial melt from atmospheric friction forming a shell over their surface.

Though the outside of meteorites is heated to melting by air friction during passage through the atmosphere, the heat does not penetrate very far into the meteorite during its brief fall, and the interior of the meteorite remains at the deeply frozen temperature of space. Even when meteorites were handled right after they fell, they were found to be only warm to the touch. There are two reports of meteorites that fell on hot summer days, one in Wisconsin and the other in India, both of which were quickly but briefly covered with a layer of frost caused by their very cold interior temperatures condensing water on their surfaces and then freezing it.

In the first few hundreds of millions of years after planet formation, there seems to have been a lot more debris loose in the solar system than there is now. During this period of heavy meteorite impacts on the new planets, called the Late Heavy Bombardment (see sidebar on page 53), the Earth is estimated to have received 1.5 billion pounds (700 million kg) of material per year from space. Since then, the amount of material from space that strikes the Earth each year has tapered down to estimates of 44 million–175 million pounds (20 million–79 million kg) per year. The number is believed to fluctuate. More meteorite falls, for example, were reported between 1840 and 1880 than were reported before or have been reported since that period, and the level of reporting may reflect an actual increase in falls. Eighty million kilograms per year is a large weight, but because meteorites are dense, it translates into a volume that is not overwhelming. If all the meteorites that fall to Earth each year were piled together, they would make a hill about 130 feet (40 m) high, the base of which would have a diameter of about 260 feet (80 m), or if they were piled onto a soccer field, they would make a solid layer about 20 feet (6 m) thick over the whole field.

Scientists have tried to estimate the number of meteorites larger than 2.2 pounds (1 kg) that fall to Earth each year, but the estimates fall over a wide range. It is thought that between nine and 90 meteorites larger than 2.2 pounds (1 kg) fall on every 390,000 square miles (1,000,000 km²) each year. This area is about the area of Germany and France combined, or about one and a half times the size of Texas.

With all the material falling to the Earth from space each year, it seems as though reports of meteorite injuries and deaths should be more commonplace. In actuality, there are only a few confirmed cases. In 1927, a girl in Juachiki, Japan, was struck by a falling meteorite, and in 1954 a woman in Sylacauga, Alabama, was struck on the leg and developed an immense bruise. She had been lying on a couch listening to the radio, when the 8.8-pound (4-kg) meteorite punched through the roof of her house, bounced off a table, and struck her on the leg. Among the most notable of meteorite strikes was the fall of a meteorite that came from Mars (it was originally a piece of the Martian crust that was thrown into space when another, larger meteorite struck Mars). This meteorite, called Nakhla, fell in Cairo, Egypt, on November 5, 1913, killing a dog when it touched down. There are also reports that a cow in Venezuela was killed by a meteorite strike in 1972.

THE LATE HEAVY BOMBARDMENT

There was a period of time early in solar system development when all the celestial bodies in the inner solar system were repeatedly impacted by large bolides. This high-activity period might be anticipated by thinking about how the planets formed, accreting from smaller bodies into larger and larger bodies, and so it may seem intuitive that there would be a time even after most of the planets formed when there was still enough material left over in the early solar system to continue bombarding and cratering the early planets.

Beyond this theory, though, there is visible evidence on Mercury, the Moon, and Mars in the form of ancient surfaces that are far more heavily cratered than any fresher surfaces. (Venus, on the other hand, has been resurfaced by volcanic activity, and plate tectonics and surface weathering have wiped out all record of early impacts on Earth.) The giant basins on the Moon, filled with dark basalt and visible to the eye from Earth, are left over from that early period of heavy impacts, called the Late Heavy Bombardment.

Dating rocks from the Moon using *radioactive* isotopes and carefully determining the age relationships of different craters' ejecta blankets indicate that the lunar Late Heavy Bombardment lasted until about 3.8 billion years ago. Some scientists believe that the Late Heavy Bombardment was a specific period of very heavy impact activity that lasted from about 4.2 to 3.8 billion years ago, after a pause in bombardment following initial planetary formation at about 4.56 billion years ago, while other scientists believe that the Late Heavy Bombardment was the tail end of a continuously decreasing rate of bombardment that began at the beginning of the solar system.

In this continual bombardment model, the last giant impacts from 4.2 to 3.8 billion years ago simply erased the evidence of all the earlier bombardment. If, alternatively, the Late Heavy Bombardment was a discrete event, then some reason for the sudden invasion of the inner solar system by giant bolides must be discovered. Were they bodies perturbed from the outer solar system by the giant planets there? If they came from the outer solar system, then more of the material was likely to be water-rich cometary material. If as much as 25 percent of the Late Heavy Bombardment was cometary material, it would have contributed enough water to the Earth to create its oceans. If this model is correct for placing water on the Earth, then a further quandary must be solved. Why didn't Venus receive as much water, or if it did where did the water go?

There are only a few relatively well-documented human deaths from meteorite falls: A 17th-century monk from Milan is said to have died when a fist-size meteor severed his femoral artery, causing him to bleed to death. In August 2007, police in the Indian state of Rajasthan reported that two nomads were killed by what was suspected to be a meteorite strike. A small crater was formed, and five other people were injured. Two people are also reported to have been killed in the Tunguska, Siberia, airburst of 1908. In the November 1994 issue of the journal *Meteoritics,* Kevin Yau, Paul Weissman, and Donald Yeomans of the Jet Propulsion Laboratory, Pasadena, California, argued that someone should typically be hit by a four-ounce (100-g) meteorite once every 14 years. This may result in injury or even death. There are various reports of such incidents in ancient literature, including several from China. In 616 C.E. for example, it is reported that "a large shooting star like a bushel fell onto the rebel Lu Ming-yueh's camp. It destroyed his wall-attacking tower and crushed to death more than ten people." Another account from 1341 reads, "It rained iron in Chin-ning. They damaged crops. Most of the people and animals struck by them were killed." In 1875, there was a report of a man in Ohio being killed by a meteorite. This is how the report read in the Philadelphia press at the time (*aerolite* is a archaic term for a class of meteorites):

> As David Misenthaler, the famous stockman, of Whetstone township, was driving his cows to the barn about daylight this morning he was struck by an aerolite and instantly killed. It appears as if the stone had come down from a direction a little west of south, striking the man just under or on the right shoulder, passing obliquely through him from the right shoulder to just above the left hip, burying the great portion of his body under itself in the soft earth. The stone is about the size of a wooden water bucket, and appears to be composed of pyrites of iron.

Various other unsubstantiated reports of deaths by meteorite strikes exist in newspaper records, including a report of two children killed in Chihuahua, Mexico, when their house was destroyed by a large meteorite in 1896, and a report of the death of a man named Leonidas Grover who was apparently struck by a large meteorite while sleeping in his bed in Colorado. There is statistical reasoning to believe that people should be killed by individual meteorite falls from time to time, but there is little substantiated fact of actual injuries and deaths. These stories, though, are about small meteorite falls. The more serious threat is a giant, cosmic-speed fall that can change the climate of the Earth, much as the meteorite that fell during the time of the dinosaurs seems to have done.

THE PROCESS OF GIANT METEORITE FALLS

A falling body large enough to survive atmospheric entry at its original cosmic speed is preceded by a strong shock wave of compressed air. Some energy is expended in heating this air to incandescence. The air itself literally glows with heat, and some of it is heated sufficiently that its molecules and even *atoms* disintegrate into a plasma. Depending on its mass and speed, a bolide about 300 feet (~100 m) in diameter would make a crater on the order of five miles (3 km) in diameter and form a fireball on impact that is briefly as hot as 18,000°F (10,000°C). An impact of this modest size can clearly destroy a city and, with its plume and energy flash, could burn or flatten an area the size of a state.

There are three stages of impact: compression, in which the kinetic energy of the bolide is transferred into compressing the target rocks; excavation, in which relaxation of the compression propels rock upward out of the crater and creates the ejecta blanket; and modification, in which the rocks around the crater slump into more stable shapes and the rocks beneath the crater flow back into a stable place (see figure on page 56).

The initial pressure of the shock wave hitting rock is equivalent to millions of times atmospheric pressure and enough to compress rock into about one-third of its original volume. Solid material, including rock, shocked to this extent loses all its internal strength and flows like a liquid. The intense initial compressive wave opens the initial impact cavity. The impactor is melted or completely vaporized by this process,

Shock pressures during formation of an impact crater cause the target rock to flow like a liquid for a brief period of time.

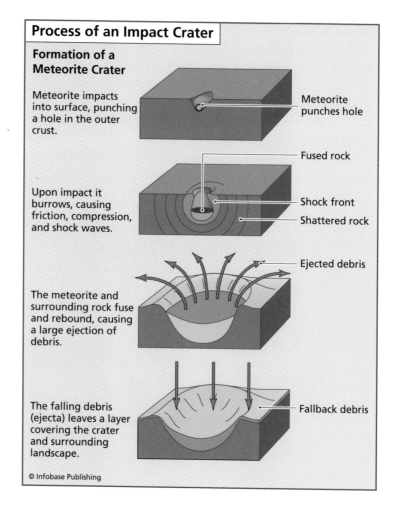

Process of an Impact Crater

Formation of a Meteorite Crater

Meteorite impacts into surface, punching a hole in the outer crust.

Meteorite punches hole

Fused rock

Upon impact it burrows, causing friction, compression, and shock waves.

Shock front

Shattered rock

Ejected debris

The meteorite and surrounding rock fuse and rebound, causing a large ejection of debris.

The falling debris (ejecta) leaves a layer covering the crater and surrounding landscape.

Fallback debris

© Infobase Publishing

lining the cavity and mixing with the target rock. The regions around the impact that are affected by pressure and heat are shown schematically in the image on this page. The higher the energy of the impact, the larger the area affected.

The intense compression is followed by decompression in which rock and impactor material is ejected as a solid or lost to the atmosphere as a vapor, when the bottom of the cavity and material to its sides spring back. Rock at the edges of the initial impact cavity is thrown back like a blanket, and additional material is ejected far from the original impact site. A small, fresh crater on Mars can be seen in the image on page 57. Its large ejecta rays are clearly visible, not having been eroded away by wind and frost. The field of view is about 1.9 miles (3 km) across.

Vaporized rock and impactor are shot upward in a super-heated plume like the cloud above a nuclear explosion. The vapor plume from a large impact will be hotter than 3,600°F (2,000°C). The vapor plume from a large hypervelocity impact would fill the entire atmosphere of the Earth with dust and particles, and the heat of impact would trigger instantaneous forest fires over a large portion of the Earth, filling the air

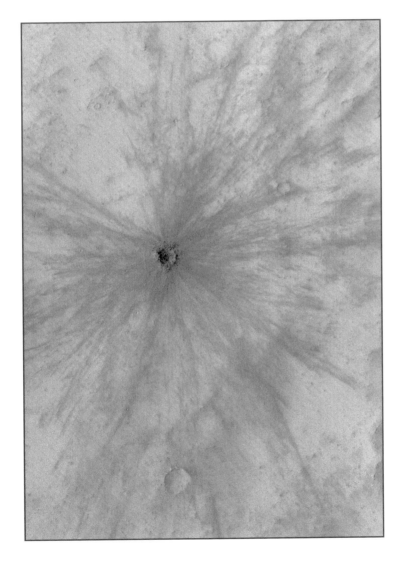

This fresh crater shows the starburst pattern of linear ejecta rays characteristic of impacts in dry material. (NASA/ JPL/MSSS)

with soot. The crater and its surroundings would oscillate downward and rebound multiple times, as in a slow-motion film of a pool of water after a pebble has fallen into it.

Some of the molten mixed impactor and raget rock are expelled from the crater site as liquid droplets rather than a vapor and fly through the atmosphere like droplets from a water gun. These spinning liquid drops cool and freeze often while still flying into dark-colored silica glass pieces, much like obsidian from a volcanic eruption. These droplets, known as tektites, have the distinctive shapes of spinning and flying liquids: droplets, dumbbells, disks, and near-toroids (similar to a doughnut without a completely punched-out hole). Though drops from explosive volcanic eruptions can attain

This frozen droplet of a lunar volcanic glass from the Apollo 15 landing site shows a dumbbell shape characteristic of a rotating, flying liquid drop, though it was not formed by an impact. (Courtesy of the author)

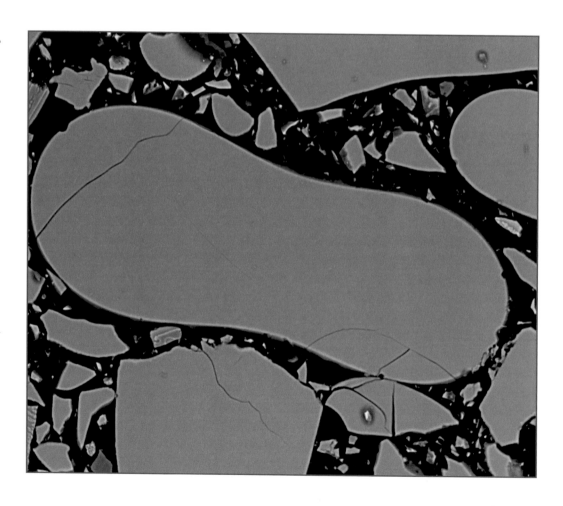

similar shapes, as demonstrated by the photomicrograph on page 58 of a drop of volcanic glass from the Moon that was spun into a dumbbell shape as it flew to land on the lunar surface, the compositions of tektites make them clearly distinct from volcanic glasses.

These tektites originated as liquid flung from the site of an unidentified large impact somewhere in Southeast Asia. Their shapes were created by forces of rotation during their flight and were preserved by the quenching of the liquid to glass. The square in the image, for scale, is one inch wide. (Courtesy of the author)

Tektites have been recognized as unusual in China for millennia and were first described in the Western scientific literature by Charles Darwin on his travels in the sailing vessel *Beagle*. Tektites come in a large range of sizes, from microscopic up to about five inches (12 cm) or more. The tektites in the photo above are from Southeast Asia and originated in an as-yet-unidentified impact event. The grey square is one inch in width.

In the first milliseconds after an impact, some of the energy of impact is released in the thermal plume and can be seen as a bright flash of light. Peter Schultz, a professor at Brown University, and his graduate students are making artificial impacts with a specially designed gun and calibrating the flashes of light that accompany the impacts. Researchers watching the Moon through telescopes during a recent Leonid meteor shower saw tiny flashes of light when the Leonid particles impacted the Moon. Using Ernst and Schultz's calibration, they may now be able to determine how large those Leonid impactors were.

After the initial seconds or minutes of liquid flow of the rock at the impact site, the crater steadies into a more final form. If the impact creates a crater on Earth less than about 4.5 miles (7 km) in diameter, the resulting crater is shaped like a bowl, called a simple crater. Meteor Crater in Arizona is an example of a bowl crater, as are the Endurance and Fram craters on Mars. The panoramic camera on NASA's Mars Exploration Rover *Opportunity* produced the image seen on page

The photo shows the energy flash that occurs when a projectile launched at speeds up to 17,000 MPH impacts a solid surface at the Hypervelocity Ballistic Range at NASA's Ames Research Center, Mountain View, California. (NASA/GRIN)

61 before *Opportunity* began its trip into the crater on July 5, 2004. Scientists sent it into the crater to study the dunes and to look for fresh volcanic rocks. *Opportunity* has made a number of important discoveries concerning the history of water on Mars in Endurance crater (seen in photo on page 61), which is about 525 feet (160 m) in diameter from rim to rim. Nearby Fram crater is only about one-tenth its size.

Larger craters undergo more complicated rebounding during impact and end with circular rims, terraced inner wall slopes, well-developed ejecta deposits, and flat floors with a central peak or peak ring. These craters are called complex craters. On the Moon (see photo on page 62), where erosion does not wear down craters as it does on Earth and the acceleration of gravity is only about 5.2 feet per second squared (1.6 m/sec²) compared to Earth's 32 feet per second squared (9.8 m/sec²), the central peaks of craters can be several kilo-

meters high. By comparison, Mount Everest is 5.5 miles, or 8.8 km, high.

A large central peak can be seen in the photo on page 63 of the Taruntius crater on the Moon. In this image, the large Taruntius crater (35 miles, or 56 km, in diameter) is in the upper left, and smaller simple craters can be seen in the lava plains below. All craters are underlain by a thick lens of broken, crushed, and mixed rock called an impact *breccia*. Most large craters also have a great sheet of crystalline rock that cooled from a pool of rock melted by impact.

While small impacts are likely to cause simple craters and giant impacts are likely to cause complex craters, other factors can affect the final shape of a crater. On Venus, about 96 percent of all craters larger than about nine miles (15 km) in diameter are complex, as shown in the images that follow on pages 64–66. Venus's exceptionally hot surface supplements the energy of the impactor and makes development of a complex crater more likely. Barton crater (named after Clara Barton, founder of the Red Cross), shown on page 66 in a radar image, is a good example of a complex crater. Barton crater has two rings and a central peak and is 31 miles (50 km) in diameter.

This panoramic image of the small Mars crater Fram was taken by the rover Opportunity. Fram shows a few dust ripples in its builder-free bottom. (NASA/JPL)

Endurance crater on Mars, imaged by the Mars rover Opportunity (NASA/JPL/Cornell)

The Lunar Orbiter 4 took this striking image of the lunar Orientale Basin, with portions of the mare basalt-filled Oceanus Procellarum visible on the upper right limb. (NASA/Lunar Orbiter 4)

Because this is a radar image and not a visible light image, the bright areas represent material that reflects radar waves efficiently and the dark areas reflect relatively fewer radar waves.

Mars's moons Phobos and Deimos are small, irregular satellites entirely unlike Earth's Moon. Their sizes and irregular orbits indicate that they are probably asteroids captured by Mars's gravity field rather than celestial bodies that formed at the same time as the planet. Phobos's significant surface feature is its huge crater Stickney, shown in the image on page 67. Stickney is six miles (9.5 km) in diameter. Like Saturn's moon Mimas, with its immense crater Herschel, the impact that caused Stickney must have almost shattered Phobos. Opposite Stickney on Phobos (this is called Stickney's antipodal point), there is a region of ridges and radial grooves. This chaotic terrain is thought to have been caused by the impact that created Stickney: The shock waves moved away from the impact and converged on the other side of the planet. This antipodal point was the focus of a lot of seismic energy coming from all sides, enough to disrupt the crust significantly. Similar antipodal terrains are found on Venus and possibly on Mars, where the Tharsis volcanic field is antipodal to the Hellas impact basin.

For some time, the remarkable roundness of impact craters confused scientists. Impacts created by bolides coming in at an angle were thought to create oblong craters. Why, then, should almost all craters have been created by vertical impacts, as the roundness of the craters implies? More detailed modeling shows, though, that all large impacts at angles between

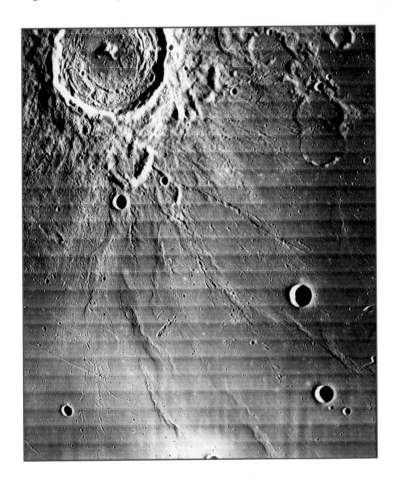

The Moon's Taruntius crater has a high central peak. (NASA/Lunar Orbiter 1/NSSDC)

20° and 90° to the Earth create round craters. Only the most oblique flight paths create oblong craters. Because such a wide range of angles of incidence all cause round craters, the rarity of oblong craters is now understood.

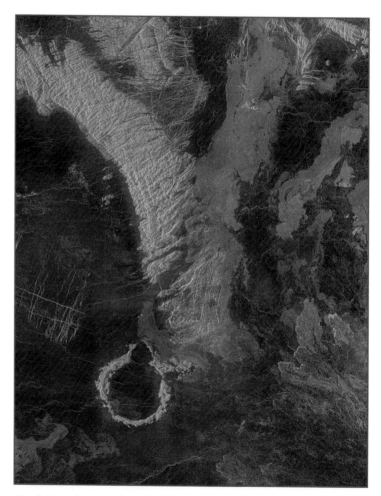

This false-color Magellan image shows a portion of Leda Planitia in the northern hemisphere of Venus. The area is 135 miles (220 km) wide and 170 miles (275 km) long. The oldest terrains appear as bright, highly fractured or chaotic highlands rising out of the plains in the upper left quadrant of the image. The circular structure, 40 miles (65 km) in diameter, is probably an impact crater. It has been given a proposed name, Heloise, after the French physician who lived from about 1098 to 1164 C.E. (NASA/JPL/Magellan)

Run-out flows from Howe, Danilova, and Aglaonice craters on Venus may be caused by the high atmospheric pressure compressing parts of the impact cloud near the surface of the planet. (NASA/Magellan/JPL)

To identify a crater and differentiate it from a round lake or a volcanic vent, a number of characteristics should be considered. A crater will be very close to perfectly round, and it will probably have a raised rim consisting of rocks that have been folded back by the outward pressure of the impact. Many craters have a central peak and pools of melted rock deep in the crater. Rocks outside the crater can be broken into cone shapes pointing inward toward the crater (called shatter cones), minerals in rocks around the crater can be deformed by the pressure of the impact, and quartz grains in rocks at the site of impact can be transformed into high-pressure phases of quartz called coesite or stishovite.

The material being impacted can affect the shape of the resulting crater. The surfaces of other planets have become better understood through studying the shapes of the craters that decorate them. Mars has an excellent example of this

Barton crater, 31 miles (50 km) in diameter, is an excellent example of a complex crater on Venus. (NASA/ Magellan/JPL)

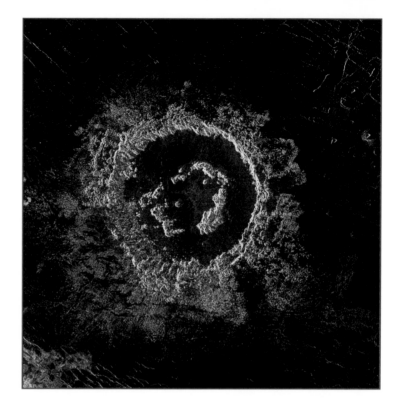

technique. Many of Mars's craters have peculiarly shaped rims that are called ramparts. Rather than a typical rim structure, many Martian craters have a splash-formed rim, thought to indicate that the impactor struck either a water- or ice-rich surface layer. Some of these craters also have splash marks on the surrounding plains. The splash-formed crater rims are somewhat visible in the image on page 69, but the flow marks on the surrounding plain are obvious. Virtually all the craters in Mars's northern hemisphere with diameters greater than about two miles (3 km) have ramparts. Because of the number of craters with ramparts and the ability to date some of the craters using Mars's relative age scale, it is thought that water was ubiquitous in the Hesperian epoch and maybe even more recently. Two rampart craters shown here have typical lobate ejecta blankets that were formed from fluidized ejecta, presumably liquid water. The crater bottoms are smooth for the same reason.

The Tharsis region on Mars has also created an odd phenomenon called perched, or pedestal, craters. These craters are
normal impact craters, but they are raised from the surrounding surface. The crater bottom is at a higher elevation than the
plain the crater lies upon. There is no cratering mechanism
that can cause this; cratering commonly creates a crater bottom that is at a lower elevation than the surroundings when

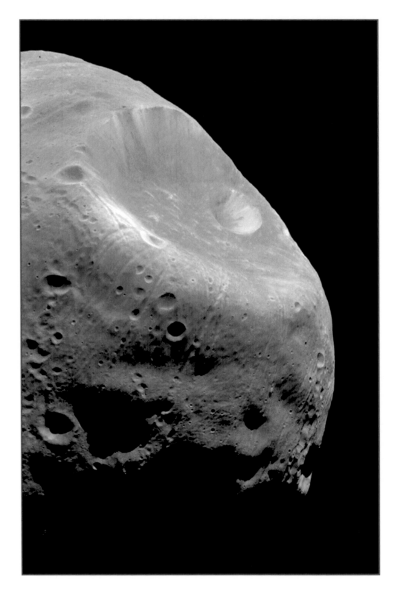

This 1998 image taken
by the Mars Global
Surveyor camera shows
Mars's moon Phobos and
its giant crater, Stickney,
with its radiating
grooves. (NASA/JPL/
MSSS)

The splash-shaped ejecta blankets from these rampart-rimmed craters are thought by some researchers to indicate that the impacts occurred in material containing water. (NASA/JPL/ Arizona State University)

the crater is excavated. The elevations of the crater bottoms have been measured and found to decrease smoothly with distance from Tharsis.

In the image at left, a rampart crater has been eroded from the base by what appears to have been flowing water, some time in Mars's distant past. Though this process could create a perched crater, the current model for perched craters calls on an immense ash fall from Tharsis that blankets all the surrounding plains with their craters. Later, the violent storms of Mars sweep over the plains and scour away all the ash and regolith from around the craters, but the crater bottoms, with their loads of ash, are relatively protected from the winds by the crater walls. The ash layers in the craters reflect the thickness of the ash fall from Tharsis and its natural decline with distance, while the plains around the craters have been scoured clean, leaving the craters perched above the new, lower plain level.

HYPERVELOCITY IMPACTS ON EARTH

The bolide that created the lunar crater Giordano Bruno is thought to have exploded with the force of 120,000 megatons of TNT (one megaton is 1 million tons, so 120,000 megatons is the same as 120,000,000,000, or 120 billion tons of TNT). The nuclear bomb that struck Hiroshima was only equivalent to 15,000 tons or 0.015 megatons of explosive, and the largest human-made explosion of all time was only 60 megatons (this was a Soviet nuclear test in

1962 on the remote Arctic island of Novaya Zemlya). For the Earth, a bolide with a radius of about 80–300 feet (25–100 m) would strike with the energy equivalent to about 15 megatons of explosive—the equivalent of a modern nuclear bomb. It would wipe out a city. A bolide with a diameter of about 600 feet to two-thirds of a mile (200 m to 1 km) would strike with the energy equivalent to 10,000 megatons of explosive, or about 5 million times that of the Hiroshima bomb. Bolides with diameters larger than about two-thirds of a mile (1 km) are the only known kind of natural disaster that can kill every living thing on Earth.

The solar system seems to contain about 2 million asteroids large enough to destroy civilization on Earth through impact, and about 1,100 of these are already in Earth-crossing orbits. The Earth's orbit passes through the orbits of about 20 million asteroids of all sizes, and as a result, the odds that the Earth will suffer a catastrophic impact in the next 100 years is about one in 5,000. The chance that an individual will be killed by a giant meteorite impact is about one in 50,000. In comparison, Americans have a one in 50,000 chance of being killed by a tornado and a one in 2 million chance of dying from botulism. Based on the known statistics of asteroid orbits and their sizes, and on the records of cratering on the Earth and Moon, it is estimated that a one-kilometer diameter bolide strikes the Earth every 800,000 years, on average (several thousand megatons equivalent of explosive on impact). A 600-foot-(200-m-) diameter object, with energy equivalent to 1,000 megatons of explosive, is estimated

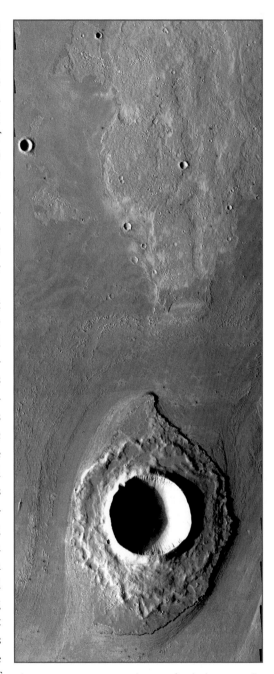

This rampart crater southwest of Athabasca Vallis has had material eroded from around its base, probably by ancient floods. (NASA/JPL/Arizona State University)

to strike the Earth every 100,000 years, and a 130-foot (40-m) object, with energy equivalent to 10 megatons, every thousand years.

In 1996, asteroid 1996 JA$_1$ came within 218,000 miles (350,000 km) of hitting the Earth, closer to the Earth than the Moon! The 300-foot (100-m) asteroid 2002 MN passed within *one-third* the distance to the Moon (75,000 miles, or 120,000 km) on June 14, 2002, and was not detected until three days after it had passed. It came from a so-called blind spot, caused by the Sun. Its approach is second only to the 30-foot (10-m) asteroid 1994 XM1, which came within 65,000 miles (105,000 km) of the Earth on December 9, 1994. Impacts by any of these bodies could have been a catastrophe.

Because there is a finite possibility that Earth will be struck by a large asteroid in our lifetimes, and because the outcome would be so catastrophic, several observatory groups are dedicated to searching for asteroids. The three largest are the California Institute of Technology and the Jet Propulsion Laboratory's Near-Earth Asteroid Tracking project (NEAT), the Massachusetts Institute of Technology and Lincoln Lab's project LINEAR, and the University of Arizona's Spacewatch. LINEAR discovered more than 50,000 minor planets by 2005, more than 10 times the number of any other team. These first-line discoverers send data on their possible new asteroids to the Minor Planet Center, in Cambridge, Massachusetts, where the initial number is assigned, and more detailed tracking ensues.

NASA's Deep Space Network antennae (DSS-14) in the desert between Los Angeles and Las Vegas accomplishes some of this more detailed tracking. DSS-14 is a white dish 24 stories high that weighs 9 million pounds (41 million kg). It was originally built in 1966 to track Mars missions, but now it spends part of its time sending radar signals toward asteroids. With a half-million watts of energy powering its radar beam, even the minute fractions that are bounced back from the asteroid are detected by the DSS-14 with enough detail to gauge the asteroid's velocity and size and sometimes even its composition and shape. Recently the National Research Council has recommended that NASA and the National Science Foundation build a giant telescope, to be called the Large Synoptic Survey Telescope, to take images of the entire sky every seven days to search for asteroids down to about 1,000 feet (300 m) in diameter. This project is scheduled to begin construction in Chile in 2010 and experience "first light," that is, the first viewed objects through the telescope, in 2015.

NASA considers a one-kilometer-diameter asteroid to be the threshold size for global disaster from an impact. In 2008, there were about 733 near-Earth asteroids (NEAs) larger than one kilometer in diameter out of the known NEA population of about 5,200. An NEA is one whose orbit crosses the Earth's orbit, but not all of these asteroids are positioned to pass near the Earth. Those that travel very close to or have a chance of colliding with the Earth are called potentially hazardous asteroids. There are about 916 known potentially hazardous asteroids of all sizes.

Computer models show that NEAs are efficiently removed from the solar system by collisions or gravitational interactions on a timescale of about 10–100 million years. Since this is so much shorter than the age of the solar system, NEAs must be continually replenished from the outer solar system or they would all have been destroyed or removed by now. They are therefore thought to be the products of collisions in the main asteroid belt or asteroids from other parts of the solar system whose unstable orbits brought them close enough to a planet to be swung inward by the planet's gravity.

The inventory of Earth-crossing asteroids larger than one kilometer in diameter is increased by about one per day, and so it is thought that the entire population of one-kilometer NEAs will be known and tracked within the next decade. Asteroids with diameters less than about 300 feet (100 m) are virtually undetectable, since they are dark objects, but they comprise the vast majority of NEAs. These asteroids would strike the Earth with the energy of a nuclear bomb, devastating the immediate area of impact and thus be devastating only if the asteroid strikes over a populated area.

Though such an asteroid would have a limited effect if it fell on land, its effect if it fell in the ocean could be far larger. A bolide falling to Earth would be most likely to fall in the ocean rather than on the land, since the oceans take up more of the surface area of the Earth than land does. A bolide 100 feet (300 m) in diameter falling into the deep ocean will instantly create a cavity in the water six miles (10 km) wide and two miles (3 km) deep. Waves will radiate away from the impact site at high velocities. In the past, some scientists have argued that these waves will all be on the wavelength of the cavity itself, that is, a couple of miles and will therefore break and fade when they strike the shallowing edge of the ocean on the continental shelf, significantly decreasing their impact on land. Newer computer modeling and theoretical calculations show, unfortunately, that water waves over a wide range of wavelengths will be created by the impact, and so tsunamis will be expected to strike all the ocean's shores. Meanwhile, the cavity blown in the ocean will collapse at supersonic speeds, smashing together and sending a plume of water beyond the *tropopause* in the atmosphere. The plume will collapse again, sending a new set of tsunamis across the oceans. This rush-in and fall-back will continue, diminishing in scale each time. Landslides are the common cause of tsunamis on Earth. The record tsunami occurred 8,000 years ago, in response to a 1,300 square mile (3,500 km^3) landslide in Norway and is thought to have reached to 65 feet (20 m) above mean sea level. Tsunamis caused by ocean impacts, however, will be larger than any created by landslides. Although the scale of water inundation on the continents cannot yet be calculated with any certainty, it is possible that a smaller impact in the oceans could be more devastating to life on Earth than a larger impact on land.

In 1997, the asteroid XF11 was predicted to have a small chance of striking the Earth in the year 2028. Though it was later determined that the calculated orbit was incorrect and the asteroid had had no chance of ever hitting the Earth, it was too late: the media had heard about the threat and a great amount of fairly hysterical press coverage followed, with headlines like "Killer Asteroid!" NASA created the Near-Earth Objects Office to handle media relations following that press nightmare. As the International Astronomical Union (IAU) states on its Web site, like all Earth-crossing asteroids, XF11 may someday hit the Earth, but this seems to be an event for the distant future. At present there is more at risk from some unknown asteroid colliding with the Earth than from XF11 or any other object already discovered. Over the coming centuries and millennia, though, the orbit of XF11 will bring it close to the Earth many times. In 2028, it may even be bright enough to be seen without telescopic aid.

One asteroid, 1950 DA, may eventually collide with Earth after 15 more near-miss passes. If it does, it will be in the year 2880. The familiar asteroid 2002 MN, which passed within one-third the distance between the Earth and Moon in the year of its discovery, also has a nonzero chance of striking the Earth on one of several orbits between the years 2070 and 2101. It is 230 feet (70 m) in diameter and would strike at about 50 feet per second (15 m/sec), creating an explosion with a similar strength to the bomb that struck Hiroshima. The likelihood of 2002 MN striking the Earth at any time in the future is now calculated at 3.3×10^{-6} to 1, in other words, highly unlikely, but possible. At the time of writing, there are about 200 NEAs that have a small but finite chance of striking the Earth at some time in the future. They are listed at the fascinating Web site http://neo.jpl.nasa.gov/risk.

The known meteorite now considered most likely to impact Earth is called 2000 SG_{344}, with a miniscule 1.8×10^{-3} probability of striking Earth after the year 2060. For a period of time after its discovery, this NEA was thought to pose a significant risk to the Earth. Image archives were searched for previously overlooked photos of 2000 SG_{344}, so that a much more accurate orbit could be calculated, and these calculations ruled out the chance of an Earth impact in that year. The closest the object can approach the Earth before 2060 will be on September 30, 2030, at 11 lunar distances from the Earth. Further in the future its orbit may pose more serious dangers.

Small asteroids are very hard to detect. On March 17, 2004, NASA announced that just two days earlier the LIN-EAR array had detected an asteroid that would make the closest approach yet of any asteroid during human observation. Detected on Monday, March 15, the 100-foot (30-m) diameter asteroid 2004 FH passed 26,500 miles (43,000 km) above the Earth on Thursday, March 18, 2004. The approach was only about three-and-a-half Earth diameters above the surface, at a height where some telecommunications and weather satellites orbit. This asteroid could be seen with binoculars. A more educated press and public hardly noticed the event, in stark comparison to the media relations nightmare NASA went through in 1997 when it wrongly predicted that XF11 might strike the Earth.

The simple probability of a strike by a given asteroid is not the whole story: A better risk assessment includes information on the size and speed of the impactor, which indicates the size of the impact itself. There are two scales used to quantify the risk of future meteorite impacts: the Palermo scale and the Torino scale. The Palermo technical impact hazard scale categorizes potential impact risks spanning a wide range of impact dates, energies, and probabilities. Palermo scale values less than −2 reflect events for which there are no likely consequences, while values between −2 and 0 indicate situations that merit careful monitoring. Higher Palermo scale values indicate greater risks. The scale compares the likelihood of the potential impact with the average risk posed by objects of the same size or larger over the years until the date of the potential impact. This average risk from random impacts is known as the background risk. For convenience, the scale is logarithmic, so, for example, a Palermo scale value of −2 indicates that the detected potential impact event is only 1 percent as likely as a random background event occurring in the intervening years; a value of zero indicates that the single event is just as threatening as the background hazard; and a value of +2 indicates an event that is 100 times more likely than a background impact by an object at least as large before the date of the potential impact in question.

The Torino scale (see table on page 75) is designed to communicate to the public the risk associated with a future Earth approach by a bolide. This scale has integer values from 0 to 10 and takes into consideration the predicted impact energy of the event as well as its likelihood of actually happening. Object 2007 VK_{184} is the only body that currently has a Torino scale rating above 0: Its rating is 1 because of a very low probability

THE TORINO SCALE OF IMPACT RISK

events having no likely consequences (white zone)	0	The likelihood of a collision is zero or well below the chance that a random object of the same size will strike the Earth within the next few decades. This designation also applies to any small object that, in the event of a collision, is unlikely to reach the Earth's surface intact
events meriting careful monitoring (green zone)	1	The chance of collision is extremely unlikely, about the same as a random object of the same size striking the Earth within the next few decades
events meriting concern (yellow zone)	2	A somewhat close but not unusual encounter. Collision is very unlikely
	3	A close encounter with 1 percent or greater chance of a collision capable of causing localized destruction
	4	A close encounter with 1 percent or greater chance of a collision capable of causing regional devastation
threatening events (orange zone)	5	A close encounter with a significant threat of a collision capable of causing regional devastation
	6	A close encounter with a significant threat of a collision capable of causing global catastrophe
	7	A close encounter with an extremely significant threat of a collision capable of causing a global catastrophe
certain collisions (red zone)	8	A collision capable of causing localized destruction. Such events occur somewhere on Earth between once per 50 years and once per 1,000 years
	9	A collision capable of causing regional devastation. Such events occur between once per 1,000 years and once per 100,000 years.
	10	A collision capable of causing global climatic catastrophe. Such events occur once per 100,000 years or less often.

This description of the Torino scale is provided by the Jet Propulsion Laboratory at the California Institute of Technology.

of impact after the year 2048. The body has a Palermo scale rating of −1.82.

Though the possibility of a catastrophic impact on Earth is remote, the effects of such an impact are potentially so severe that all the time and effort put into tracking asteroid orbits is well invested. Here, then, is another effect of the development of technology: Because better and better telescopes have been made, a new threat has been detected (nearby asteroids) and a new field of science (near-Earth-object tracking and investigation) developed.

Asteroids and Meteorites

3

With the advancement of telescopes and other instruments, thousands of asteroids have been detected and their orbits described. In recent years, some information about their compositions has been obtained through both remote sensing and space missions to asteroids. Asteroid compositions are now known to vary with distance from the Sun, moving to higher ice contents with distance from the Sun. At the same time, scientists and adventurers are combing the Earth for meteorites, and so the database of meteorite compositions is constantly growing. Meteorites can be divided into groups according to how much processing they experienced in the early solar system: Some are clearly parts of planetesimals that formed iron *cores* and then were broken apart in catastrophic collisions, while others appear to be pieces of the primordial matter from which the solar system formed. In this chapter, the classifications of the asteroids and meteorites are described, along with some fascinating evidence that the parent bodies of some meteorites have been identified, still orbiting the Sun, minus the small pieces that fell to Earth and were found by humans.

The first orbiting asteroid was discovered in 1801; more discoveries quickly followed. The largest object in the main asteroid belt between Mars and Jupiter is the dwarf planet Ceres, at ~590 miles in diameter (960 km). The second largest is 2 Pallas, at 350 miles in diameter (570 km), and the third is 4 Vesta, at 326 miles (525 km). Though Vesta is not the largest asteroid, it is the brightest (reflecting 38 percent of incident light), and it is the only asteroid that can be seen with the naked eye from Earth.

The numbering of asteroids refers to the order of their discovery, which was roughly in the order of their size because larger asteroids are normally easier to see in a telescope. The asteroid belt appears to have evolved from perhaps 50 large planetesimals that accreted until they were in the range of several hundred miles in diameter. The large number of big bodies means that they were more vulnerable to mutual collisions and have all broken up. There are 33 known asteroids that are larger than 120 miles (200 km) in diameter, and there are about 1,200 in the main belt alone that are larger than 19 miles (30 km). Even the largest body in the asteroid belt, 1 Ceres, has a radius of only about one-third of the Moon's.

Asteroids orbit the Sun and rotate on their axes, just as planets do, although asteroids may tumble rather than rotate. Those that rotate on a consistent axis have day lengths (periods) from three hours to several Earth days. The average is nine hours, which is about 1 Ceres's rate. On opposite ends of the rotation spectrum, Mathilde rotates in 17 days and Florentina in three hours. The rotation rate of asteroids is usually determined by taking measurements of their brightness over time and creating a plot called a light curve that shows brightness over time. The brightness of a nonspherical asteroid varies according to the size of the area facing the viewer, so the curves of brightness correspond to rotation. The period of an asteroid's rotation depends upon its size and its history of collisions, as well as gravitational interaction with other bodies.

Recent images have shown that asteroids are often not solid blocks of rock. Those asteroids that are single, intact blocks of rock are now called monoliths. Those that have enough cracks to reduce their tensile strength (the maximum amount of force that the body can withstand before breaking) are called fractured bodies if their original structure is mainly intact and shattered bodies if their original structure has been disrupted by breakage. Bodies that have been completely shattered and reassembled are called *rubble piles* (a term actually used in scientific papers). Rubble piles are loosely held together by self-gravity. As the ability to take high-resolution images of asteroids has increased, it has become apparent that a large fraction of asteroids fall under these latter categories and that in fact many asteroids have their own attendant swarms of smaller asteroids, forming disaggregated rubble piles.

Because they are the broken fragments of larger bodies, asteroids can come in many shapes. One famous example obtained from a radar image is 216 Kleopatra, which can be seen clearly as a tumbling body shaped uncannily like a dog bone. Kleopatra is about 135 miles (217 km) long and about 58 miles (94 km) wide, or about the size of New Jersey. It is one of several dozen asteroids whose coloring suggests metallic content. A team of astronomers observing Kleopatra used the 1,000-foot (305-m) telescope of the Arecibo Observatory in Puerto Rico to bounce radio signals off Kleopatra. Using computer analysis techniques, they transformed the radar echoes into images and produced a computer model of the asteroid's shape. The images were obtained when Kleopatra was about 106 million miles (171 million km) from Earth, but this model is still accurate to within about nine miles (15 km).

WHERE DO ASTEROIDS ORBIT?
Asteroids in the Inner Solar System

The inner solar system is a crowded place, filled with gravitational interactions between the planets and the Sun. Asteroids traveling through the inner solar system are seldom in stable orbits because they are constantly being deflected by the gravitational fields of planets. Asteroids in unstable orbits will not trace the same path over and over again but will experience gradual deflections that cause their orbits to wander, until they experience a larger gravitational pull and impact a planet, fall into the Sun, or, less likely, are expelled into the outer solar system. In addition, all small bodies in the solar system, except those locked into special stable orbits, slowly spiral toward the Sun under the influence of a force called the Poynting-Robertson effect. This is caused by reflecting and reradiating solar radiation, which slows the body by tiny, tiny amounts, gradually causing its orbit to decay to be closer to the Sun.

With so many effects making orbits unstable, most asteroids in the inner solar system have only a limited life span here. Over time, some small bodies are added to the inner solar system from the outer solar system, but many more are lost into the Sun, impact planets, or are flung into the outer solar system. The population of small bodies in the inner solar system might be expected to be much smaller so long after the solar system began, except that there are specific regions where their orbits are stable. The two major ways that asteroids can safely orbit near planets are through *resonance* of orbits, and by orbiting at Lagrange points.

Orbital periods can differ from each other by an integer multiple. For example, the period of one orbit is two years and the other six, differing by a multiple of three; this means that every three years the two bodies will have a close encounter. Even asteroidal orbits that differ by an integral multiple from the orbit of the large planet are usually cleared of asteroids by the gravitational field of the large planet. However, some special integral multiples of orbits actually stabilize the orbits of the asteroids, maintaining them in place indefinitely. These stabilizing multiples are called resonances, and the unstable multiples eventually are depopulated of asteroids, creating gaps.

The Jupiter system has good examples of both resonances and gaps. One group of Jovian asteroids, the Trojans, are at 1:1 (meaning that their orbit and Jupiter's are the same). Another group, the Hildas, are at 3:2 (meaning that they orbit the Sun three times for every two Jupiter orbits), and the asteroid Thule orbits at 4:3. There are gaps at 1:2, 2:3, 1:3, 3:1, 5:2, 7:3, 2:1, and 5:3. Gaps in the asteroid belt that are cleared out by gravitational interactions with Jupiter have the special name of "Kirkwood gaps" because they were first observed in 1886 by Daniel Kirkwood, a professor of mathematics at Indiana University.

The second type of stable orbit is named for its discoverer, Joseph-Louis Lagrange, a famous French mathematician who lived in the late 18th and early 19th centuries. He calculated that there are five positions in an orbiting system of two large bodies in which a third small body, or collection of small bodies, can exist without being thrown out of orbit by gravitational forces. More precisely, the Lagrange points mark positions where the gravitational pull of the two large bodies precisely equals the centripetal force required to rotate with them. In the solar system, the two large bodies are the Sun and a planet, and the smaller body or group of bodies, asteroids.

Of the five Lagrange points, three are unstable over long periods, and two are permanently stable. The unstable Lagrange points, L1, L2 and L3, lie along the line connecting the two large masses. The stable Lagrange points, L4 and L5, lie in the orbit of the planet, 60 degrees ahead and 60 degrees behind the planet itself (see figure on page 98).

The L4 and L5 points are stable orbits so long as the mass ratio between the two large masses exceeds 24.96. This is the case for the Jupiter-Sun, Earth-Sun, and Earth-Moon systems and for many other pairs of bodies in the solar system. Objects found orbiting at the L4 and L5 points are often called Trojans after the three large asteroids Agamemnon, Achilles, and Hektor that orbit in the L4 and L5 points of the Jupiter-Sun system. (According to Homer, a Greek historian and writer from the eighth or ninth century B.C.E., Hektor was the Trojan champion slain by Achilles during King Agamemnon's siege of Troy.)

There are hundreds of Trojan-type asteroids in the solar system. Most orbit with Jupiter, but others orbit with Mars. The first Trojan-type asteroids for Mars were discovered in 1990 and named 5261 Eureka. Saturn has co-orbital asteroids as well, and Uranus is suspected to have its own Trojans. Neptune has recently discovered Trojans, including 2001 QR$_{322}$, which is in a particularly stable and long-lived orbit. No large asteroids have been found at the Trojan points of the Earth-Moon or Earth-Sun systems. However, in 1956, the Polish astronomer Kazimierz Kordylewski discovered dense concentrations of dust at the Trojan points of the Earth-Moon system.

There are at least two regions of resonance in the inner solar system where, theoretically, long-lived stable belts of asteroids can orbit the Sun without being disrupted by the gravitational pulls of planets. One theoretical belt lies between the Sun and Mercury and is named Vulcan, after the mythical planet once thought to orbit there. This region is theoretically stable for asteroids, but none have yet been found. The Vulcanoid region extends from 0.09 to 0.20 astronomical units (AU), with gaps at 0.15 and 0.18 AU that correspond to destabilizing resonances with Mercury and Venus. Here debris left over from the solar nebula may still orbit, perhaps along with material knocked off Mercury by large impacts. N. Wyn Evans and Serge Tabachik, researchers at Oxford University, have estimated that the largest Vulcanoids likely orbit between 0.16 and 0.18 AU, and they recommend sky searches in that area to locate larger asteroids. Other scientists are searching for Vulcanoids by scanning photos taken by fighter planes at high altitudes at dusk and dawn. Discovery of Vulcanoids may need to wait for the MESSENGER mission to Mercury, launched in 2004 and flying by and orbiting Mercury between 2008 and 2012. There also may be stable orbits between the Earth and Mars (at least one scientist has suggested that, according to physical calculations, a planet should have formed there).

Most of the asteroids that potentially threaten the safety of Earth are in unstable orbits and are classified according to their distance from the Sun. Those that have orbits crossing the orbits of other planets, particularly the Earth, are of special interest. These asteroids have the highest probability of creating a catastrophic impact, should the planet and the asteroid both happen to be at that crossing point in their orbits at the same time.

While the characteristics of an ellipse drawn on a sheet of paper can be measured by hand (see the sidebar "Describing Orbits" on page 83), orbits in space are more difficult to characterize. The ellipse itself has to be described, and then the ellipse's position in space, and then the motion of the body as

(continues on page 86)

DESCRIBING ORBITS

All orbits are ellipses, not circles. An ellipse can be thought of simply as a squashed circle, resembling an oval. The proper definition of an ellipse is the set of all points that have the same sum of distances to two given fixed points, called foci. To demonstrate this definition, take two pins, push them into a piece of stiff cardboard, and loop a string around the pins (see figure below). The two pins are the foci of the ellipse. Pull the string away from the pins with a pencil and draw the ellipse, keeping the string taut around the pins and the pencil all the way around. Adding the distance along the two string segments from the pencil to each of the pins will give the same answer each time: The ellipse is the set of all points that have the same sum of distances from the two foci.

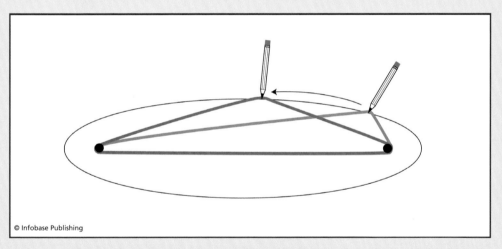

© Infobase Publishing

Making an ellipse with string and two pins: Adding the distance along the two string segments from the pencil to each of the pins will give the same sum at every point around the ellipse. This method creates an ellipse with the pins at its foci.

The mathematical equation for an ellipse is

$$\frac{x^2}{a^2} + \frac{x^2}{b^2} + 1,$$

(continues)

(continued)

where x and y are the coordinates of all the points on the ellipse, and a and b are the semimajor and semiminor axes, respectively. The semimajor axis and semiminor axis would both be the radius if the shape were a circle, but two are needed for an ellipse. If a and b are equal, then the equation for the ellipse becomes the equation for a circle:

$$x^2 + y^2 = n,$$

where n is any constant.

When drawing an ellipse with string and pins, it is obvious where the foci are (they are the pins). In the abstract, the foci can be calculated according to the following equations:

Coordinates of the first focus

$$= (\sqrt{a^2 - b^2}, 0)$$

Coordinates of the second focus

$$= (- \sqrt{a^2 - b^2}, 0)$$

In the case of an orbit, the object being orbited (for example, the Sun) is located at one of the foci (see figure below).

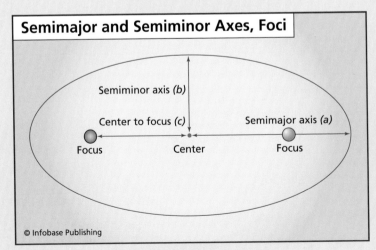

Semimajor and Semiminor Axes, Foci

Semiminor axis *(b)*

Center to focus *(c)*

Semimajor axis *(a)*

Focus

Center

Focus

© Infobase Publishing

The semimajor and semiminor axes of an ellipse (or an orbit) are the elements used to calculate its eccentricity, and the body being orbited always lies at one of the foci.

An important characteristic of an ellipse—perhaps the most important for orbital physics—is its eccentricity, a measure of how different the semimajor and semiminor axes of the ellipse are. Eccentricity is dimensionless and ranges from 0 to 1, where an eccentricity of zero means that the figure is a circle, and an eccentricity of 1 means that the ellipse has gone to its other extreme, a parabola (the reason an extreme ellipse becomes a parabola results from its definition as a conic section). One equation for eccentricity is

$$e = \sqrt{1 - \frac{b^2}{a^2}},$$

where a and b are the semimajor and semiminor axes, respectively. Another equation for eccentricity is

$$e = \frac{c}{a},$$

where c is the distance between the center of the ellipse and one focus. The eccentricities of the orbits of the planets vary widely, though most are very close to circles, as shown in the figure here. Pluto has the most eccentric orbit at 0.244, and Mercury's orbit is also very eccentric, but the rest have eccentricities below 0.09.

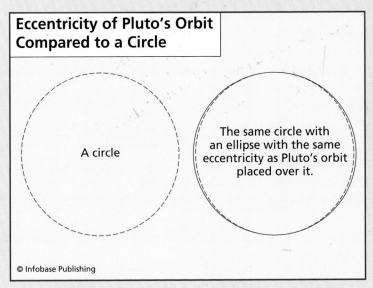

Eccentricity of Pluto's Orbit Compared to a Circle

A circle

The same circle with an ellipse with the same eccentricity as Pluto's orbit placed over it.

© Infobase Publishing

Though the orbits of planets are measurably eccentric, they deviate from circularity by very little. This figure shows the eccentricity of Pluto's orbit in comparison with a circle.

(continued from page 82)
it travels around the ellipse. The shape of the ellipse and its relation to the Sun help determine the seasons, though the tilt of the planet on its axis is the most important determinant of seasons.

Inner Planet—Crossing Asteroids: The Aten, Amor, and Apollo Families

Aten asteroids have orbital periods of less than one year and orbits that average less than 1 AU and therefore may overlap the Earth's orbit. The original Aten asteroid, 2062 Aten, with a diameter of 0.56 miles (0.9 km), was discovered in 1976 by Eleanor Francis Helin, a researcher at the Jet Propulsion Laboratory. 2062 Aten has an orbit slightly smaller than Earth's but more eccentric, and its orbit crosses Earth's orbit. There are now about 516 known asteroids that have an orbital period of less than one year and average less than 1 AU from the Sun. These are all called Aten asteroids.

Apollo asteroids have orbits that overlap the Earth's orbit, as Aten asteroids do, but Apollo asteroids have periods longer than one year. More than 3,133 Apollo asteroids are known. The largest Apollo asteroid is 1685 Toro, with a diameter of about 7.5 miles (12 km). There are about 13 Apollo asteroids with diameters larger than three miles (5 km). One curious Apollo asteroid also shows characteristics of a comet: Asteroid 4015 Wilson-Harrington was discovered on November 15, 1979, by Eleanor F. Helin at the Palomar Observatory. This asteroid was later discovered to be the same object as a short-period comet discovered by Albert Wilson and Robert Harrington, also at the Palomar Observatory. When Wilson and Harrington observed it, it had a cometlike tail, but when Helin observed it, it was gasless. 4015 Wilson-Harrington is one of the enigmatic asteroids that has a gassy coma when at perihelion and therefore bridges the gap between asteroids and comets. It has an orbital period of four years, 107 days and is about 1.5 miles (2.5 km) in diameter. (There are now five objects classified as both asteroids and comets.)

Amor asteroids, the third class of asteroids that most endanger the Earth, orbit near but outside the Earth's orbit. Amor asteroids all have perihelia between 1.0 and 1.3 AU and are named after 1221 Amor, the first such discovered. There are more than 1,648 known Amor asteroids. Amors often cross the orbit of Mars, but they do not cross the orbit of Earth. The two moons of Mars, Deimos and Phobos, appear to be Amor asteroids that were captured by Mars's gravity field. Deimos has a strange, shiny surface, but Phobos, the larger of Mars's moons, appears to be very similar to other Amor asteroids.

433 Eros, another Amor asteroid, is one of the most elongated asteroids known, with estimated dimensions of 20.5 × eight × eight miles (33 × 13 × 13 km). Eros is one of only three NEAs a diameter above six miles (10 km). It orbits the Sun in 1.76 years at an inclination of 10.8 degrees to the ecliptic. Its orbit carries it close to the Earth, with a perihelion distance of 1.13 AU; its *aphelion* (farthest distance from the Sun) is 1.78 AU. The closest approach of Eros to Earth in the 20th century

NEAR Shoemaker *settles into the orbit shown and then landed on asteroid Eros in 2001.* (NASA/JPL/JHUAPL)

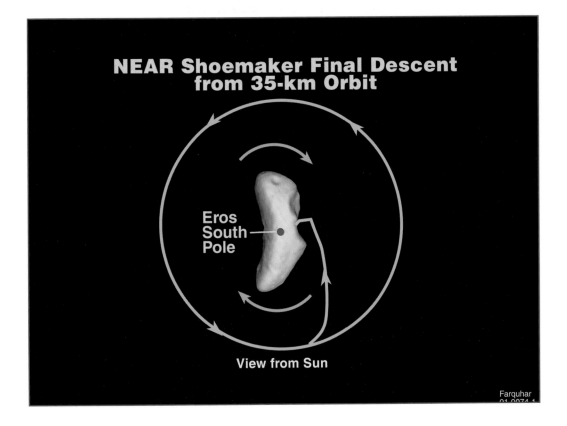

NEAR Shoemaker Final Descent from 35-km Orbit

Eros South Pole

View from Sun

Farquhar

was on January 23, 1975, at approximately 0.15 AU. Previous close approaches occurred in 1901 and in 1931. Because of its repeated close encounters with Earth, Eros has been an important object historically for refining calculations of the mass of the Earth-Moon system and the value of the AU. The asteroid rotates in 5.27 hours and has an albedo of 0.16, bright among asteroids. Eros is thought to be compositionally varied: One side appears from spectrographic inspection to have a higher pyroxene mineral content and the other a higher *olivine* mineral content.

Because of Eros's close approaches to Earth and its interesting surface appearance it has been the subject of a space mission culminating with an actual spacecraft landing. The NEAR Shoemaker mission craft orbited the asteroid and then touched down on February 12, 2001.

Far from being a bare rock, this asteroid has its own regolith, the rocks and dust that form the "soil" on rocky celestial bodies. The crater shown in the figure on page 90, Psyche, is the largest on Eros. A large boulder perched on the crater wall illustrates Eros's unusual gravity: Because of its elongated shape the regions with lowest gravity on Eros are not necessarily in the bottoms of craters. The boulder appears to rest on the sloping wall of the crater instead of rolling down to the floor. These and the other NEAR Shoemaker mission craft photos were groundbreaking in the understanding of asteroids; these missions have provided data detailed enough to create an image of what standing on the asteroid might be like. Daytime temperature is about 212°F (100°C), the boiling point of water on Earth, while at night the temperature falls to −238°F (−150°C). Gravity on tiny Eros is of course weak: A 100-pound (45-kg) object on Earth would weigh about an ounce on Eros.

The largest asteroid that is a potential Earth hazard is 4179 Toutatis. This asteroid is nearly one mile (1.6 km) long. Its orbit makes it particularly dangerous, since it lies almost perfectly in the same plane as the Earth's, inclined from it by less than a half degree. No other hazardous asteroid larger than 0.6 mile (1 km) has been found that moves around the Sun in an orbit so nearly coplanar with Earth's. The more coplanar

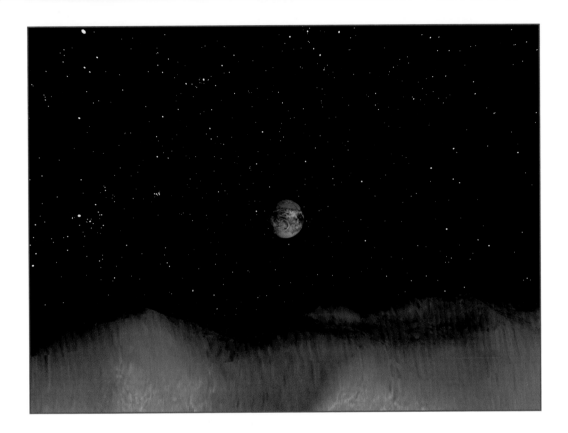

the orbits, the more likely a collision. Toutatis's orbit extends from just inside Earth's orbit to a point deep within the main asteroid belt. On September 29, 2004, Toutatis passed within just four times the distance from Earth to the Moon. For a previous close approach, a computer-generated image was made of the Earth as it would appear from Toutatis, demonstrating graphically how close the objects come.

A meteorite a half mile (1 km) in diameter striking the Earth at 13 miles per second (21 km/sec), near the slower end of the possible range of meteorite velocities, will create a crater with a diameter of about 15 miles (25 km). The estimated population of asteroids with diameters larger than one kilometer in Earth-crossing orbits leads to an estimate of impact likelihood on the Earth of about three impacts per million years. Mercury has fewer asteroid impacts than the Earth but more cometary impacts. Impacts are also harder on Mercury

The Earth appears near and large as seen from the asteroid Toutatis, in this computer-generated image. (NASA/JPL)

Crater Psyche, photographed from a range of 62 miles (100 km), is 433 Eros's largest crater. (NASA/JPL/ JHUAPL)

because objects are moving faster as they near the Sun. Mars is being struck by a population of asteroids whose orbits do not cross the Earth's, so Martian cratering and Earth's are not as closely related as Earth's and Mercury's.

Another family of main belt asteroids is called the "shallow Mars-crossers." There are about 20,000 of these bodies. They are probably pieces left over from planetary *accretion* (the accumulation of smaller bodies into a larger body) of Mars, and they have a 50:50 chance, over the age of the solar system, of either hitting Mars or being thrown out of the solar system.

Most of the near-Earth asteroids are in orbits that are unstable over the long term. In the section "Asteroids in the Inner Solar System," on page 79, two simple examples of stable orbits are described, but there are other, far more complex possibilities. Recently Paul Wiegert at the University of Western Ontario and his colleagues Kim Innanen and Seppo Mikkola have shown that four asteroids share the Earth's orbit in a most strange resonance. The asteroids 3753 Cruithne, 1998 UP1, 2000 PH5, and 2002 AA29 share the Earth's orbit while orbiting, not in an ellipse, but in a horseshoe pattern. The simplest version of this kind of orbit involves the asteroids switching from just inside to just outside the Earth's orbit whenever they come near, so that the asteroids never pass the Earth. The asteroids fall just outside the Earth's orbit and slow down, but just before the Earth overtakes them, they swing across the

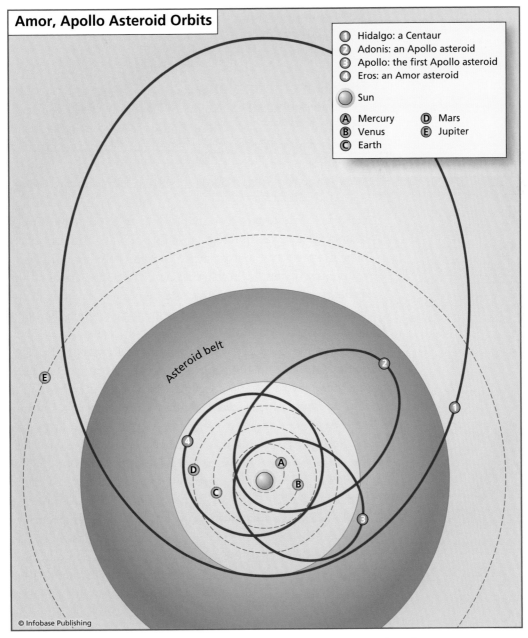

Amor, Apollo Asteroid Orbits

1. Hidalgo: a Centaur
2. Adonis: an Apollo asteroid
3. Apollo: the first Apollo asteroid
4. Eros: an Amor asteroid

Sun

A. Mercury   D. Mars
B. Venus   E. Jupiter
C. Earth

Asteroid belt

© Infobase Publishing

Amor, Aten, and Apollo asteroids have orbits that approach or cross Earth's orbit.

Earth's orbit, drawn by its gravity and the Sun's, into an orbit closer to the Sun. In this closer orbit, they speed up, but just before they lap the Earth on the inside, they are drawn behind the Earth across its orbit into an orbit outside the Earth, and they slow down again. In this way, they never collide with the Earth and, in fact, never pass the Earth. The asteroids follow a similar horseshoe pattern, but they constantly spiral around the Earth's orbit as they go.

The Main Asteroid Belt

Asteroids are usually thought of as coming from the main asteroid belt, the collection of celestial bodies with orbits lying between Mars and Jupiter. About 95 percent of asteroids reside in this main belt, which stretches from 1.7 to 4 AU from the Sun. Based on modern studies using infrared imaging, there seem to be between 1.1 million and 1.9 million main belt asteroids larger than a half mile (about 1 km) in diameter. Many millions or perhaps billions of smaller asteroids also orbit in the main belt. Though there are millions of individual bodies in the asteroid belt, the total mass of all the asteroids is less than one 10th of a percent of the mass of the Earth and was probably only a few times that when the asteroid belt was new. If all the bodies now in the asteroid belt were accumulated into one planetesimal, it would be only about 900 miles (1,400 km) in diameter, much smaller than the Moon.

Johannes Kepler, the prominent 17th-century German mathematician and astronomer, first noticed the large gap between Mars and Jupiter where the main belt resides, but the development of the telescope was required before the first bodies in this gap were discovered. Though it was thought that a planet had formed in the gap and was subsequently destroyed, it is now clear that Jupiter's disrupting gravity field is so strong that no planet could ever have formed in that orbit. The material of the asteroid belt must have formed near its current location in the solar nebula because its combination of rocky and metallic materials is consistent with an inner solar system origin. Some material from the asteroid belt (notably, the carbonaceous *chondrites,* discussed later) has clearly never been heated above 70°F (20°C) or so and therefore must never have been very close to the Sun.

Though some asteroids in the main belt seem to contain water (see the sidebar "Spectrophotometry and Mineral Absorption Bands" on page 157), others appear completely dry. Inside 2.5 AU from the Sun, all objects are dry. This distance, 2.5 AU, is sometimes called the "snow line." Inside 2.5 AU, temperatures in the solar nebula are too high to allow ices to condense. (The ice condensation temperature is reached at just about 2.5 AU.) Not coincidentally, the snow line also marks the boundary between the inner, rocky planets and the outer planets that are rich in ice and gas.

All asteroids orbiting between 1.7 and 4 AU are considered to be in the main belt, but asteroids are not distributed evenly over the width of the belt. Some regions of the belt have distinct populations with similar properties that are thought to be fragments of a common large parent body. Main belt families include the Hungaria, Flora, Cybele, and Hilda families (described below), as well as the Phocaea, Koronis, Eos, and Themis families. Studying these families gives scientists a chance to gather statistics on impact, collision, and disruption rates in the solar system. This information is the closest thing to knowing what happened in early asteroid history, when the larger, original bodies of the main belt were colliding and breaking up. By studying families, scientists can calibrate their models for how a body breaks up when it experiences a catastrophic collision.

Mars orbits at 1.52 AU. Shortly beyond Mars lies the Hungaria group, the innermost group of asteroids in the main belt. The Hungarias orbit between 1.78 and 2.0 AU, in orbits with eccentricities below about 0.2. The Flora family orbits from 2.1 to 2.3 AU, with eccentricities up to 0.9 and orbital inclinations up to 11°; beyond the Flora family lies the bulk of the main belt, between 2.3 and 3.25 AU. (In general the eccentricities of the orbits go down with distance from the Sun.)

Gaspra is a Flora-family asteroid with a cratered body about 10 miles (17 km) long. In the image above, Gaspra (right) is shown with Ida (left), a main belt asteroid in the Koronis family (discussed below). Shown at the same scale, both

The main belt asteroids Gaspra (right) and Ida (left) show craters and a regolith layer on their surfaces. (NASA/JPL/USGS)

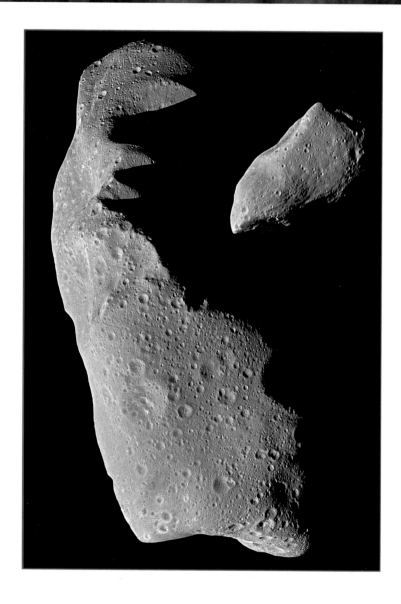

objects are irregular in shape, suggesting that they are pieces derived from larger bodies by catastrophic collisions. Craters are more abundant on Ida, suggesting that it formed earlier than Gaspra. Both asteroids have linear depressions more than a thousand feet wide in places and a hundred feet or so deep, which may be where loose soil has partly fallen into fractures. These asteroids show evidence of having such a fragmental layer, which on Ida may be 165–330 feet (50–100 m) in depth.

The Koronis family orbits within the main belt. More than 200 asteroids are now identified as members of the Koronis family, orbiting at about 3 AU. 243 Ida, an asteroid famous for having its own orbiting moonlet, Dactyl, is a Koronis family member. Dactyl is the first confirmed and photographed natural satellite of an asteroid. The tiny moon is about 0.75 × 0.87 × 1 mile (1.2 × 1.4 × 1.6 km) across. Its name is derived from the Dactyli, a group of mythological beings who lived on Mount Ida. The Dactyli protected the infant Zeus after the nymph Ida hid and raised the god on the mountain.

The first full picture showing both asteroid 243 Ida and Dactyl, newly discovered at the time, is shown in the image below. The *Galileo* spacecraft took this image from a range of 6,755 miles (10,870 km). The moon is not identical in spectral properties to any area of Ida, though its overall similarity in reflectance and general spectral type suggests that it is made of the same basic rock types.

Ida itself is an irregular Type-S asteroid, with dimensions of 35 ×15 × 13 miles (56 × 24 × 21 km). Dactyl's orbit allowed scientists to calculate Ida's mass, since given the dimensions of each of the objects and their orbital period and distance the density can be calculated.

After 3.25 AU there is a distinct gap before reaching the Cybele family of asteroids at 3.3 AU. The Cybele-family

243 Ida is an irregularly shaped main belt asteroid that was the first asteroid confirmed to have its own moonlet. The tiny moonlet Dactyl is only about one mile (1.6 km) in its longest dimension. (NASA/JPL/Galileo)

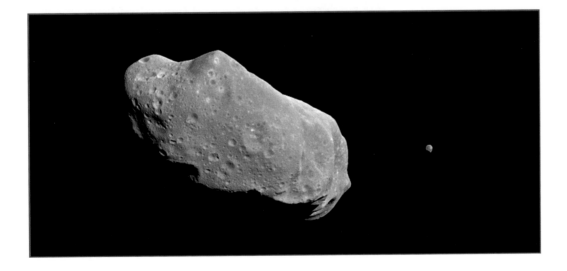

Distribution of Asteroids in the Main Belt

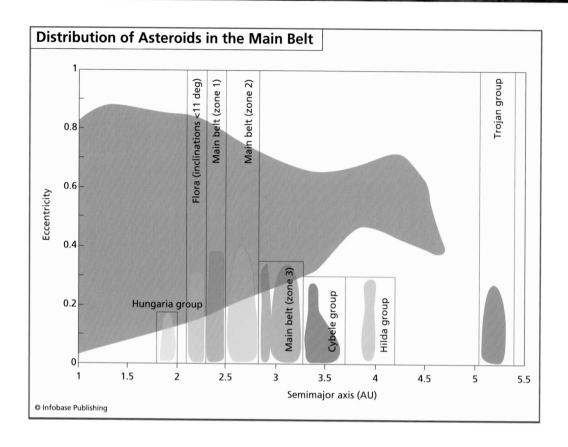

© Infobase Publishing

Asteroids in the main belt are divided into a series of families that may have originated as large bodies, later fragmented through impacts.

asteroids orbit between 3.3 and 3.5 AU. Like the Hungarias before them and the Hilda family after them, the Cybele asteroids have relatively low orbital eccentricities, below 0.3. The Cybeles appear to have formed from a large, common parent body that was broken up in the distant past. This family is named after 65 Cybele, the seventh-largest known asteroid, with a diameter of 192 miles (308 km). Another especially interesting Cybele-family asteroid is 121 Hermione. This asteroid was discovered by James C. Watson at Ann Arbor in 1872 and has a diameter of about 130 miles (209 km). 121 Hermione is notable because it has its own tiny moon, like the asteroid Ida and its tiny moon Dactyl. Hermione's tiny moon is about eight miles (13 km) in diameter and was discovered by William Merline at the Southwest Research Institute and his colleagues in 2002 using the Keck II 10-meter telescope.

The Hilda family asteroids are in the outermost part of the main belt and have orbits protected by a resonance with Jupiter: They orbit at 3.9 to 4.2 AU from the Sun, with an orbital period of eight years. This places them at a 3:2 resonance with Jupiter. Beyond the Hilda family there is a gap from 4.2 to 5.05 AU with very few asteroids, and then come the orbits of the Trojan-family asteroids, which share their orbit with Jupiter.

Asteroids in the Outer Solar System
Jupiter- and Saturn-Family Asteroids

Though Jupiter and Saturn have immense gravity fields, there are safe, stable orbits near them for small bodies. As described above, asteroids can survive if their orbits are inside the giant planets' and in certain integer multiples of the large planets' periods. A second safe set of orbits lie in the same orbit as the giant planets, but 60° ahead of or behind the planets. These stable points are called Lagrange points (see figure on page 98), and these orbits hold the majority of the stable Jupiter- and Saturn-family asteroids. There are also as many as 13,000 unstable Jupiter-crossing asteroids. These bodies can have orbital inclinations up to 90° and very eccentric orbits. They are good candidates for disruption into the inner solar system.

The asteroids that orbit in the Lagrange points of Jupiter are called Trojan asteroids. Asteroid 624 Hektor orbits 60° ahead of Jupiter and was the first Trojan asteroid to be discovered, in 1907. 624 Hektor is 186 by 93 miles (300 by 150 km), the largest of all the Trojans. There are about 1,200 Trojan asteroids now known. These asteroids are named after the Greek besiegers of Troy in the Trojan War and for the Trojan opponents. As these asteroids are discovered, they are named for the men in the battles: Those at the Lagrange point L4 are all meant to be named after Greeks, and those at L5 after Trojans. Unfortunately a few errors have been made, placing people on the wrong side of the battle, and some astronomers affectionately refer to these misnamed asteroids as spies. 617 Patroclus, for example, named after a prominent Greek hero, is in the L5 Trojan Lagrange point.

There are five positions, called Lagrange points, relative to Jupiter in which small bodies can orbit stably. Jupiter's Lagrange points L4 and L5 hold collections of asteroids called the Trojans.

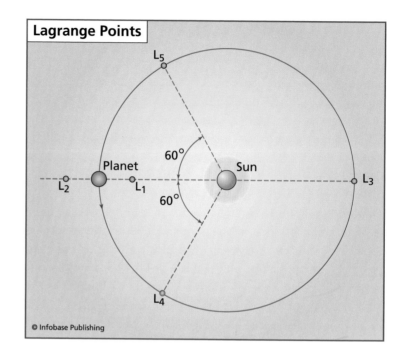

Because of the Sun's immense gravity, planets are almost never hit by objects that orbit closer to the Sun than they do. Jupiter is mostly struck by extinct comets, Jupiter-family comets, and by long-period comets. It is not a surprise that the one object witnessed striking Jupiter was a comet. Saturn is also struck by members of these families but more often by Saturn-family comets.

Centaurs: Near Jupiter and Saturn

A population of small bodies called Centaurs orbit in the outer solar system. Centaurs' orbits approach or cross the orbits of Jupiter and Saturn but also carry them beyond these planets. Many of the Centaurs are thought to be objects that have migrated in from the Kuiper belt, the population of bodies that orbit with and beyond Pluto. These planet-crossing orbits are unstable and will not persist forever without being perturbed. Their orbits will further degrade until they collide with a gas giant planet, are drawn into the inner solar system, or, less likely, are flung back into a more distant orbit. The Centaurs identified to date are large bodies, probably more because of the high visibility of large objects than because there are few small Centaurs.

Charles Kowal, now at the Space Telescope Science Institute, discovered the first Centaur, 2060 Chiron, in 1977. 2060 Chiron has an orbit that crosses Saturn's and Uranus's orbits and is considered unstable or chaotic. Its perihelion is inside Saturn, at about 8.5 AU, and its aphelion is near Uranus, at about 18.9 AU. It has a radius of about 50 miles (85 km). This enigmatic minor planet has a gassy coma when near its perihelion, and since its coma was observed, Chiron is officially now both an asteroid and a comet under the designation 95P/Chiron.

Other Centaurs include 944 Hidalgo, which crosses the orbits of both Jupiter and Saturn. It is probably an extinct comet, judging from its orbit. Its perihelion is inside Mars, at about 2.0 AU, and its aphelion is near Uranus, at 9.7 AU. Hidalgo is not the only Centaur with a highly eccentric orbit: 5335 Damocles' orbit ranges from near Mars to beyond Uranus, and 5145 Pholus orbits from Saturn to past Neptune.

Trans-Neptunian Objects

Trans-Neptunian objects, orbiting beyond Neptune, are a class of objects that was discovered in 1992. This category includes all small bodies orbiting beyond Neptune, at 30 AU, including isolated asteroids as well as those in the Kuiper belt. The Kuiper belt is a large collection of bodies that orbit between 30 and 49 AU. Since 1993, more than 700 trans-Neptunian objects have been found, and new objects in this class are being found at the rate of about 10 per month.

Short-period comets are thought to originate in the Kuiper belt, though only one trans-Neptunian object has been found that displays a spectrum indicating the presence of water. Most of the objects probably consist of rocky material and ices other than water. Their varying colors indicate that their compositions vary. Judging from luminosity, the total mass of these objects may be about 20 percent of Earth's mass. Though this is a small mass by solar system standards, it is still about a hundred times the mass of the main asteroid belt.

The orbits of objects outside the Kuiper belt are variable, with some displaying resonance with the nearby planets and others being scattered. Numerical modeling of orbits and masses also indicates that some trans-Neptunian objects may be perturbed into orbits that place them between Jupiter and Neptune, where they would be classified as Centaurs. They can be further perturbed by the gravity fields of passing planets to become Jupiter-family short-period comets. Thus, trans-Neptunian objects are thought to be the source of some short-period comets.

Pluto and its moon Charon reside in the Kuiper belt. Until 2006, Pluto was officially the ninth planet, but change was in the air: In 2005 a team of scientists found a Kuiper belt object larger than Pluto. This object, Eris, is about 5 percent larger than Pluto. Immediately the question was raised, is Eris a new planet? Or in fact, is Pluto not a planet? The decision was made by the International Astronomical Union (IAU) to demote Pluto to the status of a dwarf planet and reduce our official number of planets to eight. (See the sidebar "How the Discovery of Eris Caused Pluto to Lose Its Status as a Planet.")

There are thought to be thousands of bodies in the Kuiper belt with diameters of at least 600 miles (1,000 km), 70,000 objects with diameters larger than 60 miles (100 km), and at least 450,000 bodies with diameters larger than 30 miles (50 km). The orbits of these bodies were first thought to merge into those of the Oort cloud, the immense cloud of comets that forms the outer solar system (described below), but better observations show there is a clear outer edge to the Kuiper belt and a gap of about 11 AU before the Oort cloud begins. The Kuiper belt thus forms a contained population.

In 1992, David Jewitt at the Institute for Astronomy in Honolulu found the first Kuiper body after Pluto by using the Mauna Kea telescope. Its preliminary minor planet designation was 1992 QB$_1$, and it is about 150 miles (240 km) in diameter. The discoverers wished to name 1992 QB$_1$ Smiley, after a character from novels by John le Carré, but an asteroid had already claimed that name. Jewitt named a subsequent Kuiper belt discovery Karla, another le Carré character. A number of researchers are searching for Kuiper belt objects, and their searches have resulted in many discoveries. Kuiper belt object 28978 Ixion is at least 580 miles (930 km) across, about the same size as the largest inner solar system asteroid, 1 Ceres. It appears to consist of a solid mixture of rock and ice.

Other large Kuiper belt objects (aside from Eris and Pluto) include 2003 EL61, Quaoar, 2005 FY9, Charon, Orcus, Ixion, and Varuna, all thought to be a least 600 miles (1,000 km) in diameter. Pluto itself has a diameter of approximately 1,450 miles (2,320 km). With the exception of Pluto, which will not likely get a more accurate size measurement until *New Horizons* visits it, all these bodies have multiple size estimates that have been produced by different research teams using different techniques. Estimates differing by hundred of kilometers can be found dating within a couple of years of each other. Thus, with the likely exception of Eris, stating unequivocally that one is larger than the other is a matter of argument.

Saturn's moon Phoebe is a captured asteroid, as evidenced by its highly inclined and retrograde orbit. The moon has prominent icy streaks inside its craters, indicating that it is an icy body with a mantle of dust and other material. Its high ice content may indicate that it originated far out in the solar system and thus may be the first object from the Kuiper belt to be observed closely by a space mission. (Not even Pluto has been visited—though the *New Horizons* mission is meant to change that.)

In June 2002, scientists from Caltech Chad Trujillo and Mike Brown saw for the first time a Kuiper belt body that they named Quaoar (pronounced KWAH-o-wahr). Quaoar lies in an orbit about 42 AU from the Earth, far beyond Pluto. Quaoar is in a nearly circular orbit, with an eccentricity less than 0.04, meaning that its distance from the Sun only changes by about 8 percent over the course of a Quaoar year, which is 285 Earth years. This eccentricity is very different from Pluto's, which is six times higher. Because this object is so bright, within a month of discovery they were able to trace Quaoar's position back two decades in earlier telescope images. Quaoar's orbit is inclined to the ecliptic by about eight degrees. Its diameter is at least 745 miles (1,200 km), so it is as large or larger than Charon, which has a diameter of about 737 miles (1,186 km).

Since the discovery of Quaoar a number of additional large Kuiper belt objects have been found. (See the table "Selected Kuiper Belt and Oort Cloud Objects" in Approximate Size Order on page 188.) Their albedos (reflectances) vary widely, indicating that their surfaces differ. Compositions may differ, and so might freshness: 2003 EL61 appears to be a football-shaped rocky body surrounded by icy moons, so it may have been recently altered by a huge impact. Seasons also matter when considering surface qualities: The surface of Eris has among the highest albedos of any solar system object, but that may be because its atmosphere has frozen out into a frost layer, and when it reaches the parts of its orbit nearer the Sun, its atmosphere will rise again as a gas. Eris's orbital period is, unfortunately, 557 years, so none of the current researchers are likely to see this phenomenon.

New Horizons, launched on January 19, 2006, is the first of the New Frontiers program of medium-class planetary missions (the second, *Juno,* is planned to launch in 2011). *New Horizons* is planned to fly by Pluto and Charon. At the time of launch, Pluto was the last planet in the solar system never to have been visited by a spacecraft; eight months later Pluto was demoted to a dwarf planet, but the importance of its visit is not diminished.

On its way to the Kuiper belt, where Pluto and Charon orbit, *New Horizons* received a gravity assist from Jupiter in February 2007. Passing at 51,000 km/hour (23 km/sec), the craft was only 32 Jupiter radii away from the planet, about three times closer than the *Cassini* spacecraft. *New Horizons* will not reach Pluto and Charon until July 2015, and after it passes them, the craft will go on to a series of Kuiper belt encounters in the years 2016 to 2020. The whole mission will encompass 10 years and 3 billion miles.

When objects in the Kuiper belt are perturbed, they can fall into orbits that bring them into the inner solar system, where the solar wind excited jets of volatiles and turns them into comets. Because of the extreme distance to the Kuiper belt and the smallness of the objects, their total number is not known; even the mass of the Kuiper belt is not known within a multiple of two or more. Compositions are equally interesting—

Kuiper belt objects are thought to be rich in organic material, the raw material from which life evolves.

Study of Mars, Venus, Mercury, and the Earth has shown that a planet's atmosphere changes in composition, mass, and temperature throughout its evolution. Mars, for example, appears to have had a thick wet atmosphere early in its development, but that atmosphere was gradually lost to space or frozen into the Martian ground. Observations of Pluto show that it loses its atmosphere continually and in such quantities that it can look like a comet, with its lost atmosphere streaming behind it in its orbit. Researchers think this is how the early atmospheres of the terrestrial planets were lost, but no process like this has been observed anywhere. *New Horizons* will measure the escape of Pluto's atmosphere along with the composition and structure of the atmosphere it is retaining.

The major mission objectives of *New Horizons* are:

1. map the surface compositions, temperature, geology, and surface features of Pluto and Charon;
2. measure the atmosphere of Pluto and any atmosphere on Charon;
3. search for rings and additional satellites around Pluto; and
4. conduct similar investigations of one or more Kuiper belt objects.

Though *New Horizons* will pass directly by Pluto and Charon without entering orbit, observations will still extend over a long period of time. The first meaningful observations of Pluto and Charon will begin five months before the closest encounter, and at 10 weeks out the images from the spacecraft will exceed the best *Hubble Space Telescope* images. Daily studies will begin at four weeks before the closest approach, and post-encounter studies will continue for a similar amount of time after the closest approach (see figure on page 104). The extended mission is planned to include one to two encounters of Kuiper belt objects, ranging from about 25 to 55 miles (40 to 90 km) in diameter.

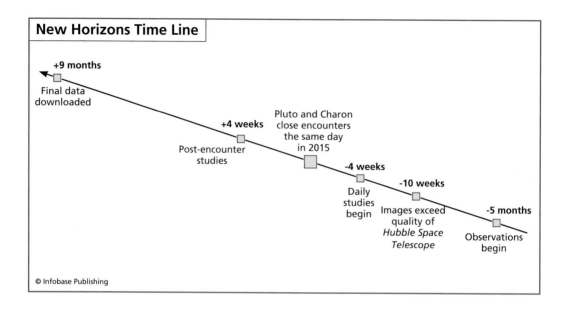

New Horizons Time Line

+9 months
Final data downloaded

+4 weeks
Post-encounter studies

Pluto and Charon close encounters the same day in 2015

-4 weeks
Daily studies begin

-10 weeks
Images exceed quality of *Hubble Space Telescope*

-5 months
Observations begin

© Infobase Publishing

This time line shows the brief, intense, 14-month New Horizons mission as the craft approaches, encounters, and passes Pluto and Charon in 2015.

The exact Kuiper belt objects to be examined by *New Horizons* cannot yet be determined. There are so many years between now and when *New Horizons* will be near them that they are far in their orbits from the rendezvous locations. All of the objects that will be in the right place at the right time are now in line with the galactic plane from our point of view and thus cannot be detected in the brightness and mass of objects. This mission is thus in the unusual position of planning to visit objects that are not yet identified!

The science payload of *New Horizons* includes seven instruments:

1. **Ralph:** Visible and infrared imager/spectrometer; provides color, composition and temperature maps.
2. **Alice:** Ultraviolet imaging spectrometer; analyzes composition and structure of Pluto's atmosphere and looks for atmospheres around Charon and Kuiper belt objects.
3. **REX:** (Radio Science EXperiment) Measures atmospheric composition and temperature.
4. **LORRI:** (Long Range Reconnaissance Imager) Telescopic camera; obtains encounter data at long

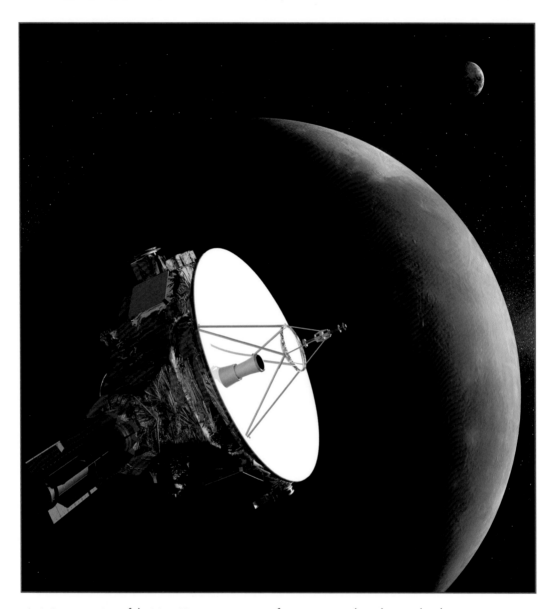

Artist's conception of the New Horizons spacecraft as it approaches Pluto and its largest moon, Charon, in July 2015. The craft's miniature cameras, radio science experiment, ultraviolet and infrared spectrometers, and space plasma experiments will characterize the global geology and geomorphology of Pluto and Charon, map their surface compositions and temperatures, and examine Pluto's atmosphere in detail. The spacecraft's most prominent design feature is a nearly seven-foot (2.1-m) dish antenna, through which it will communicate with Earth from as far away as 4.7 billion miles (7.5 billion km). (NASA/Johns Hopkins University Applied Physics Laboratory/ Southwest Research Institute)

distances, maps Pluto's far side and provides high resolution geologic data.

5. **SWAP:** (Solar Wind Around Pluto) Solar wind and plasma spectrometer; measures atmospheric escape rate and observes Pluto's interaction with solar wind.

6. **PEPSSI:** (Pluto Energetic Particle Spectrometer Science Investigation) Energetic particle spectrometer; measures the composition and density of plasma (ions) escaping from Pluto's atmosphere.

7. **SDC:** (Student Dust Counter) Built and operated by students; measures the space dust peppering *New Horizons* during its voyage across the solar system.

For more information about the New Horizons mission and to see where the spacecraft is right now, visit the mission Web site at http://pluto.jhuapl.edu/index.php.

HOW ARE METEORITES AND ASTEROIDS RELATED?

Meteorites are made, for the most part, of the same materials found in rocks here on Earth, including common minerals and iron and nickel metals. Meteorites are also small pieces of material that previously orbited the Sun with asteroids and were presumably parts of asteroids before being broken off by collisions. To understand how comparisons can be made between meteorites here on Earth, small enough to hold in your hand, and asteroids orbiting millions of miles away, Earth rock contents must be understood.

All the materials in the solar system are made of atoms or parts of atoms. A family of atoms that has the same number of positively charged particles in its nuclei (the center of the atom) is called an element. Oxygen and iron are elements, as are aluminum, helium, carbon, silicon, platinum, gold, hydrogen, and well over 200 others. Every single atom of oxygen has eight positively charged particles, called protons, in its *nucleus*. The number of protons in an atom's nucleus is called

(continues on page 110)

HOW THE DISCOVERY OF ERIS CAUSED PLUTO TO LOSE ITS STATUS AS A PLANET

On January 5, 2005, Mike Brown, Chad Trujillo, and Dan Rabonowitz discovered a slow-moving, distant object in the Kuiper belt. This object, temporarily labeled 2003 UB313, had originally been missed by computer analysis in 2003 because it was moving so slowly. The object took the informal name, Xena, and its tiny moon became known as Gabrielle. The immediate question was, how big is Xena?

Because the size of an object in the Kuiper belt is judged in part by its brightness, the albedo of the object must be known before brightness can be used to judge size. For any reasonable albedo they chose, however, this new object was going to be bigger than Pluto. This was the largest object to be discovered in the solar system in over 150 years, and it was larger than one of the planets.

As better and better measurements of the object were made, the researchers determined that it is about 1,500 miles (2,400 km) in diameter, about 5 percent larger than Pluto, and that it reflects a surprising 86 percent of light that strikes its surface. Pluto, by comparison, reflects only about 60 percent of light.

The announcement of an object larger than Pluto led to great excitement in the planetary community, and even NASA held a press conference announcing the discovery of a 10th planet! This led to increasing discussion in the scientific community about the definition of a planet, until finally the IAU took action to determine an answer. After more than a year of debate, a new committee of the IAU met in Paris in summer 2006 and developed what is currently the accepted definition:

Resolution B5: Definition of a Planet in the Solar System

Contemporary observations are changing our understanding of planetary systems, and it is important that our nomenclature for objects reflect our current understanding. This applies, in particular, to the designation "planets." The word "planet" originally described "wanderers" that were known only as moving lights in the sky. Recent discoveries led us to create a new definition, which we can make using currently available scientific information.

The IAU therefore resolves that planets and other bodies, except satellites, in our solar system be defined into three distinct categories in the following way:

(1) A "planet"[1] is a celestial body that
   (a) is in orbit around the Sun,

(continues)

(continued)

     (b) has sufficient mass for its self-gravity to overcome rigid body forces so that it assumes a hydrostatic equilibrium (nearly round) shape, and

     (c) has cleared the neighborhood around its orbit.

(2) A "dwarf planet" is a celestial body that

     (a) is in orbit around the Sun,

     (b) has sufficient mass for its self-gravity to overcome rigid body forces so that it assumes a hydrostatic equilibrium (nearly round) shape[2],

     (c) has not cleared the neighborhood around its orbit, and

     (d) is not a satellite.

(3) All other objects[3], except satellites, orbiting the Sun shall be referred to collectively as "Small Solar System Bodies."

Notes:

1. The eight planets are: Mercury, Venus, Earth, Mars, Jupiter, Saturn, Uranus, and Neptune.

2. An IAU process will be established to assign borderline objects into either dwarf planet and into other categories.

3. These currently include most of the solar system asteroids, most Trans-Neptunian Objects (TNOs), comets, and other small bodies.

As a corollary to Resolution B5, the IAU then issued Resolution 6, which declared that Pluto is no longer a planet.

Resolution 6: Pluto

The IAU further resolves:

Pluto is a "dwarf planet" by the above definition and is recognized as the prototype of a new category of Trans-Neptunian Objects[1].

Note:

1. An IAU process will be established to select a name for this category.

Source note: This material was picked up from an International Astronomical Union booklet.

Resolutions B5 and 6 of the 2006 General Assembly of the IAU can be found at the URL: http://www.iau.org/administration/resolutions/general_assemblies/.

After hearing that he was no longer a discoverer of the 10th planet, Mike Brown posted the following heartfelt text on his Web site:

When I discovered it and realized that it was, indeed, bigger than Pluto, I immediately called my wife and excitedly told her "I found a planet!"

Right after the astronomical vote yesterday, I made the same phone call again. I had to tell her that the 10th planet was being buried alongside Pluto. Her voice dropped. Really? She said. Really. My wife was already mourning the little planet that we had gotten to know so well. I think her reaction was like that of the many Pluto fans out there who feel an emotional attachment to Pluto. See, to us Xena was more than just "the tenth planet." We had gotten to know her quite well over the past year. We knew about her tiny moon (Gabrielle, of course), her incredibly shiny surface, and her atmosphere frozen in a thin layer all around the globe. We had discussed her name, her orbit, and how many more like her might be out there.

Brown went on to say that he thought the IAU had done the right thing; after all, Pluto and 2003 UB313 are both significantly smaller than the other planets and do share their orbits with many other like objects.

Brown, Trujillo, and Rabonowitz suggested "Eris" as the official name for 2003 UB313, and the name was accepted by the IAU on September 13, 2006. In Greek mythology, Eris is the goddess of warfare, and she stirs up jealousy to cause fighting among men. In the astronomical world, as Brown points out, Eris stirred up a great deal of trouble among the international astronomical community when the question of its proper designation led to a solar system with only eight planets. Eris's moon has received the official name Dysnomia, who in Greek mythology is Eris's daughter and the demon spirit of lawlessness.

Around the world people objected to the new designation of Pluto—the object has been entirely cemented into modern culture as a planet, and it has a large sentimental following. Bumper stickers were seen around the United States proclaiming "Honk If Pluto Is Still a Planet." Clearly, in the hearts of people, Pluto is still just as important as it ever was, despite the first-ever scientific definition of a planet, from which it is excluded. On the other hand, Pluto has entered an even more exclusive category, that of the dwarf planet. The IAU recognizes only three at the moment, Pluto, Eris, and Ceres. However, about an additional 40 objects are under consideration for the designation.

(continued from page 106)

its *atomic number:* All oxygen atoms have an atomic number of eight, and that is what makes them all oxygen atoms.

Naturally occurring nonradioactive oxygen, however, can have in its nucleus, in addition to the eight protons, either eight, nine, or 10 uncharged particles, called neutrons. Different weights of the same element caused by addition of neutrons are called isotopes. The sum of the protons and neutrons in an atom's nucleus is called its *mass number.* Oxygen can have mass numbers of 16 (eight positively charged particles and eight uncharged particles), 17 (eight protons and nine neutrons), or 18 (eight protons and 10 neutrons). These isotopes are written as ^{16}O, ^{17}O, and ^{18}O. The first, ^{16}O, is by far the most common of the three isotopes of oxygen.

Atoms, regardless of their isotope, combine to make molecules and compounds. For example, carbon (C) and hydrogen (H) molecules combine to make methane, a common gas constituent of the outer planets. Methane consists of one carbon atom and four hydrogen atoms and is shown symbolically as CH_4. Whenever a subscript is placed by the symbol of an element, it indicates how many of those atoms go into the makeup of that molecule or compound.

The quantities of elements in the various planets and moons, and ratios of isotopes, are important ways to determine whether the planets and moons formed from the same or different materials. Oxygen, again, is a good example. If the quantities of each of the oxygen isotopes are measured in every rock on Earth, and a graph is made of the ratios of $^{17}O/^{16}O$ versus $^{18}O/^{16}O$, the points on the graph will form a line with a certain slope (the slope is half the value, in fact). The fact that the data form a line means that the material that formed the Earth was homogeneous; beyond rocks, the oxygen isotopes in every living thing and in the atmosphere also lie on this slope. The materials on the Moon also show this same slope. By measuring oxygen isotopes in many different kinds of solar system materials, it has now been shown that the slope of the plot $^{17}O/^{16}O$ versus $^{18}O/^{16}O$ is half for every object, but each object's line is offset from the others by some amount. Each solar system object lies along a different parallel line.

At first it was thought that the distribution of oxygen isotopes in the solar system was determined by their mass: The more massive isotopes stayed closer to the huge gravitational force of the Sun, and the lighter isotopes strayed farther out into the solar system. However, studies of very primitive meteorites called chondrites, thought to be the most primitive material in the solar system, showed that they have heterogeneous oxygen isotope ratios, and, therefore, oxygen isotopes were not evenly spread in the early solar system. Scientists then recognized that temperature also affects oxygen isotopic ratios: At different temperatures, different ratios of oxygen isotopes condense. As material in the early solar system cooled, it is thought that first aluminum oxide condensed, at a temperature of about 2,410°F (1,320°C), and then calcium-titanium oxide ($CaTiO_3$, at a temperature of about 2,260°F (1,240°C), and then a calcium-aluminum-silicon-oxide ($Ca_2Al_2SiO_7$), at a temperature of about 2,180°F (1,190°C), and so on through other compounds down to iron-nickel alloy at 1,780°F (970°C) and water, at −200°F (−130°C) (water freezes on Earth at less than 32°F or 0°C because it is in the relative vacuum of space). Since oxygen isotopic ratios vary with temperature, each of these oxides would have a slightly different isotopic ratio, even if they came from the same place in the solar system. Despite these details, though, the basic fact remains true: Each solar system body has its own line on the graph of oxygen isotope ratios.

The key process that determines the oxygen isotopes available at different points in the early solar system nebula seems to be that simple compounds created with ^{18}O are relatively stable at high temperatures, while those made with the other two isotopes break down more easily and at lower temperatures. It is therefore thought that ^{17}O and ^{18}O were concentrated in the middle of the nebular cloud, while ^{16}O was more common at the edge. Despite these details, each of the types of meteorites lies on its own line, indicating a different origin in the early solar system.

Most atoms are stable. A carbon-12 atom, for example, remains a carbon-12 atom forever, and an oxygen-16 atom remains an oxygen-16 atom forever, but certain atoms eventually disintegrate into a totally new atom. These atoms are said to be "unstable" or "radioactive." An unstable atom has excess internal energy, with the result that the nucleus can undergo a spontaneous change toward a more stable form. This is called radioactive decay.

Unstable isotopes (radioactive isotopes) are called radioisotopes. Some elements, such as uranium, have no stable isotopes. The rate at which unstable elements decay is measured as a *half-life,* the time it takes for half of the unstable atoms to have decayed. After one half-life, half the unstable atoms remain; after two half-lives, one quarter remain, and so forth. Half-lives vary from parts of a second to millions of years, depending on the atom being considered. Whenever an isotope decays, it gives off energy, which can heat and also damage the material around it. Decay of radioisotopes is a major source of the internal heat of the Earth today. The heat generated by accreting the Earth out of smaller bodies and the heat generated by the giant impactor that formed the Moon have long since conducted away into space.

In rocks the atoms are arranged into minerals. A mineral is a naturally occurring crystalline material with definite compositional and physical characteristics that make it recognizable. A crystal is a substance made of regular repeating patterns of bonded atoms. Salt is a crystal, for example, and is made of alternating sodium and chloride atoms arranged in a square lattice, like a three-dimensional chess board.

Many common rock-forming minerals have a basic structure made of silica tetrahedras, that is, four oxygen atoms arranged like a triangular-based pyramid, with a silicon atom in its middle. The four oxygens are negatively charged ions, and the silicon is a positively charged ion; together they make a neutral molecule. Quartz is pure silica. Other minerals combine the silica molecules with other atoms in many ways. The crystals can be made of many individual units stacked together, or by chains of units piled together, or sheets bonded together, or three-dimensional networks. Mica and clay minerals are good examples of sheet-type minerals. Sheets of strongly bonded silica and oxygen are held together by fillings of weakly bonded water and potassium, with other elements thrown in to make the differences among the types of micas and clays.

Other rock-forming minerals have no silica in them but are combinations of sulfur, phosphorus, carbonate (CO_3), nitrogen, or other atoms. Even metals, like the iron and nickel found in iron meteorites, are crystalline materials. Each of these minerals has specific conditions under which it can form, and all have been studied here on Earth.

Two of the common minerals found in meteorites that are also found in terrestrial rocks are olivine and pyroxene. Olivine and pyroxene are commonly associated with rocks that crystallized from a liquid (*igneous rocks*), whether formed on Earth or in the asteroid belt. The particular alloys of iron and nickel that are found in meteorites, called taenite and kamacite, are also found on Earth but are rare (at least at the surface; something similar may be found in the Earth's core). Some minerals have been identified for the first time in meteorites and have never been found on Earth; for example, schriebersite (iron nickel phosphide), oldhamite (calcium sulfide), osbornite (titanium nitride), and sinoite (silica nitrogen oxide). These, however, are rare even in meteorites. For the most part, meteorites consist of minerals that are also found in Earth rocks.

Because meteorites are similar to Earth rocks, they are sometimes hard to tell apart from Earth rocks. The presence of fusion crusts or regmaglypts (see the section "The Process of Small Meteorite Falls" on page 47) is definitive in identifying meteorites, but they are not present on all meteorites. Inspection under a microscope and compositional analyses are often necessary. There are about 14,000 known meteorites on Earth right now, of which almost three-quarters are obtained through special annual meteorite-hunting expeditions to the ice fields of Antarctica. Of the meteorites found on continents other than Antarctica, only about one-third were seen to fall.

Antarctica is a perfect place to hunt for meteorites because of its vast ice fields. In fact 90 percent of the Earth's ice is in Antarctica. In 1969, Japanese glaciologists discovered nine meteorites near the Yamato Mountain Range, and the Japanese began annual expeditions to Antarctica to search for meteorites in 1973. The United States began its annual expeditions in 1976, and other countries have searched in Antarctica for meteorites as well. The best places to search are the Yamato ice field and the Allan Hills ice field. These are meteorite "stranding surfaces": As ice builds at the top of a glacial ice field, it slowly compacts and flows downhill like a very thick syrup, pressed by the new ice forming above it. If the ice sheet has a clear path, it slowly flows down to the sea, where it breaks apart to form icebergs. If, instead, the ice field flows down to an obstruction like a mountain range such as Yamato or Allan Hills, the ice builds up where it presses against the mountains, and sublimates into the atmosphere, leaving behind on its surface all the meteorites it has collected in its slow creep. It has been shown that meteorites found on stranding surfaces in Antarctica fell between a few thousand and 900,000 years ago; it took them that long to be carried through the ice sheets to the surface once again.

Modern understanding of the conditions of the early solar system, the material that built the planets, the compositions of asteroids, and the dynamics of solar and planetary formation come largely from the study of meteorites. Without meteorites, it would be much more difficult to determine the age of the solar system. New kinds of meteorites are still being discovered, and they bring new insights into the conditions of the early solar system. The scientific community, therefore, is always eager to learn of new finds and to examine and study new kinds.

Private meteorite collections are popular, and wealthy buyers from the private sector are driving up prices beyond what academics can afford. Academic researchers have often agreed to classify meteorites for dealers in return for a portion of the meteorite, usually 2g or 40 mass percent whichever is larger. Some dealers are now learning to make their own classifications, and so academics have far less access to the meteorites found in African deserts and other non-Antarctic areas. ("Classification" means to identify the meteorite class, for example, ordinary chondrite, or enstatite chondrite, or achondrite, and to further classify the sample within the class.)

The Antarctic Search for Meteorites (ANSMET) is a program that sends scientists and other interested participants to Antarctica every fall, where they spend about six weeks searching for meteorites on the ice. This program is the only regular, reliable source for new meteorites for the scientific community, and it has been running since 1976, funded by the U.S. National Science Foundation (NSF). Over the years the program has returned more than 10,000 meteorites.

Ralph Harvey, the principal investigator of the project, has to choose a team for the year's search. He picks candidates from paper application letters he receives (not accepting e-mail applications has significantly cut down on applicants and therefore on his workload). These candidates are almost all graduate students or established scientists. Between six and 12 people are chosen for the team, and they join Ralph for the expedition.

The team flies to Christchurch, New Zealand in November, just before Thanksgiving. At the NSF Office of Polar Programs (OPP) center, all participants are given the necessary clothing. The team then gets on an uncomfortable National Guard plane for the six-hour flight to McMurdo Base, on Antarctica. After a week of training, they take off onto the ice with snowmobiles for six weeks of camping and collecting meteorites.

Each meteorite found on the ice is photographed in place, packaged individually with a field number and a brief description, and kept frozen. For some time any sample that looked special in the field would be given a special field number— that is how ALH 84001 obtained its important "001" number. All the meteorites are shipped on a freezer ship to California and then driven in a freezer truck to the Johnson Space Center. There, they are finally thawed, but only using a freeze-dry process, so the sample never soaks in terrestrial water. After freeze-drying, a chip of each sample is sent to the Smithsonian to be classified. The most interesting-looking material comes first, usually by the summer following the search.

ANSMET, though originally funded only by the NSF, is really a cooperative process between NASA (which curates the bulk of the meteorites), NSF, and the Smithsonian. These organizations work in concert to run the searches, process and classify the meteorites, and make them available to the scientific community. On average, the team members find about

300 meteorites in a season, though in one recent year they found almost 1,500. NASA has also funded an additional four people to be a reconnaissance team, to move ahead of the main team and guide them to the richest areas.

The team members always find travel and life on Antarctica an intense experience. Two people stay in each tent, partly for heat, and partly for safety. The tents are heated with small camping stoves, and as the season wears on the stoves can begin to malfunction. It is not uncommon to see, while walking through camp, a tent open suddenly and a flaming stove soar out into the snow. The deliberate pace of operations and the vagaries of weather and equipment require utmost levels of patience and flexibility. Cari Corrigan, a geologist with the Smithsonian Institution and member of the permanent ANSMET team, explains that team members learn to accept things that would otherwise be miserable or frustrating, and they learn to accept delays without irritation (see the following sidebar). To learn more about ANSMET, see maps for the coming season's search, and learn about what to pack when you are going to Antarctica, see URL: http://geology.cwru.edu/~ansmet/.

Though the bulk of meteorites are found in Antarctica, they do fall more or less evenly over the whole Earth. They are simply easier to recognize in Antarctica. The Nullabor desert in Australia and areas of New Mexico and the Sahara are also fruitful places to search. Meteorites are usually named after the place where they fall, but so many are found in Antarctica that a special system has been developed for their naming. An example is ALH84001, perhaps the most famous of all the meteorites proven to have come from Mars because it is the meteorite that may contain evidence for life on Mars. The "ALH" stands for Allan Hills, the place where the meteorite was found; "84" is the year of its finding; and "001" is the order of its find in that year.

Meteorites are divided into four major classes: chondrites, achondrites, iron, and stony-iron meteorites. Chondrites are thought to contain the most primitive solar system material, while achondrites, iron, and stony-iron meteorites are thought to represent portions of larger asteroids that have undergone differentiation and other changes since solar system formation. Each of the major classes of meteorites contains many subclasses, often named after the fall location of the first example found, and in other cases, differentiated according to mineral grain size, alteration by water, or other descriptive means. The major subclasses are described below, but there are many smaller subclasses of esoteric and sometimes poorly understood meteorites that are not described in this volume.

About 85 percent of meteorites now falling to Earth are chondrites (this number is calculated from observed meteorite falls, not from collected samples). Nonetheless, proportionally somewhat more iron and stony-iron meteorites are found because they do not look as much like terrestrial rocks and so are easier to recognize. Iron meteorites also tend to be larger than stony meteorites. Many iron meteorites weigh more than 9,000 pounds (4,000 kg), while stony meteorites rarely weigh more than 1,100 pounds (500 kg), though one stony meteorite weighing 3,920 pounds (1,750 kg) fell in China in 1976. In the world meteorite collection of about 9,000 samples, about 7,100 are chondrites, about 600 short of 85 percent. By mass the discrepancy between iron and chondrite meteorites is far more disproportionate.

As described above, some asteroids are spherical solids (these are likely to be called dwarf planets), some are piles of rubble, and others are irregularly shaped. Remote sensing techniques also show that asteroids can differ greatly in their interior structure and composition. If achondrites and stony-iron meteorites are thought to represent portions of larger asteroids that have somehow separated their stony material from their metallic material, then there must be some logical process that allow this differentiation to occur. First, there are three main characteristics of a body that determine whether or not it will become round:

1. The first is its *viscosity,* that is, its ability to flow. Fluid bodies can be round because of surface tension, no matter their size; self-gravitation does not play a role. The force bonding together the molecules on

(continues on page 120)

CARI CORRIGAN AND THE ANTARCTIC SEARCH FOR METEORITES

In 2008, Cari Corrigan joined the Smithsonian Institution as a geologist. Cari has studied meteorites and planetary science since she was an undergraduate, and now she has landed in the nerve center of meteoritical science, where all the meteorites from the ANSMET searches come for classification.

As a child Cari took many walks in the woods, which prompted her interest in natural science. When she asked her mother about geology, her mother advised her to avoid it, claiming it would be tedious to analyze rocks and mud. So while studying at Michigan State University, Corrigan focused on archaeology. However, she took a class on astronomy and loved it enough to ask her professor for recommendations of similar classes. He advised her to take geology, and so she did. She liked the field so much she declared it her major, but Cari ultimately wanted to combine astronomy and geology. How to do it? Her adviser, Michael Velbel, happened to be the only faculty member at the university linking the subjects, as he worked on weathering (chemical and physical breakdown) of terrestrial rocks and meteorites. Cari started on her meteorite work.

After her undergraduate work, Cari worked as an intern at the Lunar and Planetary Institute (LPI) just south of Houston, Texas, near the Johnson Space Center. The institute has a very successful and long-running internship program, in which undergraduate students work with scientists at the LPI doing original research. It is a very effective introduction to the field and to the community of scientists.

Cari worked on meteorites and meteor impacts on the Earth and Mars and for her master's thesis she studied the Chicxulub impact crater, formed by the meteor that may have been responsible for the extinction of the dinosaurs. After her master's, Cari spent a year teaching at Central Michigan University, which convinced her that she wanted to go back for her Ph.D. and stay in academic science (with only a master's degree positions in science are very limited).

Through the community of scientists she had met at the Johnson Space Center, she knew Ralph Harvey, the current principal investigator on the Antarctic Search for Meteorites. Cari went to Case Western Reserve, where Ralph is on the faculty, and began her Ph.D. research. The project she was given focused on the famous meteorite ALH 84001, the oldest known Martian meteorite, and the one that some researchers have argued has evidence for life on the planet. (Though exceptionally exciting, most of the scientific community agrees that the evidence is not on its own convincing.)

Cari was given five or six samples of the meteorite, a treasure trove. Her particular interest was in the carbonate minerals in the meteorite—these are minerals built in part from the CO_3^{2-} molecule, and on Earth they are created mostly in shallow oceans. She had to learn a complete arsenal of analytical techniques to study them. She took classes in materials science and learned how to use a transmission electron microscope. This room-sized instrument uses electrons instead of light to make an image of an object, and, because electrons are so much smaller than the wavelength of light, a transmission electron microscope can magnify 1,000 times more than the best light microscope. For other kinds of analysis, she had to travel to other universities and research centers; at first this was intimidating and a little inconvenient, but she quickly realized that the opportunities to meet other scientists and see other facilities was spectacularly valuable.

At the University of Chicago, Cari used the electron microprobe, another room-sized instrument that uses an electron beam to energize a small volume of a sliver of the meteorite. The energized atoms release their energy as X-rays, which have wavelengths that are characteristic of the kind of atom that released them. By measuring the X-rays, the machine determines the exact composition of the part of the mineral in the meteorite that the electron beam struck.

Cari continued to Washington University in St. Louis, where she used an instrument called an ion probe to measure very low concentrations of rarer elements in the carbonate minerals, then she was off to Arizona State and UCLA to measure the ratios of oxygen isotopes in the carbonate minerals. Finally, she visited the Smithsonian where she used a mass spectrometer to make a compositional map of the minerals. This mass spectrometer, called the Time of Flight Secondary Ion Mass Spectrometer, identifies elements by their "time of flight" or how long they take to get from the surface of the material being analyzed, to the detector. It takes a spectrum from each point it analyzes, and those mass spectra are built into an image where each pixel provides chemical information.

Through all these micoanalytical techniques, Cari found a relatively large single crystal of carbonate that was intact, and the internal growth rings of the crystal could be seen. Crystals growing from a liquid or a vapor sometimes grow in layers, like the growth rings in a tree, and by measuring the differences in composition of the layers, the changing environment of growth can be measured. This way the environment of the

(continues)

(continued)

rock during its formation can be understood a little bit. This "relatively large" crystal was still very, very small—the meteorite has only very small mineral grains—with a diameter of only a few microns! Nonetheless, the layers in the tiny grain showed that the carbonate mineral had grown in a low-temperature water-rich environment and only experienced high temperatures at the end of growth, perhaps indicating the shock of the meteor impact on Mars that launched the rock off Mars and started it on its space travel to Earth.

After several short jobs in related areas of science, Cari got her current permanent job with ANSMET at the Smithsonian, as geologist at the Smithsonian Department of Mineral Sciences, a position funded by a special trust. Cari has a great position in the world of meteorites: She is the liaison between the Johnson Space Center and the Smithsonian, and she is in charge of the Antarctic meteorites that return from the ANSMET searches. She also has a permanent position on the Meteorite Working Group, the committee of scientists who receive all the requests for meteorite samples from all over the world and who decide who gets which samples and in what amounts. Over the years, more than 10,000 samples have gone to over 24 countries. The Meteorite Working Group also publishes a newsletter twice a year, which lists all the recently classified meteorite finds from the ANSMET search. (The *Meteoritical Bulletin* is another publication that lists recent finds from all areas; these two publications are the main ways that scientists learn about new meteorite finds.)

Much of the job is classifying the meteorites that come in from the ANSMET searches. Since the great majority of meteorite finds are the kind called ordinary chondrites, Cari and her colleagues search through the collection and pick out samples that look unusual or at least not like ordinary chondrites for early classification. Thus the exciting finds get classified and published first, and the more common samples get classified as time allows. The 2004 Antarctic search was so successful that the classifications were not complete until four years later. In 2008, the last of the 2006 ordinary chondrites were classified, and soon the most exciting finds from the next season will come in, and shortly scientists will start clamoring for samples, and new information will be gained about the earliest times in the solar system.

(continued from page 117)

the outside of a fluid drop pull the surface into the smallest possible area, which is a sphere. Solid material, like rock, can flow slowly if it is hot, so heat is an important aspect of viscosity. When planets are formed it is thought that they start as agglomerations of small bodies and that more and more small bodies collide or are attracted gravitationally, making the main body larger and larger. The transformation of the original pile of rubble into a spherical planet is helped along significantly by the heat contributed by colliding planetesimals: The loss of their kinetic energy acts to heat up the main body. The hotter the main body, the easier it is for the material to flow into a sphere in response to its growing gravitational field

2. The second main characteristic is density. Solid round bodies obtain their shape from gravity, which acts equally in all directions and therefore works to make a body a sphere. The same volume of a very dense material will create a stronger gravitational field than a less dense material, and the stronger the gravity of the object, the more likely it is to pull itself into a sphere

3. The third characteristic is mass, which is really another aspect of density. If the object is made of low-density material, there just has to be a lot more of it to make the gravitational field required to make it round.

Bodies that are too small to heat up enough to allow any flow, or to have a large enough internal gravitational field, may retain irregular outlines. Their shapes are determined by mechanical strength and their response to outside forces such as meteorite impacts, rather than determined by their own self-gravity. The largest asteroids, including all 100 or so that have diameters greater than about 60 miles (100 km), and the larger moons are round from self-gravity.

There is another stage of planetary evolution after attainment of a spherical shape: internal differentiation. All asteroids and the terrestrial planets probably started out made of primitive materials, such as those that make up the class of asteroids and meteorites called CI or enstatite chondrites. The planets and some of the larger asteroids then became compositionally stratified in their interiors, a process called differentiation. In a *differentiated body,* heavy metals—mainly iron with some nickel and other minor impurities in the case of terrestrial planets, and rocky and icy material in the case of the gaseous planets—have sank to the middle of the body and formed a core.

Terrestrial planets and differentiated asteroids are therefore made up, in a rough sense, of concentric shells of materials with different compositions. Some bodies in the solar system, though, are not differentiated; the material they are made of is still in a more primitive state, and the body may not be spherical. Undifferentiated bodies in the asteroid belt have their metal component still mixed through their silicate portions; it has not separated and flowed into the interior to form a core.

Among asteroids, the sizes of bodies that differentiated vary widely. Iron meteorites, thought to be the differentiated cores of rocky bodies that have since been shattered, consist of crystals of iron and nickel. The size of the crystals depends upon their cooling rate, which in turn depends upon the size of the body that is cooling. Crystal sizes in iron meteorites indicate parent bodies from six to 30 miles (10 to 50 km) or more in diameter. Vesta, an asteroid with a basaltic crust and a radius of 326 miles (525 km), seems to be the largest surviving differentiated body in the asteroid belt. Vesta has a huge crater, 430 km in diameter, thought to have been caused by a projectile 40–60 kilometers in diameter. Vesta alone among the large asteroids has a surface covered with basalt, a common igneous rock created by solidification of a magma. Vesta is therefore the only remaining large portion of an early planetesimal remaining in the asteroid belt. The basalt is evidence that it once was part of a body large enough to have internally differentiated and heated to the point of internal melting. A number of achondritic meteorites found on Earth are thought to have originated as part of Vesta, further evidence of its breakup and of its origin as a large differentiated body.

Before it was given the classification of dwarf planet, 1 Ceres was the largest asteroid in the inner solar system. Ceres's mass is equivalent to about 30 percent of the sum of the masses of all main belt asteroids. Though Ceres is unevenly shaped, approximately 577 by 596 miles (930 by 960 km), it is nearly three times the size of Vesta, and it seems from spectro-scopic analyses to be largely undifferentiated. Based on its size and density, Ceres should be round through self-gravitation, but it is an irregular body, and based on its shape and composition, it appears to be a primitive material that has never differentiated (see figure on page 124). The higher percent-ages of volatiles available at the distance of Ceres's orbit may have helped it cool faster and prevented the buildup of heat required for differentiation. Compositionally, it is a type of chondrite called "CM," described below, and it has a density of about 162 pounds per cubic foot (2,600 kg/m^3). Ceres and Vesta are thought to be among the last surviving "protoplan-ets," and that almost all asteroids of smaller size are the shat-tered remains of larger bodies.

Where does the heat for differentiation come from? The larger asteroids generated enough internal heat from radioac-tive decay to melt (at least partially) and differentiate. Gener-ally bodies need to be larger than about 300 miles (500 km) in diameter to be insulated enough to trap the heat from radioac-tive decay so that melting can occur. If the body is too small, it cools too fast and no differentiation can take place.

A source for heat to create differentiation, and perhaps the main source, is the heat of accretion. When smaller bodies, often called planetesimals, are colliding and sticking together to create a single larger body (perhaps a planet), they are said to be accreting. Accretion need not depend on random chance collisions: A larger body may have enough gravity itself to begin altering the paths of passing planetesimals and attracting them to it. In any case the process of accretion adds tremendous heat to the body, by the transformation of the kinetic energy of the planetesimals into heat in the larger body. To understand kinetic energy, start with momentum, called p and defined as the product of a body's mass m and its velocity v:

$$p = mv.$$

Sir Isaac Newton called momentum "quality of movement." The greater the mass of the object, the greater its momentum, and likewise, the greater its velocity, the greater its momentum.

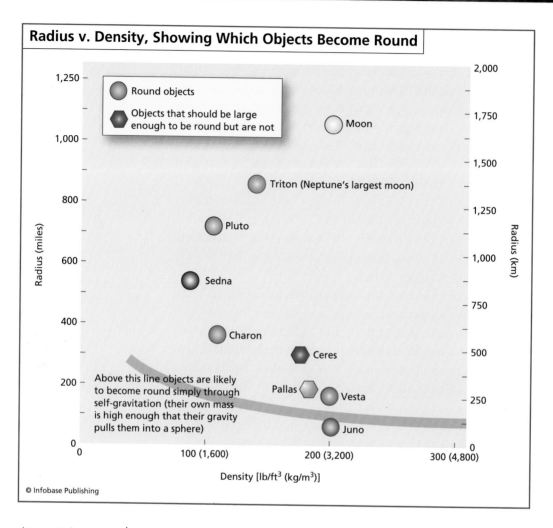

Radius v. Density, Showing Which Objects Become Round

Round objects

Objects that should be large enough to be round but are not

Moon

Triton (Neptune's largest moon)

Pluto

Sedna

Charon

Ceres

Above this line objects are likely to become round simply through self-gravitation (their own mass is high enough that their gravity pulls them into a sphere)

Pallas

Vesta

Juno

Radius (miles)

Radius (km)

Density [lb/ft³ (kg/m³)]

© Infobase Publishing

At a certain mass, solar system bodies should become round due to self-gravitation. This general rule works for some bodies, but others have remained irregular despite what should be a large enough mass.

A change in momentum creates a force, such as what a person feels when something bumps into him or her. The object that bumps into him or her experiences a change in momentum because it has suddenly slowed down, and the person experiences a force. The reason the person feels more force when someone tosses a full soda can to him or her than when they toss an empty soda can is that the full can has a greater mass, and therefore momentum, than the empty can, and when it hits him or her, it loses all its momentum, transferring to the person a greater force.

How does this relate to heating by accretion? Those incoming planetesimals have momentum due to their mass and velocity, and when they crash into the larger body, their momentum is converted into energy—in this case heat. The energy of the body, created by its mass and velocity, is called its kinetic energy. Kinetic energy is the total effect of changing momentum of a body, in this case as its velocity slows down to zero. Kinetic energy is expressed in terms of mass (m) and velocity (v):

$$k = \frac{1}{2} mv^2.$$

Students of calculus might note that kinetic energy is the integral of momentum with respect to velocity:

$$K = \int mv\,dv = \frac{1}{2} mv^2.$$

The kinetic energy is converted from mass and velocity into heat energy when it strikes the growing body. This energy, and therefore heat, is considerable, and if accretion occurs fast enough, then the larger body can be heated all the way to melting by accretional kinetic energy. If the larger body is melted even partially, it will differentiate.

How is energy transfigured into heat, and how is heat transformed into melting? To transfer energy into heat, the type of material has to be taken into consideration. Heat capacity describes how a material's temperature changes in response to added energy. Some materials increase in temperature easily in response to energy, while others need more energy to get hotter. Silicate minerals have a heat capacity of 245.2 cal/°lb (1,256.1 J/°kg), meaning that 245.2 calories of energy are required to raise the temperature of one pound of silicate material one degree. Here is a sample calculation. A planetesimal is about to impact a larger body, and the planetesimal is one kilometer in radius. It would weigh roughly 3.7×10^{13} pounds (1.7×10^{13} kg) if its density were about 250 pounds per cubic foot (4,000 kg/m³). If it was traveling at six miles per second (10 km/sec), then its kinetic energy would be

$$K = \tfrac{1}{2}\, mv^2 = (1.7 \times 10^{13} kg)\, (10{,}000 \text{ m/sec})^2$$
$$= 8.5 \times 10^{20}\, J = 2 \times 10^{20}\, cal.$$

Using the heat capacity, the temperature change created by an impact of a given mass can be calculated:

$$8.5 \times \frac{10^{20}\, {}^{\circ}kg}{1{,}256.1\, J\,/\,{}^{\circ}kg} = 6.8 \times 1017\, {}^{\circ}kg = 8.3 \times 10^{17}\, {}^{\circ}lb.$$

How many kilograms of the larger body are going to be heated by the impact? Once this quantity is known, it can be divided by the number of kilograms being heated to determine how many degrees they will be heated. How widespread is the influence of this impact? How deeply does it heat and how widely? Of course, the material closest to the impact will receive most of the energy, and the energy input will go down with distance from the impact, until finally the material is completely unheated. What is the pattern of energy dispersal? Energy dispersal is not well understood, even by scientists who study impactors. Here is a simpler question: If all the energies were put into melting the impacted material evenly, how much could they melt? To melt a silicate completely requires that its temperature be raised to about 2,700°F (1,500°C), as a rough estimate, so here is the mass of material that can be completely melted by this example impact:

$$6.8 \times \frac{10^{17}\, {}^{\circ}kg}{1{,}500^{\circ}} = 4.5 \times 10^{14} kg = 9.9 \times 10^{14} lb.$$

This means that the impactor can melt about 25 times its own mass ($4.5 \times 10^{14}/1.7 \times 10^{13} = 26$). This is a rough calculation, but it does show how effective accretion can be in heating a growing body and how it can therefore help the body to attain a spherical shape and to internally differentiate into different compositional shells.

Meteorites contain minerals that hold clues about how long it took them to crystallize and therefore how rapidly the material cooled. The original meteorite material was apparently quite hot in many cases, well above 1,800°F (1,000°C), since in some cases it started as a complete melt. In other cases, temperatures this high are required to allow certain trace atoms to diffuse and move through crystals as they apparently have in these bodies. Since the original bodies were hot and stayed hot for some time, they were necessarily large, from the arguments that can be made about heat of accretion of the bodies. This reasoning leads to the inevitable conclusion that the meteorites started as parts of larger bodies, planetesimals of some sort, which were then broken up by catastrophic impacts and the smaller pieces then cooled rapidly in the freezer of space. The large original body that accreted from the solar nebula is known as the parent body of the smaller pieces that fall into the Earth's atmosphere today.

In many cases the size of the original body, the time of breakup, and the speed of cooling can be calculated from the meteorite fragments found on Earth. Dynamical studies of asteroids show that large asteroids, those 120 miles (200 km) in diameter or larger, are likely to be broken by impact within tens of billions of years. Right now, 21 asteroids this large are known in the solar system. In the early solar system, there may have been a thousand times more of these large asteroids. Four hundred of these original 2,000 or so bodies should have been destroyed by collisions in the first million years of the solar system. The meteorite record shows that many of the parent bodies of the meteorites that land on Earth broke up very early in the solar system, consistent with these estimates for sizes and populations of asteroids. And though evidence shows that the parent bodies of meteorites were in some cases hundreds of kilometers in diameter, there is no evidence that bodies even as large as the Moon existed in the early asteroid belt.

When minerals in a meteorite indicate that the material cooled slowly inside the parent body before it was broken up, there is another clever way to determine how large the parent body was. Plutonium 244 (^{244}Pu) is a radioactive isotope that ejects a large particle with a lot of energy when it decays. The flying particle breaks through the crystal structure of the mineral of which the plutonium is a part. The path of the particle can be seen as a curving track if the mineral is polished and etched with acid; these curving paths are called fission tracks. If the mineral grain is reheated sufficiently after fission tracks are formed, the crystal reorganizes itself into a clean crystal structure, and the fission track is erased. This process is called annealing. Each mineral has a different temperature at which annealing can occur. Pyroxene loses its fission tracks, or anneals, at about 570°F (300°C), while a calcium mineral called whitlockite anneals at 210°F (100°C). By counting the density of fission tracks in different minerals, the speed of cooling between the annealing temperatures of the different minerals can be calculated.

The size of the parent body of the meteorite can be calculated using this cooling rate. Rock is an insulating material that holds its heat for a long time. The larger the body, the more slowly the interior cools. The mass of rock needed to transfer heat at a given rate can be calculated. In this way the likely size of a chondrite parent body has been calculated to be a couple of hundred miles (several hundred km).

The idea that meteorites were fragments of material from the asteroid belt came long before the radiogenic heating and cooling evidence discussed above. In the early 1800s, scientists were already suggesting that meteorites came from asteroids. Now, there is proof: In some cases the compositions of meteorites that have fallen to Earth can be shown to match the compositions of asteroids. In some cases these asteroids are thought to be the large remnants of the even larger parent bodies of both asteroids and meteorites; in other cases the meteorites that fell to Earth may simply have been smashed off the asteroid by smaller impacts.

Because meteorites originate with asteroids that formed in different parts of the solar system and through different processes, meteorites themselves have a wide range of compositions and appearances. In the next section, the types of meteorites and what can be learned from them are described, beginning with the most primitive type, the chondrites.

CHONDRITES: PRIMORDIAL MATERIAL

To guess which meteorite composition represents the most primitive material, scientists have compared the elements in the meteorite with the elements that make up the Sun. The

Sun, since it contains more than 99 percent of the material in the solar system, is probably a good measure of an average solar system composition. Other materials have been processed by being smashed by other impactors, by being partly melted and having the solid and melted portions separated, perhaps repeatedly, or by being mixed and heated with water. Thus, material from planets, and even most material from asteroids and meteorites, does not represent the initial bulk composition of the solar system.

Chondrites have compositions very similar to the Sun's, except for the very volatile elements like helium and hydrogen. If the abundance of elements in the Sun is plotted against the abundance of elements in chondrite meteorites, the plot forms almost a straight line. Other meteorites and especially planetary materials do not have comparable elemental abundances to the Sun.

The chondrite meteorites are named after tiny round bodies that they contain, called *chondrules*. Chondrules are rounded, heterogeneous bodies that contain both crystal and glass. Because they are rounded, they are thought to have cooled before being incorporated into the meteorites (otherwise their round, smooth outlines would have been shaped by the crystals around them). They are further thought to be droplets that condensed from a liquid. They reminded their first researchers of volcanic glass. These droplets are thought to represent the earliest solar system material. They are not like any other material yet found in the solar system. Radioisotopic dating shows that chondrules formed at approximately 4.568 billion years before present, and that is the age of the solar system, the time when material first began to condense.

Experiments to reproduce chondrules indicate that they formed by heating to 2,700°F (1,500°C) or higher, followed by rapid cooling. This may reflect transient, hot areas in the very early solar system, or perhaps these are simply the very first materials to condense from the solar nebula. Some chondrules also contain special pieces of material called calcium-aluminum inclusions (CAIs). These special inclusions often consist of concentric shells like an onion and contain minerals that form at very high temperatures, such as melilite and spinel. Some also have nuggets of rare metals such as platinum (these nuggets were named *fremdlinge* by early German petrologists, meaning "little strangers"). Forming a CAI requires temperatures of 3,100°F (1,700°C) or more, with slow cooling. CAIs may be the very earliest of the early material, since they formed before the chondrules themselves and consist of materials that condense at the highest temperatures.

Chondrites contain relatively little oxygen compared to other solar system materials. On Earth and the other terrestrial planets, elements such as calcium, manganese, magnesium, zinc, iron, and chromium usually bind together with oxygen to balance their electric charges and produce a neutral particle. In chondrites, these elements bind with sulfur or even nitrogen because of the lack of oxygen. This lack of oxygen is also consistent with being a very primitive material.

Chondrites show differing amounts of evidence for processing (heating, or exposure to water) after their early formation but while still in space. The material can be heated by the heat of accretion of a parent body and also by radionuclides. Radioactive elements release heat when they decay. This is still an important source of heat in planets today, but it was even more important in the very early solar system because of short-lived radioactive elements that are now gone. In particular, ^{26}Al was a highly radioactive heat-producing isotope of aluminum, but its half-life is only 700,000 years. ^{26}Al has long been gone from the solar system. Its stable daughter element, a particular isotope of magnesium that can be still measured, proves the original presence of ^{26}Al in material billions of years old. The heat of decay of now-extinct radionuclides may have been an important source for heating early solar system materials. CAIs, those very primitive inclusions inside chondrules, have especially high concentrations of the magnesium daughter product of ^{26}Al. This high concentration is further evidence that CAIs are the most primitive materials and formed earlier than any others.

Chondrite meteorites generally consist of chondrules and the minerals olivine and pyroxene, with a fine-grained matrix filling in the gaps. Some chondrites show evidence of heating in the fuzzy outlines of their mineral grains: The grains were heated to the point that they started to diffuse quickly

RADIOACTIVE ISOTOPES USED FOR DATING

Parent	Daughter	Half-life of the parent
^{87}Rb (rubidium)	^{87}Sr (strontium)	48.8 billion years
^{143}Nd (neodymium	^{143}Sm (samarium)	106 billion years
^{238}U (uranium)	^{206}Pb (lead)	4.47 billion years
^{235}U (uranium)	^{207}Pb (lead)	0.704 billion years
^{232}Th (thorium)	^{208}Pb (lead)	14.01 billion years
^{187}Re (rhenium)	^{187}Os (osmium)	42.3 billion years
^{176}Lu (lutetium)	^{176}Hf (hafnium)	35.4 billion years
^{40}K (potassium)	^{40}Ar (argon)	11.93 billion years
^{14}C (carbon)	^{14}N (nitrogen)	5,700 years
^{129}I (Iodine)	^{129}Xe (xenon)	15.7 million years
^{26}Al (aluminum)	^{26}Mg (magnesium)	0.7 million years

or almost melt at their edges. This indicates that temperatures reached about 1,800°F (1,000°C). Other chondrites have minerals containing water in veins through the meteorite, as well as minerals such as carbonates, sulfates, and magnetite, which have to form in water. This is fascinating evidence that liquid water existed in large bodies in the asteroid belt even early in solar system evolution.

If chondrites can be shown to be primordial solar system material, then they should have an age of formation that is close to the age of the solar system. Dates of the Allende meteorite show an age of approximately 4.566 billion years before present, now considered to be the age of the solar system, the age at which the planets began to form. These numbers are obtained by measuring the decay rates of radioactive elements.

When rocks form, their crystals contain some amount of radioactive isotopes (see table above). Different crystals have differently sized spaces in their lattices, so some minerals are more likely to incorporate certain elements than are others. The mineral zircon, for example, usually contains a measurable amount of radioactive lead (atomic abbreviation Pb). When the crystal forms, it contains some ratio of parent and daughter atoms. As time passes, the parent atoms continue to decay according to the rate given by their half-life, and the population of daughter atoms in the crystal increases. By measuring the concentrations of parent and daughter atoms, the age of the rock can be determined.

Consider the case of the radioactive decay system ^{87}Rb (rubidium). It decays to ^{87}Sr (strontium) with a half-life of 48.8 billion years. In a given crystal, the amount of ^{87}Sr existing now is equal to the original ^{87}Sr that was incorporated in the crystal when it formed, plus the amount of ^{87}Rb that has decayed since the crystal formed. This can be written mathematically as:

$$^{87}Sr_{now} = {}^{87}Sr_{original} + \left({}^{87}Rb_{original} - {}^{87}Rb_{now}\right).$$

The amount of rubidium now is related to the original amount by its rate of decay. This can be expressed in a simple relationship that shows that the change in the number of parent atoms n is equal to the original number n_0 times one over the rate of decay, called λ (the equations will now be generalized for use with any isotope system):

$$\frac{-dn}{dt} = \lambda n_0,$$

where dn means the change in n, the original number of atoms, and dt means the change in time. To get the number of atoms present now, the expression needs to be rearranged so that the time terms are on one side and the n terms on the other. Integrated, the final result is:

$$n_0 = ne^{\lambda t}.$$

The number of daughter atoms formed by decay, D, is equal to the number of parent atoms that decayed:

$$D = n_0 - n.$$

Also, from the previous equation, $n_0 = ne^{\lambda t}$. That can be substituted into the equation for D in order to remove the term n_0:

$$D = n(e^{\lambda t} - 1).$$

Then, finally, if the number of daughter atoms when the system began was D_0, then the number of daughter atoms now is

$$D = D_0 + n(e^{\lambda t} - 1).$$

This is the equation that allows geologists to determine the age of materials based on radiogenic systems. The material in question is ground, dissolved in acid, and vaporized into an instrument called a mass spectrometer. The mass spectrometer measures the relative abundances of the isotopes in question, and then the time over which they have been decaying can be calculated.

The values of D and n are measured for a number of minerals in the same rock, or a number of rocks from the same outcrop, and the data are plotted on a graph of D versus n (often D and n are measured as ratios of some stable isotope, simply because it is easier for the mass spectrometer to measure ratios accurately than it is to measure absolute abundances). The slope of the line the data forms is $e^{\lambda t} - 1$. This relation can be solved for t, the time since the rocks formed. This technique also neatly gets around the problem of knowing D_0, the initial concentration of daughter isotopes: D_0 ends up being the y-intercept of the graph.

Radiodating, as the technique is sometimes called, is tremendously powerful in determining how fast and when processes happened on the Earth and in the early solar system. Samples of many geological materials have been dated: the lunar crustal rocks and basalts returned by the Apollo and Luna missions, many kinds of meteorites—including those from Mars—and tens of thousands of samples from all over the Earth. While the surface of the Moon has been shown to be between 3.5 and 4.6 billion years old, the Earth's surface is largely younger than 250 Ma (million years old). The oldest rock found on Earth is the Acasta gneiss, from northwestern Canada, which is 3.96 billion years old.

If the oldest rock on Earth is 3.96 billion years old, does that mean that the Earth is 3.96 billion years old? No, because scientists believe older rocks have simply been destroyed by the processes of erosion and plate tectonics and also have reason to believe that the Earth and Moon formed at nearly the same time. The ages of the chondritic meteorites, 4.56 billion years old, appears to be the age of the solar system. How is it known that this is when the solar system formed and not some later formation event?

The answer is found by using another set of extinct nuclides (nuclide is a synonym for isotope). An important example is ^{129}I (an isotope of iodine), which decays into ^{129}Xe (xenon) with a half-life of only 16 million years. All the ^{129}I that the solar system would ever have was formed when the original solar nebula was formed, just before the planets began to form. If a rock found today contains excess ^{129}Xe, above the solar system average, then it must have formed very early in solar system time, when ^{129}I was still live. The meteorites that date to 4.56 Ga (billion years) have excess ^{129}Xe, so 4.56 Ga is the age of the beginning of the solar system.

The Allende chondrite and others have ages of 4.566 Ga (billion years). The scientific community is convinced through many examples of radiodating and thorough proofs that the technique works and that 4.56 Ga is the age of the solar system. Though the solar system began forming then, the process of forming the planets took some time. Studies of other isotopic systems can put constraints on how long it took the terrestrial planets to form their cores and begin to look the way they do today. The Earth and the Moon both show an age of about 4.515 Ga. Mars seems to have formed at about 4.536 Ga. Some meteorite parent bodies also formed a little later than the very beginning of the solar system, and even very early parent bodies sometimes hold records of later processing.

Uranium radioisotope dating indicates that most chondrite meteorites cooled within the first 60 million years of the solar system. At some point after cooling the parent bodies, impacts broke the larger parent bodies into the smaller pieces that now fall to Earth. About 20 percent of chondrites also contain or are completely made of breccia, indicating strong impact forces broke the material presumably while breaking the parent body. The breccia indicates that pressure of impact may have reached 75 GPa, the equivalent of 750,000 times atmospheric pressure on Earth.

The times of impact can be dated with some accuracy using the radioisotope ^{40}K (potassium), which decays into ^{40}Ar (argon). Argon is highly volatile and doesn't fit well into rock-forming minerals. As the ^{40}K decays, ^{40}Ar builds up in the rock. When the body is broken by a catastrophic impact, it is also heated by the shock of impact. This heat is thought to be sufficient to release all the ^{40}Ar that has built up in the rock. After impact and breakup, the ^{40}Ar begins to build up again because ^{40}K continues to decay. The concentration of ^{40}Ar can therefore be used to calculate the time between present and the time of shock heating. For chondrites, the catastrophic impacts that broke up the parent bodies seem to have occurred between 100 million and 4.1 billion years ago, almost the entire range of the age of the solar system.

A few chondrite meteorite falls have been photographed. With enough photographs, their original orbits can be calculated. All the orbits for chondrites now known have their aphelions (the point farthest from the Sun) between Mars and Jupiter, so at the moment, scientists believe that all the chondrites may come from the asteroid belt.

The chondrites are divided into classes, which are sets of groups that have similar compositions or textures and may have formed in the same area of the solar system, and then into groups, each of which may be from a single parent body. The principal classes are the ordinary chondrites, the carbonaceous chondrites, and the enstatite chondrites. There are other minor classes, mostly represented by only one meteorite fall. Groups are designated by letters, such as C, L, I, and H, which are described within the classes below. In the 1960s, the scientists Randy Van Schmus of Kansas University and John Wood of the Smithsonian Astrophysical Observatory added numbers to designate the degree of alteration of the chondrite after its initial formation. Numbers 1 and 2 have been altered by water, 3 is the least altered, and numbers 4 and 5 indicate heat alteration. The number 2 indicates heating to about 70°F (20°C), number 3 to 120°F (50°C), and 4 and 5 to much higher temperatures.

Though the numbers were first developed to indicate alteration by heat and water, they also appear to correlate with numbers of chondrules: 1 indicates no chondrules, 2, sparse chondrules, 3 and 4, abundant and distinct chondrules, and 5 and 6, increasingly indistinct chondrules. Types 3 and 4 are thought to be the most primitive material known in the solar system.

PRESOLAR GRAINS

Though chondritic meteorites are among the oldest objects in the solar system, many of them dating to the beginning of this solar system, scientists have discovered materials still older. Rocks must be dissolved in acids in order to be analyzed in an instrument called a mass spectrometer, which measures the abundances of elements in the rock. Scientists discovered in the 1970s that chondritic meteorites would not completely dissolve, no matter how many iterations of hot hydrofluoric acid baths and pressurized baths of aqua regia (a mixture of nitric and hydrochloric acid) were used. In the bottom of the beaker there was always a small quantity of tiny dark grains.

These tiny grains are less than 20 microns in diameter (0.00002 m), meaning that they are in the size range of pollen grains and bacteria. Analyzing these grains required the development of new technologies; only the largest could be analyzed with ion or electron microprobes, the analytical instruments of choice. These grains turn out to be tiny diamonds, silicon carbide (SiC), graphite, and a few other carbon-rich phases. They make up less than a few hundred parts per million in chondrites and exist in varying quantities in all chondrites, embedded in the matrix between the mineral grains and chondrules.

Diamonds in meteorites? The formation of diamonds requires intense heat and pressure, far more than is projected to have existed in the solar nebula. Where did these diamonds come from? In the end, the only possible answer is that they were formed in processes that occurred previous to this solar nebula and then were incorporated in

Ordinary chondrites (groups H, L, LL) seem to have originated in parent bodies 50–60 miles (85–100 km) in radius. All chondrites contain evidence of very early impacts, showing they had already formed by the time these very early impacts occurred. The group names H, L, and LL refer to how much oxygen is bound into the crystals in the meteorite (the meteorite's oxidation state): H chondrites are highly oxidized, L chondrites have low oxidation, and LL even lower. Highly oxidized meteorites may even have water bound into their minerals.

Carbonaceous chondrites (groups CI, CM, CR, CO, CV, CK) are given their name because they contain hydrocarbons and

the nebula when it formed. These grains are actually considerably older than this solar system and originated in supernova or a specific kind of star known as a Wolf-Rayet star, which is far hotter and 20 or more times as massive as the Sun. This revelation also has the implication that these materials were incorporated into the Earth when it formed, and some of their carbon joined the rest of the carbon on Earth, meaning that some tiny fraction of the carbon in our own bodies was made in distant stars before the beginning of the solar system.

Scientists hope to learn more about star formation and isotopic ratios in the universe by studying the composition of presolar grains. Recently scientists at the University of Chicago and Fermi Labs have developed an innovative way to analyze these tiny grains, bypassing the problems of size and also losing material in the mounting process for ion probes and during dissolution for mass spectrometers. They hold the tiny grain aloft in a strong magnetic field under a vacuum and shoot it with a laser strong enough to turn the grain into a plasma of unattached atoms and ions. Each element gives off a maxium of energy when it is struck by energy of a particular wavelength, and when the atom gives off energy, that discharge can be counted using an X-ray counter. After the grain is made into a plasma, the scientists shoot lasers of different wavelengths into the plasma and count the resulting X-rays emitted by the atoms. In this way they can literally count every single atom in a grain and know its composition perfectly, even for diamonds as small as a few thousand atoms in total.

other organic material. Some of this material can be attributed to contamination after landing on Earth, but much of it is primary material that the meteorite carried with it. The carbonaceous material includes hydrocarbons in rings and chains, and amino acids. These are the early building blocks of life, but no evidence for life has been found in meteorites. The parent bodies for carbonaceous chondrites must have been smaller than for some other classes of chondrites because the hydrocarbons in these materials would not survive much processing. The groups of carbonaceous chondrites are named after the principal meteorite fall that defined their group. The CI chondrites, for example, are named after the meteorite Ivuna, which fell in Tanzania.

Enstatite chondrites (groups EH and EL) contain tiny sulfide minerals that show that the meteorite material cooled in a matter of days. This rapid cooling rate requires that the original material was in small pieces and therefore was broken by violent impacts from a larger, hotter body. Impact *breccias* (material that has been shattered) are also common in these meteorites.

ACHONDRITES

Achondrites are igneous rocks, that is, meteorites that have crystallized from a silicate melt. They do not contain chondrules or the other markers of early, undifferentiated solar system material. These meteorites are the remnants of larger bodies that formed early in the solar system and at least began the processes of differentiation and evolution. They are envisioned as miniature planets, in that they had silicate mantles, metallic iron and nickel cores, and basaltic crusts. These early, differentiated bodies are called planetesimals or planetary embryos, though those that survive in the solar system today (notably the asteroid Vesta) are likely to be designated dwarf planets. All early markers like chondrules and *calcium-aluminum inclusions (CAIs)* have been remixed into the bulk of these planetesimals, and the body had at least begun to melt internally and produce magmas that later crystallized. Achondrites therefore carry critical clues to the speed of accumulation and size of early bodies in the solar system. About 6 percent of meteorite falls to Earth are achondrites.

Some of the parent bodies of achondrites have been identified. Some achondrites originated on the Moon or Mars (clearly differentiated bodies with silicate surfaces), were launched into space by giant meteorite impacts onto these parent bodies, and eventually encountered the Earth's gravity field and were pulled to its surface. (See the sidebar "Breaking Rocks off Other Planets and Sending Them to Earth as Meteorites.") The meteorites from Mars were not identified as being from Mars for many decades after the first were found. They have been named for the places on Earth the first three were found: Shergotty (from Shergoti, India), Nakhla (the Nakhla region of Alexandria, Egypt), and Chassigny (from Chassigny, Haute-Marne, France). Subsequent finds of Martian meteorites have been classified according to which of these original meteorites they resemble: the Shergottites are *basalts* very similar to those from Earth; the Nakhlites are high-calcium pyroxene-rich rocks with some other fine-grained basaltic minerals; and the Chassignites are olivine-rich rocks, called cumulates, probably formed by minerals that settled out of a cooling magma. Collectively they are called SNC (popularly pronounced "snick") meteorites.

The first evidence that these meteorites are from Mars is their young crystallization ages. When dated using radioactive isotopes, these meteorites were found to have cooled and crystallized from between 150 million and 1.3 billion years ago. Only a large planet could have remained volcanically active for so long after its formation at 4.56 billion years ago. These meteorites, therefore, did not come from the asteroid belt and were not related to chondrites and other primitive meteorites. Later, the gases from bubbles trapped in the meteorites were carefully extracted and analyzed, and it was found that their compositions and isotopic ratios matched those from the Martian atmosphere measured by the *Viking* lander and in no way resembled Earth's atmosphere. These gas bubbles are believed to have been formed in the meteorites by the shock of the impact that ejected them from Mars; each of the Martian meteorites had to have been ejected from Mars as splashes from

EETA79001

EETA79001 provided the first strong proof that meteorites could travel to the Earth from Mars. (NASA/JSC/JPL/ Lunar Planetary Institute)

a large impactor striking Mars. Mathematical calculations show that the chances of ejecta from Mars falling to Earth are high and the time of passage between the two planets can be short. It is likely, in fact, that many pieces make the transit from Mars to the Earth in less than 2 million years. Based on damage done to the surface of the meteorites by cosmic rays while they were passing through space, the SNC meteorites found on Earth seem to have been ejected in one or more impacts on Mars within the last 1 million to 20 million years.

The Martian meteorite EETA79001, named for the Elephant Moraine location of its find in 1979 in Antarctica, is a basaltic rock that melted from the Martian interior and so holds important clues about the composition of Mars. The image of EETA79001 above shows a sawn face of the rock with gray, fine-grained minerals and black areas of glass. The glass in EETA79001 contained the first gas bubbles analyzed that showed the clear signature of the Martian atmosphere and thus proved that the meteorite came from Mars.

The table on page 142 lists the 71 Martian meteorites known to date. Though some meteorites may still linger undiscovered in existing meteorite collections, most new Martian meteorites are discovered on collecting trips.

The scientist Curt Mileikowsky from the Royal Academy in Stockholm and his colleagues calculated that over the age of the solar system a billion tons of material has been ejected from Mars by meteorite impacts and come to Earth. Very little of it, therefore, has been found. Meteorites are commonly found in deserts or in the Antarctic, not because they fall there with any more frequency than anywhere else, but because in deserts and on ice sheets stray rocks are easier to spot and are much more likely to be meteorites than anything else. In the deserts of northern Africa, nomadic tribes collect rocks and bring them to local dealers, who sort them and sell them to meteorite dealers from other continents. These dealers are increasingly aware of the possibility of finding Martian meteorites, and, after analysis, new Martian meteorite finds are regularly announced by scientific groups from around the world.

All the SNC meteorites are igneous rocks, either high-magnesium lavas or rocks derived from high-magnesium lavas. This makes them useful for inferring information about the Martian mantle, where these rocks must have originated. One important Martian meteorite ALH84001 is estimated to have taken about 3 million years to make it from Mars to Earth, moving through space on an indirect path. Mileikowsky estimates that every 100,000 years a rock makes it straight from Mars to Earth in under a year and, on the strength of this argument, suggests that if Mars developed life, its transfer to Earth was likely.

A further class of achondrites is lunar rocks that have traveled to the Earth after being ejected from the Moon's gravity field by a large impact. Fewer lunar meteorites are known than Martian meteorites. About 112 lunar meteorites are known. The importance of these meteorites pales in comparison to the Martian meteorites, since there are 856 pounds (382 kg) of carefully selected lunar samples that were brought to Earth by the American Apollo and Soviet Luna missions, but they are extensively studied nonetheless and continue to add to our understanding of the Moon. The first lunar meteorite was recognized in 1979, and all but two of the lunar meteorites have been collected in Antarctica. The suite of lunar meteorites includes basaltic breccias, anorthositic breccias, and mare basalts (samples of the great dark pools of lava that fill the lunar impact basins).

Three groups of achondritic meteorites, the howardites, eucrites, and diogenites (HED group), are known to be related

(continues on page 146)

KNOWN MARTIAN METEORITES AS OF MID 2009

Meteorite Name	Location Found	Date Found or Purchased from Local Dealer	Mass (g)	Type
Chassigny	France	October 3, 1815	~4,000	dunite
Shergotty	India	August 25, 1865	~5,000	basalt
Nakhla	Egypt	June 28, 1911	~10,000	clinopyroxenite
Lafayette	Indiana, USA	Before 1931	~800	clinopyroxenite
Governador Valadares	Brazil	1958	158	clinopyroxenite
Zagami	Nigeria	October 3, 1962	~18,000	basalt
Allan Hills (ALH) A77005	Antarctica	December 29, 1977	482	peridotite
Yamato 793605	Antartica	1979	16	peridotite
Elephant Moraine (EET) A79001	Antarctica	January 13, 1980	7,900	basalt
Allan Hills 84001	Antarctica	December 27, 1984	1,939.9	orthopyroxenite
Lewis Cliff 88516	Antarctica	December 22, 1988	13.2	peridotite
Queen Alexandra Range (QUE) 94201	Antarctica	December 16, 1994	12.0	basalt
Dar al Gani 735	Libya	1996-1997	588	basalt
Dar al Gani 489	Libya	1997	2,146	basalt
Dar al Gani 670	Libya	1998-1999	1,619	basalt
Dar al Gani 476	Libya	May 1, 1998	2,015	basalt
Dar al Gani 876	Libya	May 7, 1998	6.2	basalt
Dar al Gani 975	Libya	August 21, 1999	27.55	basalt
Dar al Gani 1037	Libya	1999	4,012.4	basalt

Meteorite Name	Location Found	Date Found or Purchased from Local Dealer	Mass (g)	Type
Yamato 980459	Antarctica, Yamato Mtns	December 4, 1998	82.46	basalt
Los Angeles 001	California, USA	October 30, 1999	452.6	basalt
Sayh al Uhaymir 005	Oman	November 26, 1999	1,344	basalt
Sayh al Uhaymir 008	Oman	November 26, 1999	8,579	basalt
Sayh al Uhaymir 051	Oman	August 1, 2000	436	basalt
Sayh al Uhaymir 094	Oman	February 8, 2001	233.3	basalt
Sayh al Uhaymir 060	Oman	June 27, 2001	42.28	basalt
Sayh al Uhaymir 090	Oman	January 19, 2002	94.84	basalt
Sayh al Uhaymir 120	Oman	November 17, 2002	75	basalt
Sayh al Uhaymir 150	Oman	October 8, 2002	107.7	basalt
Sayh al Uhaymir 125	Oman	November 19, 2003	31.7	basalt
Sayh al Uhaymir 130	Oman	January 11, 2004	278.5	basalt
Sayh al Uhaymir 131	Oman	January 11, 2004	168	
Dhofar 019	Oman	January 24, 2000	1,056	basalt
Grove Mountains 99027	Antarctica	February 8, 2000	9.97	peridotite
Dhofar 378	Oman	June 17, 2000	15	basalt
Northwest Africa 2737	Morocco	August, 2000	611	dunite
Northwest Africa 480	Morocco	November 2000	28	basalt
Northwest Africa 1460	Morocco	November 2001	70.2	basalt
Yamato 000593	Antarctica	November 29, 2000	13,700	clinopyroxenite
Yamato 000749	Antarctica	December 3, 2000	1,300	clinopyroxenite

(continues)

KNOWN MARTIAN METEORITES AS OF MID 2009
(continued)

Meteorite Name	Location Found	Date Found or Purchased from Local Dealer	Mass (g)	Type
Yamato 000802	Antarctica	January 2003?	22	clinopyroxenite
Yamato 000027	Antarctica	November 2000	9.68	Peridotite
Yamato 000047	Antarctica	November 2000	5.34	Peridotite
Yamato 000097	Antarctica	November 2000	24.48	Peridotite
Northwest Africa 817	Morocco	December 2000	104	Clinopyroxenite
Northwest Africa 4797	Morocco	2001	15	peridotite
Northwest Africa 1669	Morocco	January 2001	35.85	basalt
Northwest Africa 1950	Morocco	January 2001	797	peridotite
Northwest Africa 856	Morocco	March 2001	320	basalt
Northwest Africa 1068	Morocco	April 2001	654	basalt
Northwest Africa 1110	Morocco	January 2002	118	basalt
Northwest Africa 1775	Morocco	2002	25	basalt
Northwest Africa 2373	Morocco	August 2004	18.1	basalt
Northwest Africa 998	Algeria or Morocco	September 2001	456	clinopyroxenite
YA1075	Antarctica	before 2002	55	peridotite
Northwest Africa 1195	Morocco	March 2002	315	basalt
Grove Mountains 020090	Antarctica	January 4, 2003	7.5	peridotite
Northwest Africa 5029	Morocco	March 2003	14.7	basalt
Northwest Africa 2046	Algeria	September 2003	63	basalt

Asteroids and Meteorites 145

Meteorite Name	Location Found	Date Found or Purchased from Local Dealer	Mass (g)	Type
MIL 03346	Antarctica, Miller Range	December 15, 2003	715.2	clinopyroxenite
Roberta Massif 04261	Antarctica	2004	78.8	basalt
Roberts Massif 04262	Antarctica	2004	204.6	basalt
Northwest Africa 3171	Algeria	February 2004	506	basalt
Northwest Africa 2626	Algeria	November 2004	31.07	basalt
Northwest Africa 2646	Algeria or Morocco	December 2004	9.3	clinopyroxenite
Northwest Africa 2969	Morocco	August 2005	11.7	basalt
Northwest Africa 2975	Algeria	November 2005	70.1	basalt
Larkman Nunatak 06319	Antarctica	2006	78.6	basalt
Northwest Africa 4468	NW Africa	Summer 2006	675	basalt
Northwest Africa 4480	Morocco	Summer 2006	13	basalt
Northwest Africa 4527	Algeria	Summer 2006	10.1	basalt
Northwest Africa 2800	Morocco	July 2007	686	basalt
Northwest Africa 2800	Morocco	2007	686	basalt
Northwest Africa 2990	Morocco	2007	0.363	basalt

Notes: Entries with borders indicate they are fragments of the same meteorite; meteorites are organized by the date of finding the first piece of a given meteorite.

(continued from page 141)

because of their similar oxygen isotope systematics, which were analyzed and interpreted initially by one of the great geochemists in the field, Bob Clayton of the University of Chicago.

These meteorites are divided into classes according to their minerals. Eucrites are basalts that contain pigeonite (a kind of pyroxene mineral) and plagioclase (a kind of feldspar mineral). Basaltic magmas are made by partially melting primitive, olivine-rich rocks like those in the Earth's mantle, and so these meteorites must have originated on a body large enough to retain enough heat to create volcanism (small bodies conduct internal heat through their radii too fast for the heat to build up and melt the body internally). Diogenites are rich in orthopyroxene or olivine and probably represent subsurface accumulations of minerals that sifted out of magmas as they cooled and began to crystallize. Howardites are breccias: smashed mixtures of diogenites and eucrites, almost certainly representing the results of the giant impact that destroyed the parent body of them all. There are about 200 samples of these meteorites in collections at the present time. More than half of the samples are eucrites, the basalt member of the family, and the least represented in Earth collections are the howardites, the breccias from impact. All these meteorites seem to have broken from a parent body that was catastrophically impacted by some other body within 100 million years of the beginning of the solar system (4.4 billion years ago or longer).

The remnant of the body still existing in the asteroid belt is thought to be 4 Vesta, based on remote sensing techniques that closely link the composition of 4 Vesta to these meteorites and also based on the size of 4 Vesta. The spectra of Vesta's surface clearly shows the mineral pyroxene, indicating that Vesta has a basaltic surface that matches the eucrites. Vesta is virtually alone in that characteristic among all the asteroids in the asteroid belt—by great good fortune it is literally the only matching body.

Rick Binzel and his research group at the Massachusetts Institute of Technology made the final connection between Vesta and the HED meteorites. Jupiter's giant gravity creates bands in the asteroid belt in which any body will be disturbed by the passing Jupiter (these are called resonances) and have its orbit changed sufficiently that it may fall inward toward the Sun and potentially strike the Earth. Vesta orbits far from these resonances, and it had been thought almost impossible for any pieces of Vesta broken off to reach a resonance and be moved toward the Earth. Binzel showed that the spectroscopic signature of the HED meteorites and of Vesta was also matched by at least 12 other objects in the asteroid belt, now called Vestites, and that they formed a path between Vesta and the resonance needed to send them speeding to Earth. By working their orbits back in time, they could even be matched with Vesta's orbit.

Thus Mars, the Moon, and Vesta have been identified as parent bodies for some of the achondrites. A number of additional achondrite groups have no parent body identified, including the aubrites, ureilites, acapulcoites, lodranites, brachinites, and angrites. Hypothesizing about the formation of these meteorites is a popular topic at meteoritical and space science conferences, and progress is constantly made toward better understanding of their origins.

Both ureilites and aubrites have been thought by some to be condensates from the solar nebula that somehow have avoided obtaining chondrules, but evidence from the mineralogy in the samples does indicate that they originated in a larger body that was undergoing differentiation. Ureilites seem to have cooled at about 50°F (10°C) per hour, meaning that their parent body must have broken up catastrophically, leaving the fragments to cool quickly in the freezing vacuum of space. At the time of this catastrophic breakup, almost certainly caused by impact with another asteroidal body, the interior of the ureilite body was at about 2,300°F (1,250°C), and the impact appears to have occurred almost immediately after the formation of the solar system. Tim Grove, a scientist at the Massachusetts Institute of Technology, and his colleague Steven Singletary have created a consistent hypothesis for the formation of ureilites involving carbon and iron reactions at shallow depths in a moderately sized parent body.

Brachinites are primitive achondrites that are thought to represent the timing of the earliest igneous activity on asteroids, which provides an upper limit on the timescale of accretion of planetesimals and the actual timing of planet formation. These give an age of 4.564 Ga, meaning that planetesimals have accreted to a size that allowed them to start melting from the energy of accretion and from short-lived radioisotope decay by 5 Ma after initial solar system formation. From this evidence and from isotopic studies of the mantles of terrestrial planets, scientists have come in the last five years or so to believe that the terrestrial planets had largely finished forming by at most 15 million years after the start of the solar system.

One of the aubrite samples, the Shallowwater aubrite, has been shown to have cooled at 1,800°F (1,000°C) per hour, from what is thought to have been a catastrophic breakup of its parent body within 10 million years of the beginning of the solar system. The other classes of achondrites without identi- fied parent bodies are variously thought to represent igneous rocks, the residue of crystallizing igneous rocks, or breccias of igneous rocks. All together these miscellaneous achondrites make up only about 2 percent of worldwide meteorite collec- tions, totaling perhaps 120 samples.

IRON METEORITES

Iron meteorites are believed to represent the cores of planetes- imals that differentiated and were then fractured into pieces. These meteorites usually contain almost no silicate material and are therefore direct and unmixed samples of the cores of large, early bodies in the solar system. As such they are win- dows into core-forming processes, which remain a matter of much hypothesizing and little data since scientists cannot sample the cores of the terrestrial planets directly.

Iron meteorites consist of iron with 5–20 percent nickel and traces of gallium, germanium, carbon, sulfur, and iridium. These elements are arranged mainly into the minerals kamacite and tetrataenite, with various other minerals in small amounts (these so-called accessory minerals include martensite, awar- uite, troilite, shriebersite, and graphite). Most iron meteorites

(continues on page 150)

BREAKING ROCKS OFF OTHER PLANETS AND SENDING THEM TO EARTH AS METEORITES

As of 2009, there are more than 100 meteorites that landed on the Earth but originated on Mars or the Moon. An additional ~200 meteorites are known to have come from the asteroid Vesta and still more have come from parent bodies that have not been identified. How do these meteorites come to Earth from other planets or smaller bodies?

The parent body must have sustained its own meteor strike, an impact with sufficient energy that some of the bedrock it struck was fragmented and ejected with enough speed to escape the parent body's gravity and make it to space. How much velocity is needed to get a rock off another planet and send it to Earth? Here is an outline of the mathematics.

First, we need an expression for escape velocity, that is, the vertical speed an object needs to reach in order to escape the gravity field of the planet they were on and reach space. The minimum velocity needed is the one that balances the gravitational pull of the planet. Here we set the kinetic energy of the object equal to the gravitational potential energy of the planet:

$$\frac{1}{2}mv_{esc}^2 = \frac{GMm}{r}, \qquad (1).$$

where m is the mass of the escaping object, M is the mass of the planet, v_{esc} is the escape velocity, G is the gravitational constant, and r is the distance the object starts from the center of the planet. To simplify this expression, we can use the definition for g, the gravitational acceleration on a specific body: $g = \frac{MG}{r^2}$. Multiply the right-hand side of equation (1) by $\frac{r}{r}$ (a form of 1, so it does not change the equation) and then substitute in g, as shown here:

$$\frac{1}{2}mv_{esc}^2 = \left(\frac{GMm}{r}\right)\left(\frac{r}{r}\right) = \frac{rm}{1}\frac{MG}{r^2} = rmg. \qquad (2)$$

Now solve for v_{esc}, and we are finished:

$$v_{esc} = \left(\frac{2rmg}{m}\right)^{\frac{1}{2}} = (2rg)^{\frac{1}{2}}. \qquad (3)$$

(continues)

(continued)

As Rick Binzel and his colleague Shui Xu from MIT wrote in their analysis of the likelihood that meteorites could make it to Earth from Vesta, for a fragment of rock with mass m to escape the surface of a parent body, its velocity must be larger than the escape velocity, since it needs to reach some other independent orbit around the Sun that is appropriate for it to then be able to reach Earth. If E_{eject} is the total energy the object leaves the planet with, and E_{esc} is the kinetic energy needed for escape (as in equation 2), and E_{add} is the additional kinetic energy of the fragment beyond E_{esc}, then $E_{eject} = E_{esc} + E_{add}$. The energy for ejection can be written as

$$\frac{1}{2}mv_{eject}^2 = \frac{1}{2}mv_{esc}^2 + \frac{1}{2}mv_{add}^2, \quad (4)$$

which can be easily simplified to

$$v_{eject}^2 = v_{esc}^2 + v_{add}^2. \quad (5)$$

We know v_{esc} from equation (3), but what is v_{add}? There is a simple expression for the velocity of a body in orbit: $v_{orbit} = \left(\frac{GM}{a}\right)^{\frac{1}{2}}$, where a is the semimajor axis of the orbiting body. Therefore if we want the expelled fragment to change its semimajor axis by an amount Δa, it must change its velocity by an amount Δv, which will be that elusive amount, v_{add}, that is needed to launch the fragment into the new orbit:

(continued from page 148)

have an internal texture known as the Widmannstätten pattern, named after Alois Beckh Widmannstätten, one of its discoverers in the early 19th century. The Widmannstätten pattern is a strikingly beautiful intergrowth of narrow blades of a high-iron mineral phase (kamacite) with a high-nickel mineral phase (tetrataenite), but it can only be seen if the meteorite is highly polished and then etched lightly, usually by soaking the sample in a dilute solution of nitric acid.

The widths of the kamacite blades are highly variable among meteorites but generally consistent within a single meteorite. The sizes of the crystals in a given sample are closely related to the cooling rate of the material when it first

$$\Delta v_{orbit} = -\frac{1}{2} (GM)^{\frac{1}{2}} a^{\frac{3}{2}} \Delta a = v_{add}. \quad (6)$$

(This answer is obtained by taking the derivative of v_{orbit} with respect to a; if you have had calculus, this should make sense.) Also, v_{add} gets a negative sign because in this problem we want the new orbital velocity to be less than the old one, so the new orbit will be inside the orbit of Vesta and therefore closer to the Earth. If the fragment is meant to go into an orbit farther from the Sun, then remove the negative sign from equation (6).

Now equation (5) can be written:

$$v_{eject}^2 = \left[(2rg)^{\frac{1}{2}} \right]^2 + \left[-\frac{1}{2} (GM)^{\frac{1}{2}} a^{\frac{-3}{2}} \Delta a \right]^2 =$$

$$2rg + \frac{1}{4} GMa^{-3}(\Delta a)^2. \quad (7)$$

This is the ejection velocity that will put the fragment into an orbit Δa different in size from its parent body. Binzel and Xu found that an impactor 80 miles (130 km) in diameter was needed to strike Vesta and put the mass of material seen in the asteroid belt and found on Earth into appropriate orbits.

formed: The higher temperature forms of tetrataenite crystallize exclusively until the material has cooled to about 1,470°F (800°C). Between 1,470°F (800°C) and 930°F (500°C), kamacite nucleates and begins to grow.

The higher the nickel content of the metal, the lower the temperature at which kamacite begins to grow. The slower the cooling, the larger the kamacite can grow before the body becomes completely solid. By measuring the bulk nickel content of the meteorite and the widths of the kamacite blades, a scientist can calculate the cooling rate of the original body. This rate will in most cases apply to the cooling of the original small differentiated body early in the solar system, and therefore also imply the overall size of the body itself.

One class of iron meteorites contains iron and nickel crystals with sizes that indicate that the meteorite material cooled at about 210°F (100°C) per hour through their closure temperature, 2,200°F (1,200°C), below which little additional atomic rearrangement occurs. This cooling rate is so fast that the parent body must have cooled in less than a day! The original parent body is thought to have been about 24 miles (40 km) in radius. Another class of iron meteorites show much slower cooling, around 9°F (5°C) per year. The cooling rates obtained for iron meteorites indicate that they came from bodies that varied from about six to 105 miles (10 to 170 km) in radius.

Isotopic studies of the meteorites by a variety of researchers indicate that the cores of the parent bodies all formed within about 5 million years of the start of the solar system and that the last of the parent bodies had fully solidified by no later than 4.6 Ga. While meteorites are traveling in space, their surfaces are bombarded by cosmic rays. The amount of damage to minerals in the meteorite can be measured, and thus the length of time that the meteorite has been exposed to cosmic rays can be calculated. Cosmic-ray exposure ages from the surfaces of iron meteorites indicate that the meteorites broke up from their parent bodies and have been traveling through space for between 200 million years and 1 billion years before breaking into the pieces that eventually fell to Earth. These exposure ages imply that larger iron meteorite bodies survived intact for between 3.5 and 4.4 billion years.

Iron meteorites are divided into three broad groups: octahedrites, hexahedrites, and ataxites. When kamacite begins to grow within the matrix of the high temperature form of tetrataenite, the kamacite aligns itself along the faces of the octahedral tetrataenite crystals. Iron meteorites within a range of iron to nickel ratios that allow both tetrataenite and kamacite to grow are therefore known as octahedrites. Iron meteorites with very low nickel contents (less than about 6 percent) consist almost entirely of kamacite and therefore show no Widmannstätten pattern. Kamacite belongs to the cubic crystal class, also known as hexahedral, and so these meteorites are known as hexahedrites. On the other hand, samples with very high nickel content (above about 15 percent) grow only tiny blades of kamacite and do not develop a Widmannstätten pattern. These samples are known as ataxites.

Octahedrites are further subdivided according to the widths of the kamacite blades in their Widmannstätten patterns. Coarsest octahedrite has blades wider than 3.3 millimeters, coarse octahedrite has blades from 1.3 to 3.3 millimeters in width, medium has blades with widths from 0.5 to 1.3 millimeters, and fine octahedrites have kamacite blades from 0.2 to 0.5 millimeters in width. Those finer than 0.2 millimeters are called finest octahedrites.

Beyond the descriptive names octahedrite, hexahedrite, and ataxite and the designations indicating the sizes of their crystals, iron meteorites have been divided into a large number of classes according to their compositions. The differing germanium, iridium, and nickel contents of these meteorites indicate that they originated in different parent bodies. There are now about thirteen categories based on these elements, designated with numbers and letters such as IAB, IC, IIIAB, and IVB.

Though iron meteorites make up only about 5 percent of observed meteorite falls, and are therefore thought to make up about 5 percent of meteorites in near-Earth orbit, they make up the largest percent by mass of any meteorite group in collections. Their overrepresentation is simply explained by their durability and also their ease of recognition: While chondrites and achondrites look much like terrestrial rocks to any but the most trained eyes, iron meteorites are highly distinctive and much easier to recognize. The largest iron meteorite yet found is a meteorite in Namibia, named Hoba, which weighs 123,000 pounds (55,000 kg). The reason no larger meteorites are found is that their fall would be at cosmic speeds, not significantly slowed by the atmosphere, and the meteorite itself would be destroyed when its shock wave strikes the surface of the Earth and the meteorite explodes.

STONY-IRON METEORITES

Stony-iron meteorites consist of roughly equal mixtures of silicate material and metal phases. The metal in these meteorites closely resembles the metal of iron meteorites, and the silicate portions resemble achondrites. Stony-irons are therefore thought to represent portions of differentiated bodies that incorporated both mantle and core material. They are divided into two main classes, the pallasites and the mesosiderites.

Pallasites are among the most beautiful of all rocks in the solar system (see the image on page 155). They are thought to have originated as rocks along the boundary of the core and silicate mantle of the early planetesimals that also yielded the iron meteorites from their cores and the achondrites from their mantles and surfaces. Pallasites usually consist of a mixture of iron metal with Widmannstätten patterns and near-translucent yellow to green olivine crystals up to an inch (several centimeters) in diameter. Olivine is the most common silicate mantle mineral at low pressures and therefore represents the mantle portion of the pallasite. A few pallasites have been found with pyroxene and some other accessory crystals in addition to the olivine. The silicate and metal portions of many pallasite meteorites are not evenly distributed, reflecting the heterogeneous region in which they originated.

Pallasites are often sold and displayed as thin slices so that light can shine through the glassy olivines between the polished grey kamacite and tetrataenite crystals. Pallasites are rare, and because of their scarcity and beauty, they are particularly expensive on the meteorite market. There are about 45 pallasite meteorites known, out of the approximately 9,000 meteorites in collections worldwide. The polished, etched slice of pallasite shown here is from the Brahin meteorite, found in Brahin, Belorussia in 1810. The metal portion of this pallasite contains 8.4 percent nickel.

Mesosiderites, on the other hand, consist of silicate minerals with iron that appears never to have melted completely and recrystallized into core-like materials. They appear to consist of metal mixed with basalt or gabbro, both igneous rocks, or minerals settled from igneous rocks. Mesosiderites are far more enigmatic in origin than the pallasites. They are thought by some to represent surface-derived breccias of bodies that had not completely differentiated, the opposite end of

The Brahin pallasite was cut into slices, polished, and etched to show its shining kamacite and tetrataenite crystals and yellow-green olivine crystals. This material is thought to have formed at the core-mantle boundary of a planetesimal that was destroyed through impacts in the earliest solar system. (Courtesy of the author)

the evolution spectrum from pallasites. Still, their apparent mixture of core material (metal) with igneous rock (solidified magma that rises to the surface of a body) is unusually difficult to explain.

Isotopic ages for mesosiderites vary from about 4.4 billion years ago to 4.56 billion years, virtually the age of the solar system. The parent body or bodies are thought to have broken up at about 4.2 billion years ago, about 300 million years after solar system formation, but may have largely reassembled through gravitational attraction, since the mesosiderites themselves show cosmic-ray exposure ages indicating they were unshielded in space for only 10–170 million years. The parent body or bodies of the mesosiderites is thought to have been 60–120 miles (100–200 km) in radius, judging by the amount of heating the resulting meteorites have experienced and the rates of cooling calculated to fit the sizes of crystals that formed. The cooling rates for mesosiderites are among the slowest for all meteorites, which in itself is a difficult paradox: If they did form near the surfaces of their parent bodies, they should have cooled rapidly. More research and thought is needed to create a clear picture of mesosiderite formation.

COMPOSITIONS OF ASTEROIDS

Although meteorites are believed to be pieces of asteroids that have been destroyed, or at least fractured, there have been no sample return missions from asteroids. All the data on asteroid compositions have been obtained through remote sensing techniques.

Asteroids are classified by composition according to the shapes of their reflectance spectra, which are made by radiation reflecting off their surfaces. (See the sidebar "Spectrophotometry and Mineral Absorption Bands" on page 157.) Asteroids show a large variation in their reflectance spectra, indicating that there is a wide range of compositions even within the main asteroid belt. Parts of meteorites found on Earth have been powdered and examined in labs for their reflectance spectra. Amazingly, many of these laboratory specimens show close matches to the reflectance spectra of asteroids. In this way, in some cases a meteorite can be matched to the large asteroid that was probably its parent body.

Asteroids were originally classified according to their color, albedo, and reflectance spectra into one of three letter classes: C, for carbonaceous; S, for silica-rich; and M, for metallic. That original classification scheme, developed in 1975 by Clark R. Chapman, David Morrison, and Ben Zellner, has now been expanded to 14 classes designated by the letters A through G, P through T, V, and sometimes K.

Compositions of asteroids change roughly and gradually with their distance from the Sun. Asteroids closest to Mars are silicate S-types, while those in the middle of the belt are C-types, and those in the outer belt are dark, difficult to see D-types (see graph on page 159). These letter designations are often called spectral classes, since they are determined through spectrophotometry.

Determining the classification of an asteroid can be made more difficult by a phenomenon called *reddening*. When solar system bodies are referred to as reddened, their color appears reddish to the unaided eye, but more important, the bodies have increased albedo at low wavelengths, the "red" end of the spectrum. Old surfaces, it seems, are more reddened than new surfaces, so reddening is thought to be caused by space weathering. Craters in reddened surfaces, for example, show less reddening where fresh material is exposed. Though the cause of reddening is not fully understood, there are some reasonable theories. In one, cosmic rays from the Sun knock off a proton from organic ices, causing adjoining organic molecules to join together into long polymeric chains. These chains are thought to have redder spectra. In a second theory, cosmic

SPECTROPHOTOMETRY AND MINERAL ABSORPTION BANDS

When light shines on an object, only a fraction of the light bounces back. Some of the light is absorbed by the object itself. The reflected light is what an observer sees: It is the image of the object. The atmosphere of Neptune, for example, is composed largely of methane. When sunlight, carrying all the spectra, strikes Neptune, the methane in its atmosphere absorbs red light. The sunlight that is reflected off Neptune is therefore lacking in red and appears blue to us.

The fraction of light reflected back is called an object's albedo. A mirror reflects almost all the light that shines onto it and so has high albedo. Surprisingly, some asteroids have very low albedo and are therefore very hard to see.

The light that is reflected from an object contains information about the composition of the object. The example of Neptune makes this clear: The fact that the reflected light is lacking red wavelengths shows that Neptune contains some material that can absorb red light. Different materials can absorb light of different wavelengths, depending on the elements in the material and how they are bonded together. This idea is used to try to determine the compositions of solar system objects humankind has not yet visited.

The light reflected from the material being studied is plotted on a graph showing the intensities of light at each wavelength. This is called a reflectance spectra. On Earth, likely materials have their reflectance spectra measured in laboratories, and then the solar system object's reflectance spectra can be compared to the laboratory reflectance spectra. This technique is used for the surface of the Moon where no one has visited, as well as for the surfaces of other planets. In these cases determining composition is more of an art than a science: the minerals that may make up these bodies often have similar reflectance spectra, and qualities such as grain size, contamination, and degree of space weathering by the solar wind and micrometeorites can affect the spectra.

rays strike silicate crystals and excite iron atoms to jump out of their crystal structure (this is called "sputtering"). The iron settles on the mineral grains' exteriors, making a very thin coating. The droplets of metallic iron are called nanophase iron, because the individual droplets, and thus the thickness of the coating, are just nanometers (10^{-7} cm, or 10^{-8} inches) in diameter.

An additional problem for asteroid classification is the extreme dimness of some asteroids. Very low albedo makes obtaining a reflectance spectrum difficult. The NEAR Shoemaker mission found that asteroid 253 Mathilde is much darker than soot, reflecting only 3 percent of the sunlight that strikes it. The brightest asteroid, 4 Vesta, by comparison, reflects a bright 38 percent of incident light. The brightest object in the solar system is the moon Enceladus, with an albedo of 99 percent. This extreme brightness is thought to be caused by the high reflectance of a continually renewed layer of water ice. The second brightest object, the dwarf planet Eris, has an albedo of 68 percent, perhaps caused by the freezing out of its atmosphere in the extreme perihelion of its orbit.

Though there are some close matches between meteorite and asteroid compositions, there are many meteorites without asteroidal counterparts, and there are asteroids with no meteorite samples on Earth. Though S-type asteroids seem to be a close match for some ordinary chondrites, parent bodies for other ordinary chondrites have not been identified. The categories of asteroids described below include all but about 5 percent of known asteroids.

About 75 percent of main belt asteroids seem to be C-, G-, and B-type asteroids. 1 Ceres and 2 Pallas are both C-types. They and all C-type bodies have a distinctive absorption band in their reflectance spectra that indicates the presence of hydrous minerals. These C-type bodies seem to be made of the same material as CI and CM chondrites, which are also thought to have made up the majority of the bulk material for building the Earth and Mars. 2 Pallas is an almost perfect spectral match to CR chondrite meteorites found on Earth, and it is thought to be the actual parent body for these meteorites.

The presence of water, even bound up in minerals, is an exciting find in the asteroid belt, since it raises the possibility of the formation of life. Water is required for all known kinds of life. Though conditions on asteroids are probably not conducive to life, these asteroids have the potential to deliver both water and amino acids to planets during impact.

S-type asteroids are the second most common type, making up about 20 percent of asteroids, and include 951 Gaspra, 243 Ida, 433 Eros, and 6 Hebe. The subclass of S-type asteroids called S(IV) are the closest compositional match to ordinary chondrites, though they are a compositionally diverse group, showing varying mixes of the minerals olivine and pyroxene as well as metals. 6 Hebe itself is thought to be the actual parent body of the H chondrites. The NEAR Shoemaker mission has shown that Eros's composition is nearly identical to the L

Asteroids with similar compositions, designated with letters, tend to lie within the same radius ranges from the Sun. This organization is thought to reflect the compositional gradients in the planetary nebula.

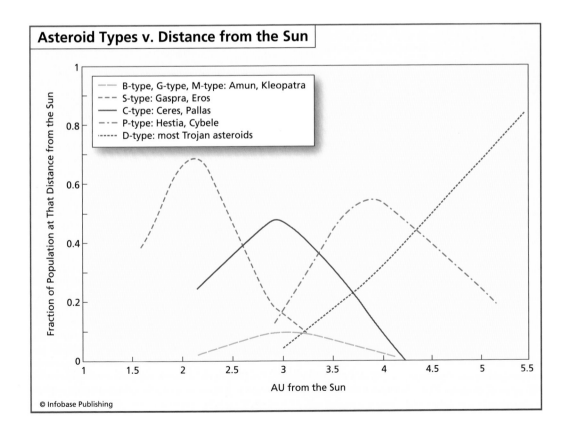

Asteroid Types v. Distance from the Sun

Legend:
- B-type, G-type, M-type: Amun, Kleopatra
- S-type: Gaspra, Eros
- C-type: Ceres, Pallas
- P-type: Hestia, Cybele
- D-type: most Trojan asteroids

Y-axis: Fraction of Population at That Distance from the Sun

X-axis: AU from the Sun

© Infobase Publishing

RELATIONS BETWEEN ASTEROIDS AND METEORITES

Type	Albedo (%)	Meteorite association	Location
E	25 to 60	aubrites	inner belt
A	13 to 40	pallasites, olivine-rich	main belt (?)
V	40	eucrites, basaltic	middle main belt, (4) Vesta and fragments
S	10 to 23	CO carbonaceous chondrites and mesosiderites	middle to inner belt
Q/R	Like S	possibly unweathered CO carbonaceous chondrites, with variable olivine and pyroxene	middle to inner belt
M	7 to 20	E chondrites, irons	central belt
P	2 to 7	unknown	outer belt
D	2 to 5	unknown	extreme outer belt, and the Trojans at Jupiter's L_4 and L_5 points
C	3 to 7	CI and CM carbonaceous chondrites	middle belt, 3.0 AU
B/F/G	4 to 9	other C subtypes	inner to outer belt

and H chondrites, except that Eros has much less sulfur. Sulfur from the surface of Eros may have been lost when it was volatilized by small impacts.

M-type asteroids consist mainly of iron and nickel, like the iron meteorites, and probably represent the cores of disrupted planetesimals. With a radius of only about 1,600 feet (500 m), 3554 Amun is the smallest known M-type asteroid, but still thought to contain a value of about $2.5 trillion in nickel, iron, and platinum. 216 Kleopatra may be the largest M-type asteroid known, a nonspherical body with radii of 67 and 29 miles (108 and 47 km).

D- and P-type asteroids are some of the darkest objects in the solar system. They have featureless spectra that are reddened (have increased albedo) at higher wavelengths. They are thought to contain large fractions of organic materials along with the iron-oxide mineral magnetite, but there are no known meteorites on Earth that correspond to these types. The Trojan asteroids that share Jupiter's orbit are mostly D-type asteroids.

The table on page 160 shows the surmised relationships among meteorites and asteroids and their positions in the solar system.

The kinds of meteorites that fall to Earth most often, the chondrites, appear to originate in the middle to inner regions of the main belt. Iron meteorites, which fall to Earth far less often, appear to originate in the central to outer belt. These results make physical sense: The meteorites that fall to Earth most often originate closest to the Earth. If the distribution of meteorite falls on Mars were known, they should be similar to those on Earth. As technology continues to improve and space missions are sent into the outer solar system, scientists will learn more about the compositions of small bodies in the region of Jupiter and beyond.

4

Comets and Other Distant Bodies

Comets were traditionally defined as solar system bodies that have tails and travel near the Earth. Ideas about comets are changing rapidly as the understanding of the solar system expands, and it is now thought that some comets remain in the outer solar system and never approach the Earth and that some rocky, asteroidal bodies sometimes have icy tails as some of their more volatile material jets out into space. Recent space missions to comets are also changing ideas about what comets are made of.

A decade or so ago, comets were thought to be the exception in the solar system—lonely travelers that flew in immense looping orbits from the outer solar system through to the inner, passing close enough to the Earth to be seen perhaps only once in a lifetime because their orbits took so long to traverse. Improved observational techniques now show that at the orbital distance of Pluto and beyond exist thousands of icy bodies, each of which would form a tail and appear as a comet if its orbit were perturbed into the inner solar system. Comets are in fact the most abundant type of body in the solar system.

The heads of most comets seem to have three parts: the nucleus, the coma (from which the tail extends), and a diffuse hydrogen cloud. The comet's nucleus may be much smaller than its tail, by 80 times or more, but cometary nuclei can still be immense. At least two comets are as large as Pluto! The ices that jet out of the head of the comet consist mainly of fragments of methane (CH_4), water (H_2O), ammonia (NH_3), HCN, and CH_3CN. Cometary tails seem to form when heat from the Sun cracks their crust and lets out volatiles like C, N, O, H. The nucleus is also thought to contain silicates, oxides, and sulfides, all rock-forming materials.

When all that could be seen of comets was their long tail, they were thought to consist mainly of ice, with some dust, and so were described as dirty iceballs. When it became clear that volatiles jetted out of cracks in the material, it was thought that they were more dust and rock and less ice, and one scientist said they were icy dirtballs, not dirty iceballs. Results from three space missions to comets indicate that cometary nuclei may be much stronger and rockier than previously thought. This further blurs the distinction between asteroids and comets: There clearly is a continuum of compositions among solar system bodies.

The coma appears when the comet is within 3 or 4 AU of the Sun because it is only within that distance of the Sun that there is enough energy from the Sun to cause the ices of the comet to sublimate (move directly from an ice state to a gas state). Cometary tails can be up to 1 AU in length (about 150,000,000 kilometers, the distance from the Sun to the Earth), and there are three distinct types of tails on each comet. One is a blue plasma tail from ionized CO, and the next is a dust tail, yellow from reflected sunlight. Dust tails are usually sweeping arcs, while plasma tails are straight but nonuniform, from the patterns in the solar wind that cause them. The third is a sodium tail, found recently on comet Hale-Bopp.

Many comets have been observed over at least several return trips to the inner solar system. Some of the most famous are listed in the accompanying table. Comets are divided into short period, those with orbits taking 200 years or less, and long period, which may have periods of tens of thousands of years or even more. Only in the last 50 years have these two

SELECTED COMETS

Name	Orbital period (years)	Next perihelion date	Orbital eccentricity	Orbital inclination (degrees)
1P Halley	76.7	2061	0.967	162.2
2P Encke	3.3	2010	0.847	11.8
6P d'Arrest	6.39	2008	0.614	19.5
9P Tempel 1	5.65	2011	0.519	10.5
19P Borrelly	6.91	2008	0.624	30.3
26P Grigg-Skjellerup	4.98	2008	0.664	21.1
55P Tempel-Tuttle	33.5	2031	0.906	162.5
75P Kohoutek	6.24	2013*	0.537	5.4
81P Wild 2	6.17	2010	0.540	3.2
95P Chiron	50.70	2046	0.38	7.0
107P Wilson-Harrington	4.30	2009	0.622	2.8
Hale-Bopp	2,380	~4,377	0.995	89.4
Hyakutake	~100,000	~102,000	0.9998	124.9

*Comet Kohoutek was not observed in 1994 or 2001, its two most recent expected returns, and may not be seen in 2013.

categories come to be understood in terms of their source populations: Comets have given us the clues necessary to predict and then find the Kuiper belt surrounding Pluto, and the far more distant Oort cloud, which reaches a great fraction of the distance to the nearest stars.

This image of comet Hale-Bopp was taken in 1997 from an island off Florida. Hale-Bopp was discovered on July 23, 1995, independently by two amateur astronomers, Alan Hale in New Mexico and Thomas Bopp in Arizona. Hale-Bopp was unusually bright and was sighted while still outside Jupiter's orbit, at 7.15 AU. Comets do not usually develop their tails until they are closer to the Sun, so the brightness of Hale-Bopp at that great distance raised hopes for a spectacular sight as it came closer to the Sun. The comet was in fact the brightest comet since comet West in 1976. In March 1996, Hale-Bopp passed within 0.8 AU of Jupiter. Jupiter's gravity altered Hale-Bopp's orbital period from its previous ~4,200 years to its current 2,380 years, setting its return date to the inner solar system to about the year 4377.

Records of comet sightings exist for as long as humankind has had the ability to create lasting archives. A bright comet makes an astonishing image, and some comets have been bright enough to see during daylight. For centuries in Europe, comets were considered evil portents, perhaps because of the coincidental passage of Halley's comet over the Battle of

Comet Hale-Bopp was photographed in the constellation Andromeda at 8:14 P.M. on March 31, 1997. During this 24-hour period, Hale-Bopp made its closest approach to the Sun. (George Shelton/NASA Kennedy Space Center)

Hastings in 1066, when the Normans invaded England. Now about 1,000 comets have been observed more than once and have at least roughly calculated orbits. About 200 of these are short-period comets that have been observed multiple times and have well-documented orbits. Astronomers await the return of an additional 200 or so that have been viewed only once. Some 20 comets have been observed once and their return predicted but have not been seen again and are considered lost. Because of gravitational perturbations of large planets and accidents and perturbations in the distant outer solar system, comets with long periods are particularly difficult to predict and track.

Some of the brightest comets seen recently are listed in the table on page 168. The *visual magnitude* given is a measure of the brightness of a celestial body as seen from Earth. This scale has no dimensions but allows comparison among objects. The lower the magnitude number, the brighter the object; a decrease of one unit represents an increase in brightness by a factor of 2.512. The brightest star is Sirius, with a magnitude of -1.4; the full Moon is −12.7; and the Sun is −26.7. The faintest stars visible under dark skies are around +6. During its recent close opposition, Mars rose to an *apparent magnitude* of −2.9, when normally it is as dim as +1.8. Comets have appeared with magnitude −10 or even brighter, meaning that they shine as brightly as the full Moon and could cast their own shadows. Comet Skjellerup-Maristany was visible in the day next to the Sun with a magnitude of only −6.

Because orbiting through the inner solar system takes time, comets can stay visible from Earth for weeks or even months, apparently stationary to the unaided eye during a single night, their tails flaming behind them as if flying while standing still. Comet Hale-Bopp was visible to the unaided eye for a year and three months, a record for visual longevity in modern astronomy. Very large and close comets have had tails that stretched across a half or more of the sky, sometimes with multiple tails visible to the unaided eye, adding considerably to their magnificence. The Great September Comet of 1882 was the brightest comet seen in at least 1,000 years, far outshining the brightest full Moon. This comet visibly broke up over the period of its visit, appearing to have several attendant small comets at times.

Halley's comet is perhaps the most famous short-period comet. It is named for Edmund Halley, Savilian Chair of Astronomy at Oxford and contemporary of Sir Isaac Newton, who predicted its return near Earth in the year 1758 based on observations people had made in 1531, 1607, and 1682. Halley noted the periodicity and predicted that these were returns of one object. The comet had also been seen and recorded many previous times. The first archive appears to be a record from China in the year 256 B.C.E., and some also accept as evidence of Halley two Babylonian clay tablets recording a cometary visit in 164 B.C.E. If the Chinese record is indeed the first, then Halley's visit in 1986 was its 30th visit recorded by human-kind. This comet has been described, painted, and observed countless times. In 1301, the remarkable Italian painter Giotto di Bondone was commissioned by the head of a wealthy family, Enrico Scrovegni, to paint frescoes in his family chapel.

Stardust Capsule Return as seen from NASA's DC-8 Airborne Laboratory, which was exploring the conditions during reentry from the light emitted by the fireball caused when the capsule streaked through the sky. (NASA)

Giotto made a highly accurate painting of Halley's comet based on its passing that year and also painted a comet in lieu of the traditional Star of Bethlehem in the depiction of the Adoration of the Magi.

Comets have existed for humankind exclusively in the realm of observational astronomy until very recently. In 1984, a large chunk of ice fell from the sky onto an agricultural field near Xishan city in eastern China. The fall was observed, and through analyses of the ice and examination of meteorological and aviation records, the ice is now definitively known to be a piece of a comet and not a hailstone nor other terres-

RECENT BRIGHT COMETS

Comet	Year of perihelion	Maximum visual magnitude
Great September Comet	1882	–17
Viscara, or the Great Comet	1901	–1
Daylight	1910	–5
Skjellerup-Maristany	1927	–6
Southern	1947	3
Eclipse	1948	1
Arend-Roland	1957	–0.5
Mrkos	1957	1
Ikeya-Seki	1965	–7
Bennett	1970	0
Kohoutek	1973	2.5
West	1976	–3
Iras-Araki-Alcock	1983	2
Hyakutake	1996	0
Hale-Bopp	1997	–0.8

trial phenomenon. Humankind has without a doubt touched a comet through this encounter. NASA and other space agencies are also sending missions to examine comets, and each science mission brings a better understanding of what comets are made of and how they change through time.

The unmanned craft *Deep Space 1* flew by comet Borrelly in 2001. The comet's nucleus is five miles (8 km) long (by comparison, the nucleus of comet Hale-Bopp is thought to be about 25 miles, or 40 km). In images from the mission, smooth, rolling plains containing brighter regions are present in the middle of the nucleus and seem to be the source of dust jets seen in the coma. The rugged areas found at both ends of the nucleus have high ridges along the jagged line between day and night on the comet. In some places, the dark material accentuates grooves and apparent faults. The nucleus of Borrelly superficially resembles any rocky asteroid from the main asteroid belt, with the exception of its high ice content.

NASA's Stardust mission flew 2.6 AU from the Earth to make a close encounter with the comet Wild 2 in 2004. Wild 2 is a new visitor to the inner solar system. By measuring its orbit, scientists were able to calculate its history and discovered that only 30 years ago it was a Kuiper belt object, but a close encounter with Jupiter perturbed its orbit so that it flew into the inner solar system.

As a new visitor to the inner solar system, Wild 2 may have fresher ices than a comet that has been traveling near the Sun for eons. The *Stardust* spacecraft is equipped with a wide-field camera (it was actually left over from the Voyager missions that were launched in the 1970s and updated for *Stardust*), and it managed to take some breathtaking photos of the comet as it passed. The spacecraft needed to come as close to the comet as possible for the best photography but stay far enough away that the chances of being struck by rocks or chunks of ice from the comet was minimized. A chunk of solid material even a centimeter across could disable the spacecraft.

Stardust took 72 photos, each either 10 or 100 milliseconds long. The short-exposure photos took clear images of the surfaces of the comet, and the long-exposure photos show the multitude of icy or gassy jets shooting out from the comet.

When viewed in close-up, the tail of the comet does not trail out of the back of the comet at all; it is made up near the comet of many small jets shooting straight up from the surface of the comet, from all sides, including the side facing the Sun and the dark back of the comet.

The photos clearly show the surface of the comet's nucleus, about three miles (5 km) in diameter, with some surprising results. Superficially, the head of the comet looks like as asteroid: a smooth surface spotted with indentations and depres-

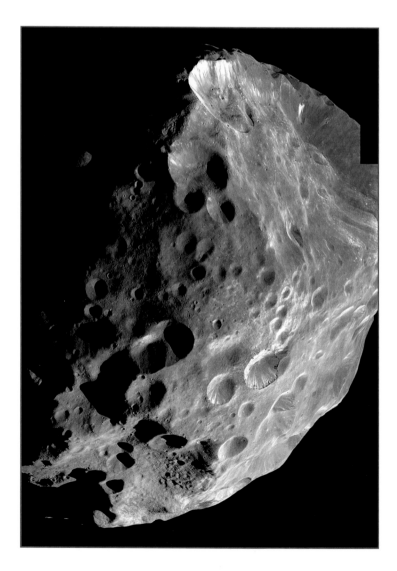

Saturn's moon Phoebe shows bright streaks on crater slopes that might be revealed by the collapse of overlying darker material from the crater wall. Aside from its bright streaks, Phoebe is one of the darkest bodies in the solar system and may be an icy Kuiper belt object captured by Saturn. (NASA/JPL/ Space Science Institute)

sions, some of which must be impact craters (see photo on page 173).

As the spacecraft flew closer, the images of the comet's nucleus became clearer. As the complexity of features on the comet became clear, the *Stardust* team named them. Though there are depressions and basins on the comet's nucleus, they are not immediately assumed to be from impacts. These depressions are distinctive and have all been named by the scientists on the mission team: Rahe, Walker, Hemenway, Mayo, and Right Foot and Left Foot, for two oblong depressions that look like footprints. One of the footprint depressions has a clearly imaged flap of material hanging from its rim over the interior of the depression, like a partial canopy. Elsewhere on the comet is a long depression with some high, thin pinnacles standing in it, each about 500 feet (150 m) high. The scientists describe this as a sort of Monument Valley. Here is the great importance of the hanging flap and the tall, thin pinnacles: previously comets had been thought of a sorts of icy rubble piles, loosely held together and continuously spewing out in the form of a tail. The hanging flap and tall pinnacle show, much to the contrary, that the material that makes up the comet is strong and continuous enough to support itself in strange, thin shapes. A rubble pile could not form tall pinnacles, because they would collapse even in the weak gravitational field of the small comet.

The jets that exit the comet to form its tail were clearly seen to be individual eruptions from specific points on the comet's surface. The composite image shown on page 176 was taken during the close approach phase of *Stardust*'s flyby. A short exposure image showing tremendous surface detail was overlain on a long exposure image taken just 10 seconds, later showing jets erupting from the comet. Together, the images show an intensely active surface, jetting dust and gas streams into space and leaving a trail millions of kilometers long. The second image on page 177 shows an artist's conception of the jets leaving the surface of the comet.

Comet tails were thought to be steadily fed from the comet and relatively thin. Observations of the nucleus of Wild 2 showed that many focused jets were the source of the comet's

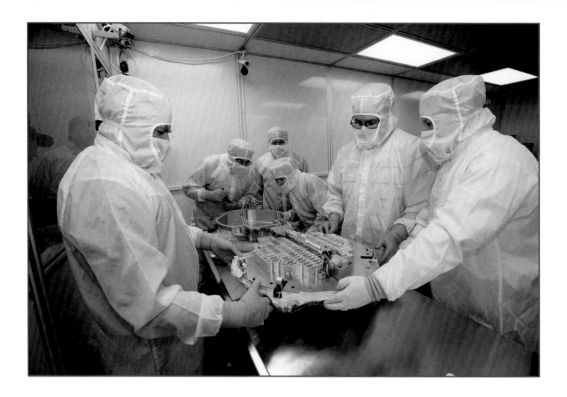

In a clean room at the Johnson Space Center, investigators from the University of Washington, Johnson Space Center, and Lockheed Martin Missiles and Space inspect a canister and sample collector from Stardust. (NASA)

tail. Many of these jets were constant and strong. The *Stardust* craft flew through this tail and encountered about 1 million particles per second streaming from Wild 2. This assault might well have damaged the craft, but it survived, despite 12 particles that were large and fast enough to punch through the top layer of the craft's shield.

"We thought Comet Wild 2 would be like a dirty, black, fluffy snowball," said *Stardust* principal investigator Dr. Donald Brownlee of the University of Washington, Seattle. "Instead, it was mind-boggling to see the diverse landscape in the first pictures from *Stardust,* including spires, pits and craters, which must be supported by a cohesive surface."

One of the goals of the mission was to collect material from the comet's tail and return it to Earth. The spacecraft carried a large round grid filled with a material called aerogel. This is a highly porous silica gel only 10 times denser than air (it has been named the world's lightest solid by the *Guinness Book of World Records*), and it has many unusual properties, such as great insulating capability. Any small particles that it encounters, even those moving at orbital speeds, will become embedded in the aerogel, leaving behind them what the Jet Propulsion Laboratory calls a carrot-shaped track, pointing to the now-trapped particle (for more on aerogel, see http://www.planetary.org/programs/projects/stardustathome/ aerogel.html).

Stardust sent the collection back to Earth, where it landed successfully in Utah in January 2006. Along with collections of meteorites and samples from the Moon, the tiny particles and dust from comet Wild 2 are housed in the planetary material curatorial facility at the Johnson Space Center in Houston. These many tiny grains of minerals and silicate glass, along with carbon-rich material, are creating a whole new story of

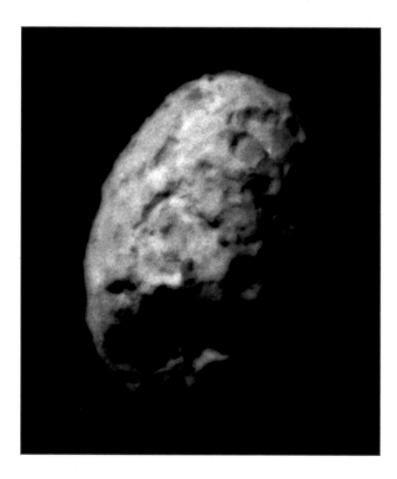

This image of the nucleus of comet Wild 2 was taken as the Stardust mission approached the comet on January 2, 2004. (NASA/Stardust/ JPL-Caltech)

planetary formation and the compositions and mixing in the early solar system.

Immediately when the scientists looked at the aerogel they saw broad, long tracks in the gel culminating in some cases in particles so large they could be seen with the unaided eye. Many of these particles turned out to be silicate crystals, which require inner solar system conditions of heat and composition to form. Some of these crystalline materials had to have formed in the vicinity of 2,300°F (1,300°C), while some other materials formed near −400°F (−240°C). These temperatures imply that the materials were made over the range of conditions in the early solar system and thus also the range of distance from the Sun, fascinating support for recent models that show significant amounts of radial mixing in the early solar system.

The aerogel also contains a number of particles smaller than a micron in size. On Earth people have spent a lot of time and money trying to make particles smaller than a micron, for industrial and commercial uses such as superefficient drug delivery for drugs being swallowed as pills. Making such tiny particles by grinding or pulverizing is incredibly difficult because at these tiny sizes electrical charges on the surfaces of the material take over and the particles clump tightly together

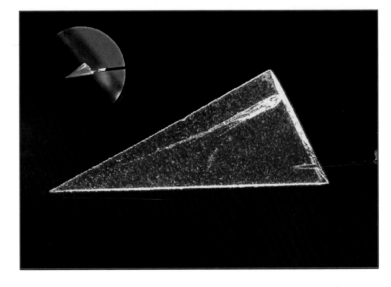

Scientists developed several ways of extracting cometary dust from Stardust's aerogel. Here, a particle and its track are cut out of the aerogel in a wedge-shaped slice called a keystone. A specialized silicon fork is then used to remove the keystone from the remaining aerogel for further analysis. (NASA)

or refuse to break down further. At some point in the grinding process, particles actually start to get larger rather than smaller. The best way to make submicron-sized particles is by allowing them to condense from a vapor. Thus, some scientists think that the tiniest particles that make up comets formed by condensation directly from the solar nebula as the solar system was forming. Additionally, the ices in a comet must never have been heated to more than about −90°C, or they would have sublimated into space.

Comets are also thought to be the contributors of an inner solar system cloud of dust that can be seen from the Earth extending along the plane of the ecliptic. The plane of the planets' orbit is also known as the zodiacal plane. The constellations of the zodiac were chosen to lie along the plane so that planets could appear to pass through them from the vantage point of the Earth. The dust particles left by passing comets shine in the approaching sunlight just before dawn and just after dusk, creating a phenomenon called gegenschein, or zodiacal light.

WHAT ARE THEIR ORBITS?

In 1950, when Dutch astronomer Jan Oort could find no other explanation for long-period comets (those with orbital periods of 200 years or more), he suggested the existence of a huge swarm of comets surrounding the solar system. He had noted that comets approach the Earth from all angles, that is, their orbits are not confined to the ecliptic plane as are the planets' orbits. Oort therefore concluded that the cloud had to be spherical rather than confined to the plane of the planets.

Oort also had enough data from watching comets pass the Earth to calculate their orbits and found that comets with long periods had perihelia about 50,000 AU from the Sun. Oort's hypothesized swarm of comets was named the Oort cloud. The theoretical comets' perihelia bring them as close as about 70 AU from the Sun, and their aphelia reach 30,000–60,000 AU. Proxima Centauri is the star closest to the Sun, 4.2 light years or about 265,000 AU away, so some Oort cloud objects travel a quarter of the way to the nearest stars.

Comet Wild 2 is about 3.1 miles (5 km) in diameter. To create this image, a short-exposure image showing surface detail was overlain on a long-exposure image taken just 10 seconds later, showing the jets that form the comet's tail, reaching millions of kilometers in length. (NASA/JPL-Caltech)

For some time following the publication of Oort's hypothesis, scientists assumed that short-period comets were created when bodies were perturbed out of the theoretical Oort cloud into orbits closer to the Sun. In 1972, Paul Joss, a professor of theoretical physics at the Massachusetts Institute of Technology, pointed out that a mass the size of Jupiter would be required to bring comets in from the Oort cloud and stabilize them in smaller orbits, and the probability of Jupiter capture is prohibitively small. A further problem then emerged: Long-period comets have orbits that are roughly randomly oriented in space, but short-period comets orbit within 30° of the ecliptic plane. The difference in the orbits of short- and long-period comets indicated that they came from different populations.

In 1943, an Irish engineer and economist named Kenneth Edgeworth had postulated that short-period comets originated in a population of small bodies past Neptune. He wrote a paper in the *Journal of the British Astronomical Association* titled "The Evolution of Our Planetary System," in which he argued that there was no reason for the solar system to suddenly stop at the end of the planets. Smaller bodies should have accreted from the scanty material further out, he reasoned, and they would occasionally visit the inner solar system as comets. This hypothesis was published seven years before Oort postulated the existence of the larger and far more distant Oort cloud and eight years before the famous Dutch astronomer Gerald Kuiper himself postulated the existence of the belt of small bodies.

Edgeworth was a minor figure in astronomy. He held no university position, though he published several papers on star formation. He spent much of his professional life as a military engineer abroad from Ireland. Kuiper, on the other hand, was an established and respected astronomer in the university research community. In 1944, Kuiper reported the first proof of an atmosphere around Saturn's moon Titan; in 1948, he discovered Uranus's moon Miranda; and in 1949, he discovered Neptune's moon Nereid. When in 1951 Kuiper hypothesized about the location of the short-period comets, his paper was widely read. Kuiper estimated how much mass had been lost from the inner solar system based on how much the planets' compositions differ from the solar composition. He assumed this mass must still exist in the solar system and postulated

This image is an artist's conception of jets leaving comet Wild 2. (NASA/ JPL-Caltech)

that it exists outside Neptune, since it is physically unlikely that the solar nebula has a sudden outer edge.

Edgeworth's paper, on the other hand, had been effectively lost from the literature (that is, not widely referenced and largely unknown and unread) in part because Kuiper neglected to refer to it in his own paper on the same subject. When a scientist publishes a paper reporting new results, they are expected to note in the text every idea or piece of data that was created by another scientist and to list all the references in a comprehensive bibliography. Careful use of this practice ensures that ideas new to a particular paper are identifiable because they bear no reference to any earlier paper. The reason for Kuiper's omission is not known, but subsequent scientists have acknowledged Edgeworth's contribution. Now his earlier hypothesis is credited as it deserves, and this population is often referred to as the Edgeworth-Kuiper belt or the Edgeworth-Kuiper disk.

By 1988, computer power had increased to the point that simulations of cometary capture from the Oort cloud could be performed. Three scientists from the University of Toronto, Martin Duncan (now at Queen's University in Ontario), Tom Quinn (now at the University of Washington), and Scott Tremaine (now at the Institute for Advanced Study, Princeton University), proved Joss's theory about the rarity of gravitational capture from the Oort cloud. They further demonstrated that comets captured from the Oort cloud would keep an approximation of their original orbital inclinations. Comets captured from the Oort cloud, in other words, would have orbits at all inclinations to the ecliptic. Short-period comets therefore could not be derived from the Oort cloud but had to reside in their own separate population. These three scientists named their postulated population of bodies beyond Neptune the "Kuiper belt."

Just before the conclusive computer modeling of Duncan, Quinn, and Tremaine, David Jewitt (now at UCLA) and Jane Luu of the University of California at Berkeley (now at MIT's Lincoln Laboratory) began an ambitious multiyear search for objects in the outer solar system. Using the large and excellent telescopes of the Mauna Kea Observatories, the scientists examined minute sections of the night sky one after the other for small moving bodies at the edge of the known solar system. After five years of fruitless searching, the first Kuiper body was found in August 1992. Its preliminary minor planet designation was 1992 QB$_1$, and it is about 240 km in diameter. 1992 QB$_1$ was the first object found beyond Neptune since Pluto was found in 1930. Suddenly the decades of theory were finished and humankind had proof that the solar system did not end with Pluto and Charon alone.

Short-Period Comets

There are about 200 well-known comets with periods of less than 200 years, the so-called short-period comets. They have their orbital aphelia near Jupiter. According to computer models, short-period comets typically remain in their orbit for less than 1 million years before they pass close to Jupiter and have their orbit perturbed by Jupiter's huge gravitational field, throwing the comet out of the solar system. Each year astronomers find about three new comets that have orbits that carry them within 1 AU of the Sun.

Neptune's orbit carries the planet from 29.8 to 30.3 AU from the Sun. Small bodies orbiting past Neptune are referred to as trans-Neptunian objects and then can be further subdivided into members of the Kuiper belt or the Oort cloud. Neptune marks the inner edge of the Kuiper belt. The Kuiper belt was originally thought to reach from 35 to 100 AU from the Sun and then to merge into the Oort cloud of comets. As study of the Kuiper belt has intensified and the orbits of more of its objects have been carefully calculated, it has become clear that the belt begins around 30 AU and that it has a sharp outer edge at 49 AU. There appears to be a gap between the edge of the Kuiper belt and the beginning of the comet-rich Oort cloud. The reason for this gap is not understood; perhaps Kuiper belt bodies become fainter or smaller with distance and cannot be seen as easily, or perhaps a sharp edge was formed by the disturbance of a passing planet or star, as unlikely as this event may be.

The Kuiper belt exists at extreme distances from the Sun. From the Kuiper belt, the radius of the Sun appears 50 times smaller than it appears from Earth, which would make the Sun look more like a very bright star than something that dominates the day. Detecting objects at that distance from Earth is exceptionally difficult and learning about their size and composition even more so. Only the most recent technology and largest telescopes allow the Kuiper belt to be explored.

The existence of the Kuiper belt had been postulated since 1943, but it remained a theory until 1992. Only the development of a highly sensitive viewing instrument called a charge-coupled device has allowed astronomers to see the tiny bodies in the Kuiper belt. George Smith and Willard Boyle invented the charge-coupled device at Bell Laboratories in 1969, and once it was refined and put into mass production, it revolutionized cameras, fax machines, scanners, and, of course, telescopes. A charge-coupled device consists of many linked capacitors, electronic components that can store and transfer electrons. When a photon strikes the surface of the charge-coupled device, it can knock an electron off the atom in the surface it strikes. This electron is captured by the capacitors. In this case the capacitors are phosphorus-doped semiconductors, one for each pixel of the image. While photographic film records a paltry 2 percent of the light that strikes it, charge-coupled devices can record as much as 70 percent of incident light. Their extreme efficiency means that far dimmer objects can be detected. This sensitivity made searching for small distant objects possible.

The preliminary minor planet designation of the first body David Jewitt and Jane Luu found after their five-year search was 1992 QB_1, and it is about 150 miles (240 km) in diameter. The discoverers wished to name 1992 QB_1 Smiley, after a character from John le Carrè's novels, but an asteroid had already claimed that name. The scientists did name the next body they found Karla, also from le Carrè's novels. By 2003, there were about 350 Kuiper belt objects known, and by 2004, more than 1,000 objects had been found. Now there are thought to be thousands of bodies in the Kuiper belt with diameters of at least 620 miles (1,000 km), about 70,000 with diameters larger than 60 miles (100 km), and at least 450,000 bodies with diameters larger than 30 miles (50 km).

Kuiper belt bodies are divided into three classes according to their orbits. Classical Kuiper belt objects have orbits with low eccentricity and low inclinations, indicating that they formed from the solar nebula in place and have not been further perturbed. These objects are sometimes called *cubewanos*. This designation includes any large Kuiper belt object orbiting between about 41 AU and 48 AU but not controlled by orbital resonances with Neptune. The odd name is derived from 1992 QB$_1$, the first Kuiper belt object found. Subsequent objects were called "que-be-one-os," or cubewanos. There are about 524 cubewanos known as of 2004, including Varuna and Quaoar, described in more detail below.

Resonance Kuiper belt objects are protected from gravitational perturbation by integral ratios between their orbital periods and Neptune's. Like Pluto, many Kuiper belt bodies have orbits in periods of 3:2 with Neptune, which allows them to orbit without being disturbed by Neptune's gravity. Because they share their resonance with Pluto, this subclass of objects are called plutinos. There are about 150 plutinos known at the time of writing and 22 other resonance objects. Models indicate that only between 10 and 20 percent of Kuiper belt objects are plutinos, meaning there are likely more than 30,000 plutinos larger than 60 miles (100 km) in diameter. Though the Kuiper belt strictly begins at around 30 AU, the region between Neptune and about 42 AU is largely empty, with the exception of the plutinos, which orbit at about 39 AU, a few bodies in the 4:3 resonance at 36.4 AU, and two objects, 1996 TR$_{66}$ and 1997 SZ$_{10}$, which seem to be in a 2:1 resonance with Neptune at 47.8 AU. These bodies in the 2:1 resonance have perihelia close to Neptune's orbit. A few more Kuiper belt bodies have been found at the 5:3 resonance near 42 AU.

The large number of bodies in resonant orbits is another paradox of the Kuiper belt. How have so many bodies fallen into these orbits? Renu Malhotra, a scientist at the University of Arizona, suggests that interactions with the gas giants early in solar system formation can explain these highly populated orbits. Computer modeling efforts as early as the 1980s indicated that gas giant planets are likely to migrate outward in the solar system early in formation. The early solar system certainly had more material in the orbits of the planets than it does now, probably including multiple bodies as large as the Earth in the orbits of the outer planets. The gas giant planets would collide with these planetesimals and scatter them either inward, toward the Sun, or outward. Planetesimals scattered outward by Neptune, Uranus, and Saturn almost certainly returned inward through the force of the Sun's gravity to be scattered again, until at last they were scattered inward toward the Sun. During each collision and scattering event, the giant planet in question had its orbit altered. Scattering a planetesimal inward toward the Sun drove the giant planet outward. Saturn, Uranus, and Neptune scattered more planetesimals inward than outward because those scattered outward returned to be scattered inward, and thus those three giant planets gradually migrated outward from the Sun. Jupiter, on the other hand, is massive enough that the planetesimals it scattered outward did not return under the Sun's gravity. Jupiter scattered slightly more planetesimals outward than inward, and so its orbit decayed slightly toward the Sun.

As Neptune, the most distant planet from the Sun, moved even further out, the locations of its resonant orbits moved outward ahead of it. These stable orbital positions thus could sweep up and capture small bodies that otherwise would never have encountered those resonant positions. Objects captured in Neptune's resonances also have their orbital eccentricities increased in a way predictable by theory. Pluto was ostensibly captured in this way, and to reach its current orbital eccentricity of 0.25, Neptune must have captured Pluto when Neptune was at 25 AU from the Sun and Pluto at 33 AU, in comparison to their current 30 and 39 AU respective distances from the Sun. Neptune continues to change the orbits of Kuiper belt bodies that are not in resonant orbits, and over the age of the solar system, Neptune is thought to have removed 40 percent of the Kuiper belt through gravitational interactions.

Both classical and resonance Kuiper belt bodies were originally thought to be orbiting at the points of their formation in the solar system, largely undisturbed since the beginning of the solar system. Unlike the randomly oriented orbits of the Oort cloud objects, Kuiper belt objects have orbits closer to the ecliptic plane. Most of the major planets' orbital planes form angles of less than a few degrees with the ecliptic plane. Neptune's orbital plane lies at just under 2 degrees from the ecliptic plane, but Pluto's orbit is the most highly inclined, at just over 17 degrees. Pluto's high inclination also marks it as a typical Kuiper belt object. A number of Kuiper belt objects have inclinations larger than 25 degrees, and the highest inclination is 31.6 degrees for 1996 RQ_{20}, a mid-range cubewano. Because the Kuiper belt objects have nonzero orbital inclinations, the Kuiper belt itself has a thickness, in contrast to the planets out to Neptune, which almost define a plane. The Kuiper belt's thickness is about 10 degrees. In addition to the range of orbital inclinations for classical and resonance Kuiper belt bodies, their orbits have eccentricities up to 0.4. These ranges indicate that these objects must have been disturbed from their original orbits, which should have been almost circular and close to the ecliptic plane. They may have been disturbed by larger bodies that existed in the early Kuiper belt but have now been destroyed through collisions, or the disturbance may have been caused by Neptune moving its orbit outward, but the dynamics of this process are not well constrained.

The third class, scattered-disk Kuiper belt objects, have large, eccentric orbits, perhaps created by gravitational interactions with the giant planets. There are about 100 known scattered-disk objects. The Kuiper belt object 1996 TL_{66} is a good example of this class, with an orbital eccentricity of 0.59 that carries it to 130 AU at aphelion. There are thought to be as many as 10,000 scattered Kuiper belt objects. The figure here shows the nearly circular orbits of the plutinos and the widely eccentric orbits of a few of the scattered objects.

Though short-period comets probably originate in the Kuiper belt, the several subpopulations of Kuiper belt bodies may be variously more stable or more likely to send comets into the inner solar system. Neptune is thought to be the main provider of the gravitational perturbations needed to throw a Kuiper belt object into the inner solar system. Kuiper belt objects that are not in stable resonant orbits are thought to experience a close encounter with Neptune on the average of once every few tens of millions of years. This low but constant

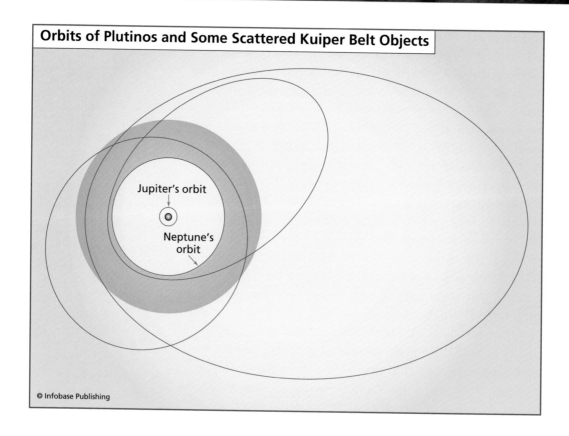

Orbits of Plutinos and Some Scattered Kuiper Belt Objects

Jupiter's orbit

Neptune's orbit

© Infobase Publishing

This sketch of the range of orbits of the plutinos and a few selected scattered Kuiper belt objects shows not only their immense distance from the Sun (compare to Jupiter's orbit) but also the wide range of orbital shapes and sizes in the Kuiper belt.

probability of Neptune encounters provides the inner solar system with a small, constant supply of short-term comets. A Kuiper belt object that comes close to Neptune has about a one-third probability of being moved into a short-period comet orbit, and it will otherwise continue in a new Kuiper belt orbit, be ejected from the solar system, or collide with a planet.

In general, a Kuiper belt object should have enough volatiles to continue producing a tail as a comet for about 10,000 years, and short-period comets have average lifetimes of about 100,000 years before colliding with a larger body or being expelled from the solar system by gravitational forces. Bodies should exist that are intermediate between comets and asteroids as they lose their volatiles. There should also be bodies in the process of moving from the Kuiper belt into short-period comet orbits. The Centaurs, bodies that orbit near Saturn and

Jupiter, are thought to be these bodies in transition. The Centaur 2060 Chiron has a cometary coma, supporting the theory that it originated in the Kuiper belt and may be perturbed into a cometary orbit.

The albedo of a body, the percent of sunlight it reflects, allows the body's size to be calculated. If the albedo is known and the sunlight intensity reflecting from the body is measured, then its size can be calculated. Most Kuiper belt objects are thought to have an albedo of about 4 percent, making them about as dark as charcoal. Based on a 4 percent albedo, the majority of Kuiper belt objects detected so far are judged to be typically about 60 miles (100 km) in radius.

The value of 4 percent albedo is a guess, however, and albedo is certain to differ among the objects. Albedo can be calculated by comparing the amount of sunlight reflected from a body with the amount of infrared radiation it emits. The infrared radiation is created by absorbed sunlight; it and the reflected sunlight should make up the total of sunlight striking the body. With a few assumptions about the material the body consists of (which controls how the sunlight heats the body and therefore its infrared emissions), the albedo of the body can be calculated.

The Kuiper belt body Varuna, for example, is thought to have an albedo of about 7 percent. For the same intensity of reflected light, a body with 7 percent albedo would be estimated to be smaller than a body with 4 percent albedo, which needs more surface area to reflect the same amount of sunlight. Pluto is exceptionally bright, with an albedo of about 60 percent. Its high albedo is thought to be created by constant cycles of ice sublimation and subsequent crystallization of fresh ice on the planet's surface as its atmosphere rises and freezes with its seasons. Young ice is highly reflective. A similar process may explain how dark Kuiper belt objects become bright short-period comets if they are perturbed into the inner solar system: Solar heating burns off the body's dark, weathered rind, and fresh icy and gassy material emerges from the interior.

Because of the extreme faintness of Kuiper belt objects, spectra are very difficult to obtain. Most inferences about

Kuiper belt objects have had to come from broadband colors, that is, the colors that the objects appear to the eye. The objects have a wide range of colors that may indicate either a range of compositions or that collisions have created fresh surfaces on some while others retain surfaces that have been weathered by millennia in space. Many of them are exceptionally red in color. When solar system bodies are referred to as "reddened," their color appears reddish to the unaided eye, but more important, the bodies have increased albedo at low wavelengths (the "red" end of the spectrum).

The unusual redness of Kuiper belt objects is not well understood, though laboratory tests show that the red spectrum of 5145 Pholus, a Centaur that orbits in the vicinity of Saturn and Uranus, can be reproduced by irradiating ices that contain nitrogen and methane. Nitrogen and methane are known constituents for Kuiper belt objects, and in fact Centaurs are likely to have been Kuiper belt objects that were perturbed from their original orbits. The complex organic molecules produced by irradiating simple organic molecules are called tholins (named by the famed Cornell University astronomer Carl Sagan after the Greek word "tholos," meaning mud). Though tholins are definitely red they unfortunately have no specific spectral absorptions and so cannot be definitively recognized remotely on Kuiper belt objects. Irradiation is certainly a significant factor in the development of surfaces in Kuiper belt objects, which have no inherent magnetic fields to shield them from cosmic rays and solar wind. When these ices are struck by high-energy particles, they lose the relatively light element hydrogen and form additional carbon-carbon bonds. Cosmic rays are highly energetic and can penetrate ices to a distance of several yards, but weak solar radiation can only penetrate a few microns.

The red color may also be caused by weathered silicate minerals, since spectral analysis of a few Kuiper belt bodies indicates that the mineral olivine may be present. Kuiper belt objects are also proven by spectral analysis to contain water ice, though it would be hard as rock at the temperatures in the Kuiper belt. These objects should also contain a large proportion of dust in addition to their ices. Comets near the

Sun eject more dust than gas, and their ratios may indicate something about the bulk compositions of Kuiper belt objects. The non-ice dust in the outer solar system is likely to be rich in radiogenic elements such as potassium (K), thorium (Th), and uranium (U). These elements emit heat when they decay, and this heat may alter the compositions and structures of the Kuiper belt bodies.

A selection of the largest outer solar system objects are listed in the accompanying table; this table includes Sedna, an object that may be the first identified body orbiting in the distant Oort cloud.

Despite their surface irradiation, Kuiper belt objects are probably the least altered objects in the solar system. Computer simulations by Matt Holman at the Harvard-Smithsonian Center for Astrophysics, Jack Wisdom at the Massachusetts Institute of Technology, and their colleagues show that Kuiper belt bodies can survive for the age of the solar system in a selection of their current, stable orbits. This study implies that Kuiper belt bodies are the remnants of the solar nebula that have stayed frozen and unaltered in the outer solar system for the last 4.56 billion years. Observations of the Kuiper belt, then, are literally observations of the original solar nebula itself.

David Jewitt and his colleagues discovered one of the first very large Kuiper belt bodies, 20000 Varuna, in November 2000 using the Spacewatch telescope in Arizona. Originally known as 2000 WR$_{106}$, Varuna is thought to be about 620 miles (1,000 km) in diameter. Its diameter is therefore less than half Pluto's. It is still larger than 1 Ceres, which is 577 by 596 miles (930 by 960 km) in diameter. Until Varuna was found, researchers thought that all Kuiper belt objects might have albedos of about 4 percent (with the exception of brilliantly bright Pluto). Varuna, though, seems to have an albedo of about 7 percent. Its brightness worked to energize the science community a little bit, since the brighter the objects are, the easier they are to find, and so more searches for Kuiper belt objects might be successful. Initially Varuna was thought to be as large as Charon, but with more refined calculations of its albedo the discovery team announced that it was in fact significantly smaller. Still, it was and is one of the larger objects

SELECTED KUIPER BELT AND OORT CLOUD OBJECTS IN APPROXIMATE SIZE ORDER

Object	Diameter [miles (km)]	Discovery and comments
Eris (2003 UB_{313})	1,500±60 (2,400±100)	Mike Brown, Chad Trujillo, and David Rabinowitz, 2003; the discovery of Eris started the dispute in the IAU that resulted in the demotion of Pluto from planet status; Eris is officially a dwarf planet and it has a moon called Dysnomia
Pluto	1,450 (2,320)	Clyde Tombaugh, 1930; Pluto is now called a dwarf planet
Haumea (2003 EL_{61})	1,200 (1,960) in its longest dimension	Mike Brown, Chad Trujillo, and David Rabinowitz, 2003; has two moons, Hi'iaka and Namaka; football-shaped
2005 FY_9	~1,070 (~1,730)	Mike Brown, Chad Trujillo, and David Rabinowitz, 2005
90377 Sedna (2003 VB_{12})	~1,000 (~1,600)	Mike Brown; may be the first object found in the Oort cloud
50000 Quaoar (2002 LM_{60})	750±120 (1,200±200)	Chad Trujillo and Mike Brown; cubewano; has one moon
Charon	754 (1,207)	James Christy and Robert Harrington, 1978
Orcus (2004 DW)	~590 (~940)	Mike Brown and Chad Trujillo; plutino; has one moon
28978 Ixion (2001 KX_{76})	~580 (~930)	Lawrence Wasserman and colleagues at the Deep Ecliptic Survey; plutino
20000 Varuna (2000 WR_{106})	560±90 (900±140)	Robert S. MacMillan, Spacewatch project; cubewano
55565 (2002 AW_{197})	555±75 (890±120)	Chad Trujillo and Mike Brown; cubewano

Object	Diameter [miles (km)]	Discovery and comments
55636 (2002 TX$_{300}$)	~440 (~700)	Jet Propulsion Laboratory NEAT program; cubewano
1999 CL$_{119}$	~270 (~430)	Most distant object in the Kuiper belt (perihelion 46.6 AU, no other perihelion farther); cubewano
15760 (1992 QB$_1$)	150 (240)	David Jewitt and Jane Luu; the definitive cubewano and first discovered Kuiper belt object

Note: Diameters marked as approximate (~) may have errors in the hundreds of kilometers; measurements are difficult, and new papers with new size measurement using new techniques are being published constantly, so a wide range of estimates are in the literature.

yet discovered. Since Varuna, there have been at least four Kuiper belt objects discovered that are larger.

In July 2001, Robert Millis and his colleagues at the Massachusetts Institute of Technology, Lowell Observatory, and the Large Binocular Telescope Observatory in Arizona discovered 28978 Ixion (originally 2001 KX$_{76}$), a large Kuiper belt object (most of these people were also on the team that discovered Uranus's rings in 1977). Along with Varuna, Ixion is larger than 1 Ceres. Ixion's size was highly uncertain when it was discovered because the telescope through which it was discovered had neither the high resolution required to measure size directly (the *Hubble Space Telescope* can do this) nor the ability to measure infrared radiation, which is related to size. At the time of discovery, the team thought Ixion was at least 750 miles (1,200 km) in diameter. This estimated size made a big media splash, since at the time it would have been the largest Kuiper belt object after Pluto, and in fact larger than Charon itself. Further study shows Ixion to be only about 580 miles (930 km) in diameter, and in the intervening years a number of larger Kuiper belt bodies have been discovered, including two that really may be larger than Charon.

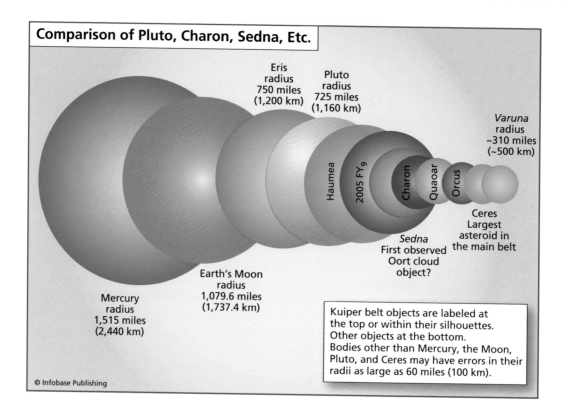

Comparison of Pluto, Charon, Sedna, Etc.

Eris
radius
750 miles
(1,200 km)

Pluto
radius
725 miles
(1,160 km)

Varuna
radius
~310 miles
(~500 km)

Haumea

2005 FY₉

Charon

Quaoar

Orcus

Ceres
Largest
asteroid in
the main belt

Sedna
First observed
Oort cloud
object?

Earth's Moon
radius
1,079.6 miles
(1,737.4 km)

Mercury
radius
1,515 miles
(2,440 km)

Kuiper belt objects are labeled at
the top or within their silhouettes.
Other objects at the bottom.
Bodies other than Mercury, the Moon,
Pluto, and Ceres may have errors in their
radii as large as 60 miles (100 km).

© Infobase Publishing

A comparison of the sizes of Mercury, the Moon, Pluto, and a series of minor planets shows that all known Kuiper and asteroid belt objects are smaller than Pluto, but even Pluto is smaller than Earth's Moon.

In June 2002, California Institute of Technology scientists Chad Trujillo (now at the Gemini Observatory) and Mike Brown saw for the first time a Kuiper belt body with the preliminary name 2002 LM₆₀, later named 50000 Quaoar (pronounced KWAH-o-wahr). Quaoar is named for the god found in the creation stories of the Tongva tribe, early inhabitants of southern California. Quaoar lies at about 42 AU from the Sun. Its orbit takes about 285 Earth years and is almost circular, with an eccentricity of only 0.04 and an inclination of about 8°. Pluto's orbital eccentricity is about six times larger than that of Quaoar's, and Pluto's inclination is about twice Quaoar's. Because Quaoar is so bright, within a month of discovery they were able to trace its position back two decades in previously taken telescope images. Quaoar has a diameter of 780 miles (1,250 km), about half the size of Pluto. Quaoar was at the time of its discovery the largest solar system body found since Pluto itself.

In February 2004, Brown, Trujillo, and their colleague David Rabinowitz from Yale University had a new announcement about the largest known Kuiper belt object, having found a new object designated 2004 DW that is still larger than Quaoar. Based on its current distance of about 48 AU from the Sun, its brightness, and its presumed albedo, 2004 DW has been estimated to be around 870–990 miles (1,400–1,600 km) in diameter, or more than half the size of Pluto. As with many other found objects, once they are identified they can then be found in photographs from sky surveys in the past. 2004 DW has been found in a First Palomar Sky Survey photograph of November 23, 1954, and in a November 8, 1951, photograph from the Siding Spring Observatory in Australia. 2004 DW appears to be a plutino with an orbit that carries it from 30.9 and 48.1 AU with an orbital inclination of about 20.6°. 2004 DW requires 248 years to complete its orbit. It reached aphelion in 1989 and will reach perihelion in 2113.

Trujillo and Brown expect to find five to 10 more large objects and perhaps some larger than Pluto. They search using a sequence of high-resolution telescope images of the same region in space, looking for objects that move relative to the starry background (the stars are moving, also, but they are so far away relative to Kuiper belt objects that their movement is undetectable over short periods of time). They spent about seven months looking using the Oschin Telescope at Palomar, California. It has a mirror diameter of 1.2 meters, which is large compared to amateur telescopes (typically ranging from 0.1 to 0.3 meters in diameter), but small compared to most professional telescopes (one to 10 meters in diameter). Although the mirror is not very large, the Oschin Telescope has a huge field of view for its size, about $(3.75°)^2$. That is about the same amount of sky area as 12 moons in each picture.

Though Jewitt and others think Kuiper belt objects as large or larger than Pluto may remain undiscovered in the outer Kuiper belt, it is unlikely that any really large Kuiper belt object exists. Any large body in the outer solar system would have perturbed the paths of the spacecraft *Voyager 1, Voyager 2,* and *Pioneer 10* as they passed the solar system and should further influence the orbit of comet Halley. To have avoided changing the orbits of these objects any remaining large Kuiper belt objects are thought to be less than five Earth masses, which in its turn is far larger than the estimated total mass of the Kuiper belt. According to Kuiper's original calculations as well as computer simulations of losses to the inner solar system and gravitational expulsions into outer space, the Kuiper belt's original mass in the beginning of the solar system was the equivalent of about 30 Earth masses. Now it is 0.2 Earth masses, or about 100 times the mass of the asteroid belt.

The density of material in the solar system decreases with distance from the Sun.

The figure below demonstrates the loss of mass from the inner solar system, particularly from the asteroid belt. The

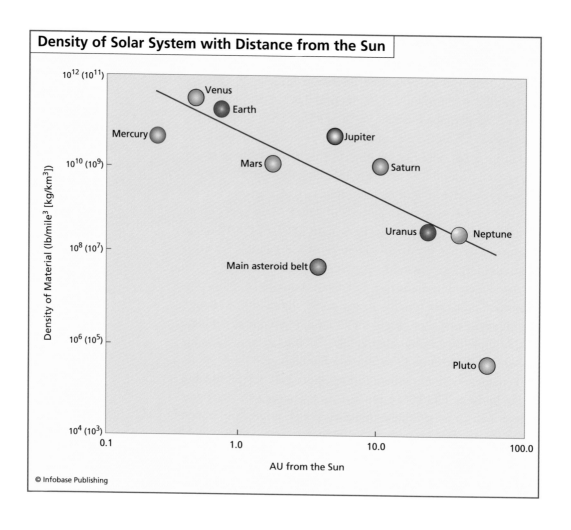

Density of Solar System with Distance from the Sun

mass of matter at a given orbit divided by the area of the orbit is plotted on the vertical axis as a measure of density of material existing at that distance from the Sun. The horizontal axis measures distance from the Sun in AU. Theories and models of the solar nebula clearly indicate that densities in the solar nebula should smoothly decrease from the Sun outward, but this graph on page 192 shows that the decrease in density is not smooth. Could the excess mass needed to smooth this graph exist in the outer solar system as more moderately large bodies, like Pluto? There may be bodies even as large as Mars remaining undiscovered in the outer solar system.

Long-Period Comets

Long-period comets are defined as those with periods of 200–300 years. This number reflects the length of time over which there is reliable orbital data, more than any inherent importance of that period for the orbital dynamics of the comets. There are about 500 comets known that have long, randomly oriented orbits. None are thought to be interstellar; all have their orbits bound by the Sun.

Long-period comets traditionally have been thought to come from a gigantic, diffuse cloud about 30,000–100,000 AU from the Earth. This region is called the Oort cloud, after the astronomer Jan Oort, who first demonstrated its existence. It is thought that most of these comets originated near Uranus and Neptune. Oort suggested that there are about 100 billion comets in the Oort cloud. Comets are thought to be perturbed out of the Oort cloud by a number of processes, including passing stars. It is thought that the heavy, early cratering on Jupiter and Saturn's satellites was caused by Oort cloud bodies. Some scientists also think that the Earth's water budget came from these bodies.

The outer edge of the Oort cloud defines the extreme edges of the solar system (see figure on page 194), where interactions with other stars and in fact the rest of the galaxy become important. This solar system is a part of a spiral galaxy called the Milky Way, which contains perhaps 100 billion stars. Stars rotate around the center of the Milky Way much as the arms of a pinwheel rotate around its center. At 30,000–60,000 AU

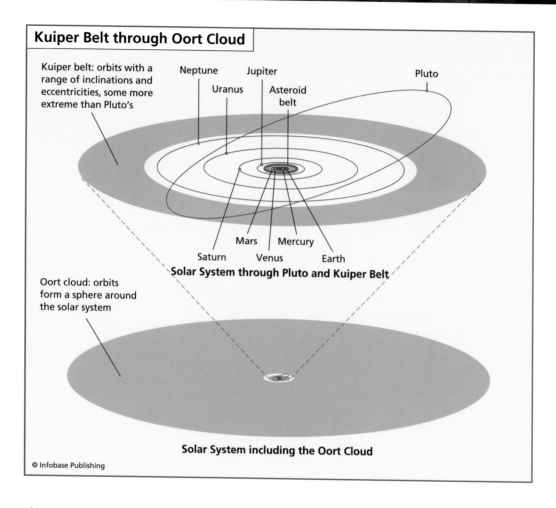

Kuiper Belt through Oort Cloud

Kuiper belt: orbits with a range of inclinations and eccentricities, some more extreme than Pluto's

Neptune

Uranus

Jupiter

Asteroid belt

Pluto

Mars

Mercury

Saturn

Venus

Earth

Solar System through Pluto and Kuiper Belt

Oort cloud: orbits form a sphere around the solar system

Solar System including the Oort Cloud

© Infobase Publishing

The Kuiper belt is vastly distant from the Sun when compared to the orbits of the terrestrial planets but miniscule when compared to the immense Oort cloud.

the comet's aphelia are so far from the solar system that the Sun's gravity is weak and the comets' orbits are perturbed by passing stars, giant molecular clouds, and even the gravitational tides of the Galactic disk and core. These gravitational perturbations sometimes divert the comets' orbits such that they pass into the inner solar system and are seen from Earth as long-term comets.

The plane in which the arms of the Milky Way rotate is called the Galactic plane. In its movements through the galaxy, the solar system oscillates above and below the Galactic plane, on a period of about 60 million years. Cometary flux from the Oort cloud is expected to vary by a factor of four over that period, as the Galactic plane exerts varying force on the bodies in the Oort cloud. The maximum cometary flux is expected to occur just after the solar system passes through the Galactic plane. The solar system has just passed through the Galactic plane, so cometary flux should now be at a local maximum.

Random close approaches of stars or giant molecular clouds (the birthplaces of stars) can cause shorter-term, much more intense spikes in cometary passages. Such a passing star could perturb a swarm on the order of 10^6 comets passing the Earth over a period of about 1 million years. Such a swarm has been suggested as a mechanism for extinctions on Earth. It is unlikely, however, that such an event would occur more frequently than once every 300 million–500 million years, and so should have occurred only about nine to 15 times in Earth history.

When Oort cloud comets are perturbed and travel into the planetary system, the gravitational fields of the planets further perturb their orbits. Scientists calculate that roughly half the comets are ejected from the solar system into interplanetary space during their first pass into the planetary system. Most of the rest are captured into tighter orbits, and only about 5 percent are returned to the Oort cloud. Some smaller fraction collides with a planet or falls into the Sun. About 10 new long-period comets are discovered each year, of which two or three pass inside the orbit of the Earth.

Because there should have been very little solar system material at the distances from the Sun where the Oort cloud now lies, some scientists think that these long-term comets originated as icy planetesimals in the vicinity of the gas giant planets. The gravitational fields of the growing gas giants expelled the smaller planetesimals beyond Pluto and into the Oort cloud. Other icy planetesimals that originated in the vicinity of Pluto were far enough from the gas giants to remain where they formed and now make up the Kuiper belt.

Some scientists estimate that 10^{12} to 10^{13} comets exist in the Oort cloud. Though the population of the Oort cloud was estimated using mathematical modeling techniques, its mass is much less certain. Even the mass of Halley's comet is not known with any precision. Its mass has to be calculated based on its size and its density, and density estimates range from 200 to 1,200 kilograms per cubic meter. The range of masses of all comets is even less well known. Masses have been estimated by using the distribution of cometary magnitudes (brightnesses) and also from estimates of masses from the Kuiper belt. A plausible average density is about 600 kg/m^3, and an average mass for a comet is about 10^{13} kg. Using these estimates, the Oort cloud contains about 20–40 Earth masses.

In 2004, the press carried a breathless story about discovering a new planet in the solar system. The planetary science community, however, was far less shocked: This was simply a large, distant object. (The press announcement occurred the week of the annual Lunar and Planetary Science Conference, the largest planetary science conference in the world, but almost no mention of the discovery was made at the conference.) The new object is named Sedna after the Inuit goddess of the ocean (it was originally designated 2003 VB12). Sedna was discovered by California Institute of Technology professor Mike Brown in November 2003 during a two-and-a-half-year sky survey for Kuiper belt objects. Each night the scientists use telescopes at the Palomar Observatory in Southern California to take three photos of a small region of the sky, one hour apart. They look for objects that move between the images and then check to see if those objects are already known. The patches of sky being examined are exceptionally tiny; Brown describes them as the size of a pinhead held at arm's length. Brown and his team had examined 15 percent of the sky in this manner before finding Sedna.

Soon after he found it, Brown realized that it was far more distant than the Kuiper belt, which reaches from 30 to 49 AU, where it has an abrupt outer edge. Sedna is currently at about 90 AU distance from the Sun and will reach its estimated perihelion of 76 AU in the year 2075. Sedna thus may be the first identified object in the Oort cloud, which up until this year was truly a theoretical construct to explain the orbits of comets. Sedna is more than twice as far from the Sun as the next closest object identified to date, which is the Kuiper belt object 1999 CL119, with a perihelion distance from the Sun of 46.6 AU. Though Sedna is not a planet, it is actually more exciting as the first known object orbiting beyond the Kuiper belt, either an inner Oort cloud object, or a member of a new population of orbiting bodies altogether.

Sedna is nearing its perihelion now, but its orbit has an eccentricity of 0.84 and carries the object to an aphelion of more than 800 AU from the Sun! This remarkable distance is 10 times farther than the Sun's magnetic field and solar wind reach. The distance carries Sedna into interstellar space, out of the field of influence of everything in the solar system except the Sun's gravity. Sedna orbits the Sun once every 10,500 years in an orbit with 12-degree inclination from the ecliptic. Sedna's radius is about 500 miles (800 km), and so it is smaller than Pluto (radius of 742 miles, or 1,195 km) and the Moon (radius of 1,079 miles, or 1,737 km). Its color is deep red, for unknown reasons, though its brightness is attributed to methane ice. It never warms above −400°F (−240°C) and so may represent some of the most primordial and unprocessed material in the solar system. It is so distant that despite its brightness it cannot be seen through any amateur telescope.

Sedna's brightness fluctuates on a 20-day cycle. Brown and his colleagues believe that the fluctuation is caused by bright and dark parts of Sedna's surface moving past as the object rotates on its cycle. A 20-day rotation is exceptionally slow: Almost every other body in the solar system rotates in hours or a day, except those bodies that are being influenced by the gravity of a moon (for example, Pluto rotates once every six days) or by the Sun if it is very close (for example, Mercury). Sedna's slow rotation was thought to be caused by a moon, but none has been seen.

Meteor Showers

The Earth travels through several major predictable dust belts each year. The dust produces tiny burning streaks as it passes into the Earth's atmosphere, burning up with the heat of entry and appearing as "shooting stars." These dust belts are left by passing comets in their orbits. Both the Eta Aquarid and the Oronid meteor showers are thought to be created from dust left by Halley's comet, the Leonids by comet P/Temple-Tuttle, and the Geminids by 3200 Phaethon.

Though the major meteor showers can produce startling numbers of meteors, dust regularly passes into the Earth's atmosphere, and meteors can be seen on any clear night of the year. The background rate of dust entering the atmosphere visible from one location on Earth creates about 10–20 meteors per hour. The rate of meteor production for each shower also varies widely from year to year. Some years the smaller showers barely rise above the background rate, but in other years the rate of meteors can verge on frightening. Several showers recorded in the last couple of centuries have produced above 100,000 meteors per hour, reportedly lighting the sky and falling near the rate of a snowstorm. In addition to the main meteor showers of the year listed in the accompanying table, there are another 70 or so minor but regular showers each year.

The meteor showers are named for the part of the sky the fire trails seem to appear from: the Geminids, for example, appear to originate from the region of the constellation of Gemini, although of course that is an optical illusion. (The dust is coming from space just outside the Earth's atmosphere and not from distant stars.)

Large observatories—notably the radar observatory at the University of Canterbury in New Zealand and the IAU Meteor Data Center in Lund, Sweden—track meteors. By analyzing the paths of meteors in the atmosphere, their original orbits can be determined. Most are found to have orbits similar to Apollo and Aten family asteroids (these are asteroids that have orbits near Earth's orbit; see below).

Although comets are the prime candidates for leaving behind the tiny dust particles that create meteor showers when the Earth moves through them, recently the near-Earth aster-oid 2101 Adonis has become a new suspect. Scientists made careful calculations about its path through the solar system and pinpointed the places where the Earth's orbit intersects the orbit of this asteroid. They found that 2101 Adonis may

MAJOR METEOR SHOWERS

Meteor shower	Approximate date	Approximate meteor rate
Quadrantids	end Dec. to beginning Jan.	60 per hour
Lyrids	mid- to end Apr.	10 per hour
Eta Aquarids	end Apr. to beginning May	20 per hour
Perseids	end July to end Aug.	75 per hour
Oronids	mid- to end Oct.	30 per hour
Leonids	mid- to end Nov.	10 per hour
Geminids	beginning to mid-Dec	75 per hour

be the source of the material that creates a number of minor meteor showers, including the nighttime sigma-Capricornids and chi-Sagittariids and the daytime chi-Capricornids. The scientist who did this calculation, Poulat B. Babadzhanov, a scientist at the Institute of Astrophysics of the Tajik Academy of Sciences, suggests that 2101 Adonis may be an old comet or an asteroid with a large ice component. Babadzhanov also suggests that the small near-Earth asteroid 1995 CS, only 50 meters in diameter, may be a fragment of 2101 Adonis, since it lies in the 2101 Adonis meteoroid stream. These interesting calculations further show that the line between asteroids and comets is blurry; this might have been expected since the asteroid belt lies between Mars and Jupiter, that is, between the last rocky planet and the first icy planet.

Missions to Comets and Asteroids

6

The first mission craft to photograph an asteroid was Galileo, in 1991. The photos taken by Galileo and those of more recent missions have completely rewritten the understanding of asteroids. These images first showed that many large asteroids are simply rubble piles and that asteroids could have their own moons. Without space missions, the science of asteroids would only be crawling slowly ahead rather than making the significant progress it is.

The minor planets have become important science; the numbers of missions reflect this interest. With at least 13 missions already completed or underway, the minor planets, taken together, have been visited more often than most of the major planets.

ICE 1978
American

The primary scientific objective of *ICE* was to study the interaction between the solar wind and a cometary atmosphere. As planned, the spacecraft traversed the plasma tail of Comet Giacobini-Zinner on September 11, 1985, and made in situ measurements of particles, fields, and waves. It also transited between the Sun and Halley's comet in late March 1986, when other spacecraft *(Giotto, Planet-A, MS-T5, Vega)* were also in the vicinity of the comet on their early March comet rendezvous missions. *ICE* became the first spacecraft to directly investigate two comets.

Vega 1 and Vega 2 1984
Soviet

These two missions to Venus and Halley's comet were launched by the Soviet Union. Two identical spacecraft, *Vega 1* and *Vega 2*, were launched December 15 and 21, 1984, respectively. After carrying Venus entry probes to the vicinity of Venus (arrival and deployment of probes were scheduled for June 11–15, 1985), the two spacecraft were retargeted using Venus gravity field assistance to intercept comet Halley in March 1986. The first spacecraft encountered comet Halley on March 6, 1986, and the second three days later. Although the spacecraft could be targeted with a precision of about 60 miles (100 km), the position of the spacecraft relative to the comet nucleus was estimated to be known only to within a few thousand kilometers.

Suisei 1985
Japanese

Suisei (the Japanese name meaning "comet") was launched by Japan's ISAS (Institute of Space and Astronautical Science) on August 18, 1985, into heliocentric orbit to fly by Halley's comet. It was identical to *Sakigake* (see below) apart from its payload: a CCD ultraviolet imaging system and a solar wind instrument. The main objective of the mission was to take ultraviolet images of the hydrogen corona for about 30 days before and after comet Halley's descending crossing of the ecliptic plane. Solar wind parameters were measured for a much longer time period. The spacecraft encountered Halley's comet at 94,000 miles (151,000 km) during March 8, 1986, suffering only two dust impacts. Limited fuel supplies prohibited the spacecraft from pursuing other mission goals.

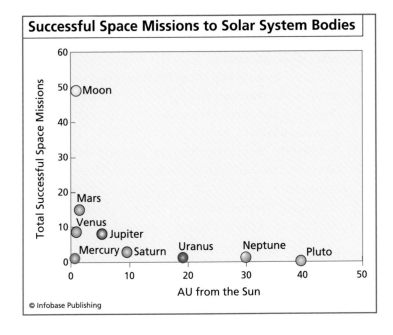

Successful Space Missions to Solar System Bodies

Total Successful Space Missions

Moon

Mars

Venus

Jupiter

Mercury Saturn

Uranus

Neptune

Pluto

AU from the Sun

© Infobase Publishing

The approximate number of successful space missions from all nations to each of the planets and the Moon shows that the Moon is by far the most visited body. Only Pluto has had no missions, and Mercury is as neglected as Uranus and Neptune. The definition of a successful mission is arguable, so totals for Mars and the Moon in particular may be disputed.

Sakigake 1985
Japanese

Sakigake ("Pioneer") was a test spacecraft similar to *Suisei*. The craft flew by Halley's comet on its sunward side at a distance of about 4,275,000 miles (7 million km) on March 11, 1986. It carried three instruments to measure plasma wave spectra, solar wind ions, and interplanetary magnetic fields, all of which worked normally.

Giotto 1985
European Space Agency

In 1986, this mission came within 375 miles (600 km) of Halley's comet. Images from this mission indicated that its surface is exceptionally black. The blackness is thought to be caused by concentrations of carbonaceous ice, but its true composition is unknown. Cracks in the black crust allow sunlight to vaporize interior ices. The major objectives of the mission were to:

1. obtain color photographs of the nucleus;

2. determine the elemental and isotopic composition of volatile components in the cometary coma, particularly parent molecules;
3. characterize the physical and chemical processes that occur in the cometary atmosphere and ionosphere;
4. determine the elemental and isotopic composition of dust particles;
5. measure the total gas-production rate and dust flux and size/mass distribution and derive the dust-to-gas ratio; and
6. investigate the macroscopic systems of plasma flows resulting from the cometary–solar wind interaction.

All experiments performed well and returned a wealth of new scientific results, of which perhaps the most important was the clear identification of the cometary nucleus. Fourteen seconds before closest approach, *Giotto* was hit by a damaging dust particle. The impact caused the spacecraft angular momentum vector to shift 0.9 degrees, enough to interrupt communications and disrupt the mission.

Galileo 1989
American

Galileo was launched by NASA on October 18, 1989, seven years after its original launch date, and its mission ended in a blaze of success on September 21, 2003. In addition to its main mission to Jupiter, Galileo passed close to two asteroids, 951 Gaspra and 243 Ida, and took the first high-resolution images of asteroids. Gaspra was photographed in October 1991 and Ida in August 1993. In these images it was discovered that Ida has its own orbiting moon, named Dactyl. Some scientists refer to the tiny moons of asteroids as "moonlets." The first asteroid thought to have a companion was 433 Eros in 1901. It and 624 Hektor have subsequently been shown to have a double-lobed shape that fooled observers into thinking they saw a main body and a moon. More than 100 suspected asteroidal moons have been reported, but many fewer have been definitively confirmed. *Galileo's* great discoveries covered the outer planets and their moons, all but eclipsing the contributions the mission made to understanding asteroids.

NEAR Shoemaker 1996
American

NEAR (Near-Earth Asteroid Rendezvous) Shoemaker was launched by NASA on February 16, 1996, and encountered asteroid 433 Eros in 1999. 433 Eros is an asteroid measuring 21 × 8 × 8 miles (33 × 13 × 13 km). Previously 433 Eros had been measured by stellar *occultation:* The passage of the asteroid in front of a distant star was observed by a number of astronomers from Earth, and the patterns of interference between the asteroid and the star were used to calculate its size. The size calculated from stellar occultation was 7 × 19 × 30 kilometers, not bad when compared with the far more accurate measurements from the *NEAR Shoemaker* mission.

NEAR Shoemaker also came within 750 miles (1,200 km) of 253 Mathilde in 1997. 253 Mathilde has a remarkably low density, only about 81 pounds per cubic foot (1,300 kg/m³), just higher than the density of water. Rock, on the other hand, varies between about 168 and 206 pounds per cubic foot (2,700 and 3,300 kg/m³). 253 Mathilde has no water in its spectrum, so its density cannot be explained by a high water content. The asteroid is now thought to be a rubble pile, about half voids and half rock, in order to achieve its very low density. The mass is held together weakly by gravity, but if it fell within the gravity field of a larger body it would immediately break into pieces. *NEAR Shoemaker*'s close encounter with Mathilde was a special bonus, since the mission was primarily designed for Eros and not for rapid flyby encounters of the type with Mathilde. Mathilde's encounter is also the first close look at a C-type asteroid.

Deep Space 1 1998
American

The Deep Space 1 mission craft was the first of a series of technology demonstration probes being developed by NASA's New

Millennium Program. The spacecraft flew by the near-Earth asteroid 9969 Braille (formerly known as 1992 KD) in July 1999 and flew by comet Borrelly on September 22, 2001. This highly successful mission has demonstrated the functionality of a number of imaging instruments and *spectrometers*. Along with its technology demonstration, the mission obtained what were at the time the best images of a cometary nucleus. In its extended mission, *Deep Space 1* visited comet Borrelly, and the spacecraft was retired in December 2001.

Stardust 1999
American

The Stardust mission traveled to the new, young comet Wild 2, took images and measurements, collected particles from the comet's tail, and returned successfully to Earth in 2006. *Stardust* had an unusually successful visit to the comet on January 2, 2004, when it flew within 147 miles (236 km) of the nucleus, taking groundbreaking images of the comet and its processes.

The *Stardust* spacecraft has been reassigned to visit comet Tempel 1 to look for changes in the comet's nucleus since it was struck by the *Deep Impact* impactor and since traveling near the Sun. This observation may allow measurement of surface movements and determine whether the surface flows like a powder: Some scientists from the *Stardust* team described the comet's surface as resembling the texture of talcum powder.

A close-up image of comet Wild 2, which was visited by the Stardust mission. (NASA)

CONTOUR 2002
American

The *Comet Nucleus Tour (CONTOUR)* spacecraft was lost early in its mission. Just as the spacecraft was igniting its solid rocket engine to leave Earth orbit contact was lost. Using Earth-based telescopes, some objects were seen in space near *CONTOUR*'s last location. These are thought to be parts of the broken spacecraft. The Comet Nucleus Tour (CON-

An artist's conception of the Stardust mission nearing comet Wild 2. (NASA)

TOUR) Discovery class mission had as its primary objective close flybys of two comets, Encke and Schwassmann-Wachmann-3.

Hayabusa (formerly known as MUSES-C) 2003
Japan

Japanese mission to collect samples from asteroid Itokawa. This mission launched in May 2003 and arrived at the asteroid in November 2005, where it was expected to land and remain for three months before return to Earth. Detailed measurements of the asteroid were returned to Earth, but the craft did not land on the asteroid and may not even have collected dust in its sampling chamber. The chamber was resealed and the craft is returning to Earth, scheduled to arrive in June 2010. Unfortunately systems on the craft have been failing, and by 2007 three of its four thruster engines were broken.

Rosetta 2004
European Space Agency

Rosetta is designed to rendezvous with comet Churyumov-Gerasimenko and study it for an extended period. The craft, designed for a long period of operation, will send a lander to the comet's surface, study the comet while orbiting it for two years, and fly through the asteroid belt for further observations. The principal goals are to study the origin of comets and what their material can reveal about the origin of the solar system. The trip to the comet will require 10 years of space travel, and to date the mission is operating normally. The craft will make its third Earth gravity assist in late 2009 and begin entering the orbit of the comet in 2014. During flight in 2007, the spacecraft was briefly mistaken for a near-Earth asteroid and given the designation 2007 VN_{84} before the error was discovered.

Deep Impact 2005
American

The idea for the Deep Impact mission came to its originators, Alan Delamere and Mike Belton of Ball Aerospace and Mike A'Hearn of the University of Maryland, when research on Halley's comet showed that the comet was black, darker than soot. The researchers began to suspect that as the ices that form the comet's tail jet away from the comet, they leave behind a growing crust of nonvolatile materials. New jets need to burst through that crust. To investigate this hypothesis, they wanted to send the "equivalent of a bullet" to crash through the crust and reveal the interior.

The impactor weighed 816 lbs (370 kg) and hit the comet at 10 km/sec after being aimed from 536,865 miles (864,000 km) away, and, to make its way, the impactor used a high-precision targeting system. Despite colliding with two dust particles on the way to the comet, each of which rotated the targeting sensors away from the comet, the impactor worked as planned. The impactor delivered the equivalent of 4.8 tons of TNT to the surface of the comet to excavate its crater.

The Deep Impact mission launched in January 2005 and reached the comet Tempel 1 on July 4, 2005. Twenty-four hours prior to impact with the comet, the craft separated an impactor and then changed its course to be out of the way of the impact when the impact happened but still able to observe it. The impact and the comet in its aftermath were also observed

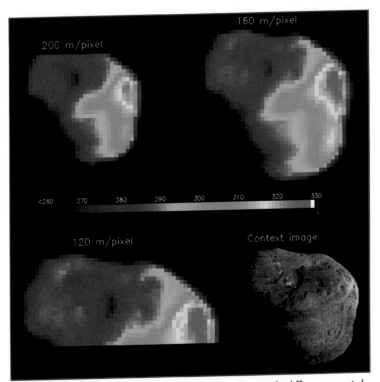

A temperature map of comet Tempel 1's nucleus with different spatial resolutions—The context image (in black and white) was taken just before impact. The color bar in the middle gives temperature in Kelvins (equal to temperature in Celsius plus 273 degrees). The Sun is to the right in all images. Shadows are the coolest temperatures, and the point directly below the Sun is hottest. (NASA/UM M. F. A'Hearn, et al., Science 310, 258 (2005); published online (9/8/05). Reprinted with permission from AAAS)

This image of comet Tempel 1 was taken 67 seconds after it obliterated Deep Impact's impactor spacecraft. Scattered light from the collision saturated the camera's detector, creating the bright splash seen here. The image reveals topographic features, including ridges, scalloped edges and possibly impact craters formed long ago. (NASA/JPL-Caltech/UMD)

by the *Spitzer Space Telescope*, along with 73 Earth-based telescopes at 35 observatories.

In the normal jets of the comet, the Spitzer Space Telescope was able to detect crystalline and glassy silicate minerals, carbon, carbonates, clay minerals, and water. These results are in agreement with the results from the Stardust mission, that comets consist of materials made at both very high and low temperatures. The mission detected a few very smooth and bright areas on the surface of the comet that proved to be water ice; despite the earlier idea that comets were largely made of water ice, this was the first real observation of water ice on a comet. The jets coming from the comet, however, were significantly rich in water, reinforcing the idea that there were richer reserves of water beneath the surface.

A brilliant flash about two-tenths of a second long occurred as the impactor struck the comet, probably resulting from the vaporization of both the impactor and part of the nucleus.

The first flash was followed by a second, possibly originating deeper within the comet. The second flash was brighter still, and it momentarily saturated some pixels in the instruments on the flyby spacecraft. An ejecta curtain of gas and dust then flew out of the crater at three to five miles/sec (5 to 7 km/sec). Though very rapid, this curtain was moving more slowly than the material in the comet's normal jets. The large amount of dust and gas indicated that the near-surface of the comet was far more powdery and weak than had been thought and therefore easier to eject.

Immediately after the impact, the brightness of the comet rose by a factor of four for about 40 minutes and returned to its original intensity by about two hours after impact. There were eight gases observed in the outflow from the crater: water (H_2O), ethane (C_2H_6), hydrogen cyanide (HCN), carbon monoxide (CO), methanol (CH_3OH), formaldehyde (H_2CO), acetylene (C_2H_2), and methane (CH_4). Only water, ethane, methanol, and hydrogen cyanide were measured both before and after the impact, indicating that the other gases are more common in the interior and represent a compositional change from the crust.

Before the impact, estimates of the crater size ranged from ~90 m to as much as 240 m, depending upon the characteristics of the material being impacted and whether the impactor exploded at or below the surface (the impactor would explode from heat and pressure, not because it was carrying explosives). After the impact, the crater was more difficult to observe than was expected, because it was obscured by the extensive amount of dust and gas. No clear images of the crater were ever obtained (though the returning Stardust mission may detect it—see below).

The *Deep Impact* spacecraft is now being reassigned to a new mission, in which it will fly by the comet Boethin and will also observe several close stars that are known to have giant planets (exoplanets) orbiting them. Meanwhile, the *Stardust* spacecraft has been reassigned to visit comet Tempel 1 and examine the changes that the comet's nucleus has experienced since being struck by the *Deep Impact* impactor and since traveling near the Sun. This observation may allow measurement of surface movements and determine whether the surface flows like a powder, as has been suggested.

New Horizons 2006
American

New Horizons launched January 19, 2006, at the highest velocity that any craft has ever left the planet. In 2007, the craft passed Jupiter and was able to photograph lightning, the development of ammonia clouds in the planet's atmosphere, and the structure of its thin rings. The mission will reach Pluto and Charon in 2015. The spacecraft will then head deeper into the Kuiper belt to study one or more of the bodies in that vast region, at least a billion miles beyond Neptune's orbit. *New Horizons* has many science partners, including the Johns Hopkins University Applied Physics Laboratory, the Southwest Research Institute, Ball Aerospace Corporation, Stanford University, and NASA. The mission includes instrumentation for visible-wavelength surface mapping, infrared and ultraviolet imaging to study surface composition and atmosphere, radiometry, and solar wind measurements.

Dawn 2007
American

Dawn is designed to orbit the asteroid 4 Vesta and the dwarf planet 1 Ceres. The objectives of the mission are to characterize the asteroids' internal structures, densities, shapes, compositions, and masses and to return information on surface patterns, cratering, and magnetism. Either or both of these bodies may be fully differentiated, that is, that heat in their early history allowed material to melt and form a metallic core and a silicate mantle. With the measurements from *Dawn*, scientists will be able to say more about the structure and history of these bodies, how hot they ever became, and whether water or carbon has been important in their formation. This information directly bears on conditions and processes of planet formation in the early solar system.

The mission launched on September 27, 2007, received a Mars gravity assist in February 2009, and will arrive at Vesta in 2011. After spending nine months with Vesta, the craft will fly an additional three years to reach Ceres, where it will spend another nine months. The plan and status of the mission can be seen at http://dawn.jpl.nasa.gov/.

In the 15 years since the first space mission visited a small body, astonishing data has been gathered. Before these missions, scientists thought of asteroids as bare chunks of rock or metal, but the images and data returned show that most asteroids are deeply fragmented, have their own regolith, and even may have their own orbiting moons. Comets were thought to be loose agglomerations of ice and dust before spacecraft traveled close enough to take clear photos of the nucleuses of Halley, Borrelly, and Wild 1 and showed dense, competent bodies with depressions resembling impact craters along with ridges and pinnacles. Future missions aim to return material from an asteroid to Earth, and from there the real detective work of linking meteorites to asteroids can continue in earnest.

7

Conclusions: The Known and the Unknown

The major planets out to Saturn have been known to humankind for millennia, into the vague shadows of prehistory. The small bodies of the solar system, including everything from dust to asteroids and comets, were not known until 200 years ago, when Piazzi saw 1 Ceres through his newly invented telescope. The discovery of these tiny bodies seemed to disrupt the natural harmonious order of the planets. Would the maker of the universe have left a gap in the order of the planets, the scientific and theological communities wondered? Briefly the idea arose that a planet had existed and was shattered, but a universe subject to such immense and capricious forces of nature was horrifying to those men of the enlightenment.

As hard as it was for society to accept the idea that the region between Mars and Jupiter was filled with small rocky bodies, the idea of meteorites falling to Earth was still harder, and the concept of catastrophic impacts creating craters more difficult still. A disorderly universe containing arbitrary and potentially fatal wandering bodies was beyond what people believed about their consistent and improving world. Craters were explained in many ways by many scientists, from the results of bursting bubbles to circular voids left when otherwise invisible volcanic activity occurred. Well into the latter half of the 20th century, scientists resisted believing that impacts made craters and were a normal and continuous process in the solar system. The ancient surfaces of the Moon and Mercury, for example, show that impacts were far more common in the distant past, near the beginning of the solar system. The acceptance of a meteorite impact ending the reign of the dinosaurs on Earth forced the community to think of impacts as events that still occur, though with less frequency than they did 4 billion years ago.

With the acceptance of the existence of a continuum of bodies in the solar system came the necessary realization that not all those bodies lie in stable orbits and that they will continue to be perturbed into orbits that will allow them to be drawn into the gravity fields of larger bodies such as the Earth. Meteorites are accepted as remnant pieces of larger bodies that separately orbited the Sun. Meteorites therefore give scientists an invaluable source of material from outside the Earth. This material in some cases has been shown to come from small planets that differentiated into iron cores and silicate mantles before being destroyed by collisions in the early solar system. Other meteorites have been proven to have traveled through space from Mars and from the Moon, blasted off their surfaces in giant impacts and eventually captured by the Earth. In other cases meteorites have been shown convincingly to be primordial undifferentiated material, the very stuff of the original solar nebula from which the planets formed.

These primitive meteorites have provided science with a wealth of information: the age of the solar system (4.556 billion years), the possible bulk composition of the Earth, and even with tiny diamonds that originated in giant stars outside this system. From the Sun to the grains of dust that comets shed, sizes in the solar system vary over perhaps 14 orders of magnitude. By comparing the inferred compositions of asteroids that were obtained through remote sensing with data on meteorites on Earth, the parent bodies of some of the meteorites now on Earth have been located in the asteroid belt.

Though asteroids are a relatively new topic in science, comets have been watched with fascination by humankind for perhaps longer than the giant planets. A comet blazing brightly enough to be seen in daylight alongside the Sun seems to be an entirely different creature than a dark, rocky asteroid that can only be seen through a high-magnification telescope, but increasingly there appears to be a continuum between the classes. Some asteroids begin to degas and produce a tiny coma and tail when they approach their perihelia (closest approach to the Sun). Since the mid-1900s, scientists have theorized that large populations of small, icy bodies orbit near Pluto, in the Kuiper belt, and well beyond the Kuiper belt, in the Oort cloud. In the last 10 years, the first members of those populations have been seen in telescopes from Earth and from the *Hubble Space Telescope*. The Oort cloud is thought to stretch a large fraction of the distance to the nearest stars.

Understanding the compositions of the small bodies in the universe, their numbers, distribution, relations to the planets, and relations to meteorites is in its infancy. Space missions will continue to bring back data important to understanding these small bodies and so will increase the understanding of solar system formation and evolution. Though asteroids and meteorites have been the last objects to command the interest of the space science community, they hold the potential to tell humankind more about the development of the solar system than the planets themselves.

Appendix 1:

Units and Measurements

FUNDAMENTAL UNITS

The system of measurements most commonly used in science is called both the SI (for Système International d'Unités) and the International System of Units (it is also sometimes called the MKS system). The SI system is based upon the metric units meter (abbreviated m), kilogram (kg), second (sec), kelvin (K), mole (mol), candela (cd), and ampere (A), used to measure length, time, mass, temperature, amount of a substance, light intensity, and electric current, respectively. This system was agreed upon in 1974 at an international general conference. There is another metric system, CGS, which stands for centimeter, gram, second; that system simply uses the hundredth of a meter (the centimeter) and the hundredth of the kilogram (the gram). The CGS system, formally introduced by the British Association for the Advancement of Science in 1874, is particularly useful to scientists making measurements of small quantities in laboratories, but it is less useful for space science. In this set, the SI system is used with the exception that temperatures will be presented in Celsius (C), instead of Kelvin. (The conversions between Celsius, Kelvin, and Fahrenheit temperatures are given below.) Often the standard unit of measure in the SI system, the meter, is too small when talking about the great distances in the solar system; kilometers (thousands of meters) or AU (astronomical units, defined below) will often be used instead of meters.

How is a unit defined? At one time a "meter" was defined as the length of a special metal ruler kept under strict conditions of temperature and humidity. That perfect meter could not be measured, however, without changing its temperature by opening the box, which would change its length, through

FUNDAMENTAL UNITS

Measurement	Unit	Symbol	Definition
length	meter	m	The meter is the distance traveled by light in a vacuum during 1/299,792,458 of a second.
time	second	sec	The second is defined as the period of time in which the oscillations of cesium atoms, under specified conditions, complete exactly 9,192,631,770 cycles. The length of a second was thought to be a constant before Einstein developed theories in physics that show that the closer to the speed of light an object is traveling, the slower time is for that object. For the velocities on Earth, time is quite accurately still considered a constant.
mass	kilogram	kg	The International Bureau of Weights and Measures keeps the world's standard kilogram in Paris, and that object is the definition of the kilogram.
temperature	kelvin	K	A degree in Kelvin (and Celsius) is 1/273.16 of the thermody- namic temperature of the triple point of water (the temperature at which, under one atmosphere pressure, water coexists as water vapor, liquid, and solid ice). In 1967, the General Conference on Weights and Measures defined this temperature as 273.16 kelvin.

thermal expansion or contraction. Today a meter is no longer defined according to a physical object; the only fundamental measurement that still is defined by a physical object is the kilogram. All of these units have had long and complex histories of attempts to define them. Some of the modern definitions, along with the use and abbreviation of each, are listed in the table here.

Mass and weight are often confused. Weight is proportional to the force of gravity: Your weight on Earth is about six times

FUNDAMENTAL UNITS *(continued)*

Measurement	Unit	Symbol	Definition
amount of a substance	mole	mol	The mole is the amount of a substance that contains as many units as there are atoms in 0.012 kilogram of carbon 12 (that is, Avogadro's number, or 6.02205×10^{23}). The units may be atoms, molecules, ions, or other particles.
electric current	ampere	A	The ampere is that constant current which, if maintained in two straight parallel conductors of infinite length, of negligible circular cross section, and placed one meter apart in a vacuum, would produce between the conductors a force equal to 2×10^{-7} newtons per meter of length
light intensity	candela	cd	The candela is the luminous intensity of a source that emits monochromatic radiation with a wavelength of 555.17 nm and that has a radiant intensity of 1/683 watt per steradian. Normal human eyes are more sensitive to the yellow-green light of this wavelength than to any other.

your weight on the Moon because Earth's gravity is about six times that of the Moon's. Mass, on the other hand, is a quantity of matter, measured independently of gravity. In fact, weight has different units from mass: Weight is actually measured as a force (newtons, in SI, or pounds, in the English system).

The table "Fundamental Units" lists the fundamental units of the SI system. These are units that need to be defined in order to make other measurements. For example, the meter and the second are fundamental units (they are not based on any other units). To measure velocity, use a derived unit, meters per second (m/sec), a combination of fundamental units. Later in this section there is a list of common derived units.

The systems of temperature are capitalized (Fahrenheit, Celsius, and Kelvin), but the units are not (degree and kelvin). Unit abbreviations are capitalized only when they are named after a person, such as K for Lord Kelvin, or A for André-Marie Ampère. The units themselves are always lowercase, even when named for a person: one newton, or one N. Throughout these tables a small dot indicates multiplication, as in N · m, which means a newton (N) times a meter (m). A space between the symbols can also be used to indicate multiplication, as in N m. When a small letter is placed in front of a symbol, it is a prefix meaning some multiplication factor. For example, J stands for the unit of energy called a joule, and a mJ indicates a millijoule, or 10^{-3} joules. The table of prefixes is given at the end of this section.

COMPARISONS AMONG KELVIN, CELSIUS, AND FAHRENHEIT

One kelvin represents the same temperature difference as 1°C, and the temperature in kelvins is always equal to 273.15 plus the temperature in degrees Celsius. The Celsius scale was designed around the behavior of water. The freezing point of water (at one atmosphere of pressure) was originally defined to be 0°C, while the boiling point is 100°C. The kelvin equals exactly 1.8°F.

To convert temperatures in the Fahrenheit scale to the Celsius scale, use the following equation, where F is degrees Fahrenheit, and C is degrees Celsius:

$$C = (F-32)/1.8.$$

And to convert Celsius to Fahrenheit, use this equation:

$$F = 1.8C + 32.$$

To convert temperatures in the Celsius scale to the Kelvin scale, add 273.16. By convention, the degree symbol (°) is used for Celsius and Fahrenheit temperatures but not for temperatures given in Kelvin, for example, 0°C equals 273K.

What exactly is temperature? Qualitatively, it is a measurement of how hot something feels, and this definition is so easy to relate to that people seldom take it further. What is really happening in a substance as it gets hot or cold, and how does that change make temperature? When a fixed amount of energy is put into a substance, it heats up by an amount depending on what it is. The temperature of an object, then, has something to do with how the material responds to energy, and that response is called entropy. The entropy of a material (entropy is usually denoted S) is a measure of atomic wiggling and disorder of the atoms in the material. Formally, temperature is defined as

$$\frac{1}{T} = \left(\frac{dS}{dU} \right)_N,$$

meaning one over temperature (the reciprocal of temperature) is defined as the change in entropy (dS, in differential notation) per change in energy (dU), for a given number of atoms (N). What this means in less technical terms is that temperature is a measure of how much heat it takes to increase the entropy (atomic wiggling and disorder) of a substance. Some materials get hotter with less energy, and others require more to reach the same temperature.

The theoretical lower limit of temperature is −459.67°F (−273.15°C, or 0K), known also as absolute zero. This is the temperature at which all atomic movement stops. The Prussian physicist Walther Nernst showed that it is impossible to actually reach absolute zero, though with laboratory methods using nuclear magnetization it is possible to reach 10^{-6}K (0.000001K).

USEFUL MEASURES OF DISTANCE

A *kilometer* is a thousand meters (see the table "International System Prefixes"), and a *light-year* is the distance light travels in a vacuum during one year (exactly 299,792,458 m/sec, but commonly rounded to 300,000,000 m/sec). A light-year, therefore, is the distance that light can travel in one year, or:

299,792,458 m/sec × 60 sec/min × 60 min/hr ×
24 hr/day × 365 days/yr = 9.4543 × 10^{15} m/yr.

For shorter distances, some astronomers use light minutes and even light seconds. A light minute is 17,998,775 km, and a light second is 299,812.59 km. The nearest star to Earth, Proxima Centauri, is 4.2 light-years away from the Sun. The next, Rigil Centaurs, is 4.3 light-years away.

An *angstrom* (10^{-10}m) is a unit of length most commonly used in nuclear or particle physics. Its symbol is Å. The diameter of an atom is about one angstrom (though each element and isotope is slightly different).

An astronomical unit (AU) is a unit of distance used by astronomers to measure distances in the solar system. One astronomical unit equals the average distance from the center of the Earth to the center of the Sun. The currently accepted value, made standard in 1996, is 149,597,870,691 meters, plus or minus 30 meters.

One kilometer equals 0.62 miles, and one mile equals 1.61 kilometers.

The following table gives the most commonly used of the units derived from the fundamental units above (there are many more derived units not listed here because they have been developed for specific situations and are little-used elsewhere; for example, in the metric world, the curvature of a railroad track is measured with a unit called "degree of curvature," defined as the angle between two points in a curving track that are separated by a chord of 20 meters).

Though the units are given in alphabetical order for ease of reference, many can fit into one of several broad categories: dimensional units (angle, area, volume), material properties (density, viscosity, thermal expansivity), properties of motion (velocity, acceleration, angular velocity), electrical properties (frequency, electric charge, electric potential, resistance, inductance, electric field strength), magnetic properties (magnetic field strength, magnetic flux, magnetic flux density), and properties of radioactivity (amount of radioactivity and effect of radioactivity).

DERIVED UNITS

Measurement	Unit symbol (derivation)	Comments
acceleration	unnamed (m/sec^2)	
angle	radian rad (m/m)	One radian is the angle centered in a circle that includes arc of length equal to the radius. Since the circumference equals two pi times the radius, one radian equals 1/ (2 pi) of the circle, or approximately 57.296°.
	steradian sr (m^2/m^2)	The steradian is a unit of solid angle. There are four pi steradians in a sphere. Thus one steradian equals about 0.079577 sphere or about 3282.806 square degrees.
angular velocity	unnamed (rad/sec)	
area	unnamed (m^2)	
density	unnamed (kg/m^3)	Density is mass per volume. Lead is dense styrofoam is not. Water has a density of one gram per cubic centimeter or 1,000 kilograms per cubic meter.
electric charge or electric flux	coulomb C ($A \cdot sec$)	One coulomb is the amount of charge accumulated in one second by a current of one ampere. One coulomb is also the amount of charge on 6.241506×10^{18} electrons.
electric field strength	unnamed [($kg \cdot m$) / ($sec^3 \cdot A$) = V/m]	Electric strength is a measure of the intensive of an electrified at a particular location. A field strength to one V/m represents a potential difference of one vol between points separated by one meter.
electric potential or electromotive force (often called voltage)	volt V [($kg \cdot m^2$)/ ($sec^3 \cdot A$)= $J/C = W/A$]	Voltage is an expression of the potential difference in charge between two points in an electrical field. Electric potential is defined as the amount of potential energy present per unit of charge. One volt is a potential of one joule per coulomb of charge. The greater the voltage, the greater the flow of electric current

(continues)

DERIVED UNITS *(continued)*		
Measurement	**Unit symbol (derivation)**	**Comments**
energy, work, or heat	joule J [N · m (= kg · m^2/sec^2)]	
	electron volt eV	The electron volt, being so much smaller than the joule (one eV = 1.6 × 10^{-17}]), is useful for describing small systems.
force	newton N (kg · m /sec^2)	This unit is the equivalent to the pound in the English system, since the pound is a measure of force and not mass.
frequency	hertz Hz (cycles/sec)	Frequency is related to wavelength as follows: Kilohertz × wavelength in meters = 300,000
inductance	henry H (Wb/A)	Inductance is the amount of magnetic flux a material produces for a given current of electricity. Metal wire with an electric current passing through it creates a magnetic field different types of metal make magnetic fields with different strengths and therefore have different inductances.
magnetic field strength	unnamed (A/m)	Magnetic field strength is the force that a magnetic field exerts on a theoretical unit magnetic pole.
magnetic flux	weber Wb [(kg · m^2)/(sec^2 · A)= V · sec]	The magnetic flux across a perpendicular surface is the product of the magnetic flux density, in teslas and the surface area, in square meters.
magnetic flux density	tesla T [kg/(sec^2 · A) = Wb/m^2]	A magnetic field of one tesla is strong. The strongest artificial fields made in laboratories are about 20 teslas. and the Earth's magnetic flux density, at its surface is about 50 microteslas (μT). Planetary magnetic fields are sometimes measured in gammas, which are nanoteslas (10^{-9} teslas)
momentum or impulse	unnamed[N · sec (= kg · m/sec]]	Momentum is a measure of moving mass: how much mass and how fast it is moving.
power	watt W [J/sec (= (kg · m^2)/sec^3)]	Power is the rate at which energy is spent. Power can be mechanical (as in horsepower) or electrical (a watt is produced by a current of one ampere flowing through an electric potential of one volt).

Measurement	Unit symbol (derivation)	Comments
pressure or stress	pascal Pa (N/m²)	The high pressures inside planets are often measured in gigapascals (10^9 pascals), abbreviated GPa. ~10,000 atm = one GPa.
	atmosphere atm	The atmosphere is a handy unit because one atmosphere is approximately the pressure felt from the air at sea level on Earth; one standard atm = 101.325 Pa; one metric atm = 98.066Pa; one atm ~ one bar.
radiation per unit mass receiving it	gray (J/Kg)	The amount of radiation energy absorbed per kilogram ofmass. One gray = 100 rads an older unit.
radiation (effect of)	sievert Sv	This unit is meant to make comparable the biological effects of different doses and types of radiation. It is the energy of radiation received per kilogram, in grays, multiplied by a factor that takes into consideration the damage done by the particular type of radiation
radioactivity (amount)	becquerel Bq	One atomic decay per second
	curie Ci	The curie is the older unit of measure but is stillfrequency seen. One Ci = 3.7×10^{10} Bq.
resistance	ohm Ω (V/A)	Resistance is a material's unwillingness to pass electric current Materials with high resistance become hot rather than allowing the current to pass and can make excellent heaters
thermal expansivity	unnamed(/°)	This unit is per degree measuring the change in volume of a substance with the rise in temperature.
vacuum	torr	Vacuum is atmospheric pressure below one atm (one torr = 1/760 atm). Give a pool of mercury with a glass tube standing in it, one torr of pressure on the pool will press the mercury one millimeter up into the tube, where one standard atmosphere will push up 760 millimeters of mercury.
velocity	unnamed (m/sec)	

(continues)

	DERIVED UNITS (continued)	
Measurement	**Unit symbol (derivation)**	**Comments**
viscosity	unnamed [Pa · sec (= kg/(m · sec)]	Viscosity is a measure of resistance to flow. If a force of one newton is needed to move one square meter of the liquid or gas relative to a second layer one meter away at a speed of one meter per second, then its viscosity is one Pa · s, often simply written Pa · s or Pas. The cgs unit for viscosity is the poise equal to 0.1Pa s.
volume	cubic meter (m³)	

DEFINITIONS FOR ELECTRICITY AND MAGNETISM

When two objects in each other's vicinity have different electrical charges, an *electric field* exists between them. An electric field also forms around any single object that is electrically charged with respect to its environment. An object is negatively charged (−) if it has an excess of electrons relative to its surroundings. An object is positively charged (+) if it is deficient in electrons with respect to its surroundings.

An electric field has an effect on other charged objects in the vicinity. The field strength at a particular distance from an object is directly proportional to the electric charge of that object, in coulombs. The field strength is inversely proportional to the distance from a charged object.

Flux is the rate (per unit of time) in which something flowing crosses a surface perpendicular to the direction of flow.

An alternative expression for the intensity of an electric field is *electric flux density*. This refers to the number of lines of electric flux passing at right angles through a given surface area, usually one meter squared (1 m²). Electric flux density, like electric field strength, is directly proportional to the charge on the object. But flux density diminishes with distance according to the inverse-square law because it is specified in terms of a surface area (per meter squared) rather than a linear displacement (per meter).

A *magnetic field* is generated when electric charge carriers such as electrons move through space or within an electrical conductor. The geometric shapes of the magnetic flux lines produced by moving charge carriers (electric current)

INTERNATIONAL SYSTEM PREFIXES

SI prefix	Symbol	Multiplying factor
exa-	E	10^{18} = 1,000,000,000,000,000,000
peta-	P	10^{15} = 1,000,000,000,000,000
tera-	T	10^{12} = 1,000,000,000,000
giga-	G	10^{9} = 1,000,000,000
mega-	M	10^{6} = 1,000,000
kilo-	k	10^{3} = 1,000
hecto-	h	10^{2} = 100
deca-	da	10 = 10
deci-	d	10^{-1} = 0.1
centi-	c	10^{-2} = 0.01
milli-	m	10^{-3} = 0.001
micro-	µ or u	10^{-6} = 0.000,001
nano-	n	10^{-9} = 0.000,000,001
pico-	p	10^{-12} = 0.000,000,000,001
femto-	f	10^{-15} = 0.000,000,000,000,001
atto-	a	10^{-18} = 0.000,000,000,000,000,001

A note on nonmetric prefixes: In the United States, the word billion means the number 1,000,000,000, or 10^{9}. In most countries of Europe and Latin America this number is called "one milliard" or "one thousand million" and "billion" means the number 1,000,000,000,000 or 10^{12}, which is what Americans call a "trillion." In this set, a billion is 10^{9}.

NAMES FOR LARGE NUMBERS

Number	American	European	SI prefix
10^9	billion	milliard	giga-
10^{12}	trillion	billion	tera-
10^{15}	quadrillion	billiard	peta-
10^{18}	quintillion	trillion	exa-
10^{21}	sextillion	trilliard	zetta-
10^{24}	septillion	quadrillion	yotta-
10^{27}	octillion	quadrilliard	
10^{30}	nonillion	quintillion	
10^{33}	decillion	quintilliard	
10^{36}	undecillion	sextillion	
10^{39}	duodecillion	sextilliard	
10^{42}	tredecillion	septillion	
10^{45}	quattuordecillion	septilliard	

This naming system is designed to expand indefinitely by factors of powers of three. Then, there is also the googol, the number 10^{100} (one followed by 100 zeroes). The googol was invented for fun by the eight-year-old nephew of the American mathematician Edward Kasner. The googolplex is 10^{googol}, or one followed by a googol of zeroes. Both it and the googol are numbers large than the total number of atoms in the universe, thought to be about 10^{80}.

are similar to the shapes of the flux lines in an electrostatic field. But there are differences in the ways electrostatic and magnetic fields interact with the environment.

Electrostatic flux is impeded or blocked by metallic objects. *Magnetic flux* passes through most metals with little or no effect, with certain exceptions, notably iron and nickel. These two metals, and alloys and mixtures containing them, are known as ferromagnetic materials because they concentrate magnetic lines of flux.

Magnetic flux density and *magnetic force* are related to *magnetic field strength*. In general, the magnetic field strength diminishes with increasing distance from the axis of a magnetic dipole in which the flux field is stable. The function defining the rate at which this field-strength decrease occurs depends on the geometry of the magnetic lines of flux (the shape of the flux field).

PREFIXES

Adding a prefix to the name of that unit forms a multiple of a unit in the International System (see the table "International System Prefixes"). The prefixes change the magnitude of the unit by orders of 10 from 10^{18} to 10^{-18}.

Very small concentrations of chemicals are also measured in parts per million (ppm) or parts per billion (ppb), which mean just what they sound like: If there are four parts per million of lead in a rock (4 ppm), then out of every million atoms in that rock, on average four of them will be lead.

Appendix 2:

Light, Wavelength, and Radiation

Electromagnetic radiation is energy given off by matter, traveling in the form of waves or particles. Electromagnetic energy exists in a wide range of energy values, of which visible light is one small part of the total spectrum. The source of radiation may be the hot and therefore highly energized atoms of the Sun, pouring out radiation across a wide range of energy values, including of course visible light, and they may also be unstable (radioactive) elements giving off radiation as they decay.

Radiation is called "electromagnetic" because it moves as interlocked waves of electrical and magnetic fields. A wave is a disturbance traveling through space, transferring energy from one point to the next. In a vacuum, all electromagnetic radiation travels at the speed of light, 983,319,262 feet per second (299,792,458 m/sec, often approximated as 300,000,000 m/sec). Depending on the type of radiation, the waves have different wavelengths, energies, and frequencies (see the following figure). The wavelength is the distance between individual waves, from one peak to another. The frequency is the number of waves that pass a stationary point each second. Notice in the graphic how the wave undulates up and down from peaks to valleys to peaks. The time from one peak to the next peak is called one cycle. A single unit of frequency is equal to one cycle per second. Scientists refer to a single cycle as one hertz, which commemorates 19th-century German physicist Heinrich Hertz, whose discovery of electromagnetic waves led to the development of radio. The frequency of a wave is related to its energy: The higher the frequency of a wave, the higher its energy, though its speed in a vacuum does not change.

Electromagnetic Waves

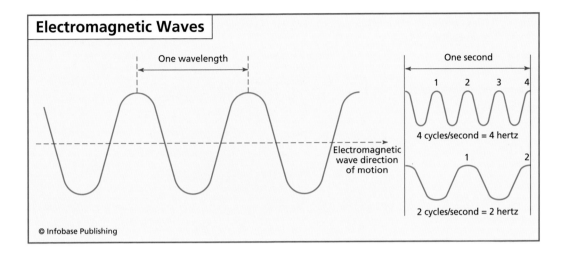

© Infobase Publishing

The smallest wavelength, highest energy and frequency electromagnetic waves are cosmic rays, then as wavelength increases and energy and frequency decrease, come gamma rays, then X-rays, then ultraviolet light, then visible light (moving from violet through indigo, blue, green, yellow, orange, and red), then infrared (divided into near, meaning near to visible, mid-, and far infrared), then microwaves, and then radio waves, which have the longest wavelengths and the lowest energy and frequency. The electromagnetic spectrum is shown in the accompanying figure and table.

As a wave travels and vibrates up and down with its characteristic wavelength, it can be imagined as vibrating up and down in a single plane, such as the plane of this sheet of paper in the case of the simple example in the figure here showing polarization. In nature, some waves change their polarization constantly so that their polarization sweeps through all angles, and they are said to be circularly polarized. In ordinary visible light, the waves are vibrating up and down in numerous random planes. Light can be shone through a special filter called a polarizing filter that blocks out all the light except that polarized in a certain direction, and the light that shines out the other side of the filter is then called polarized light.

Polarization is important in wireless communications systems such as radios, cell phones, and non-cable television. The orientation of the transmitting antenna creates the

Each electromagnetic wave has a measurable wavelength and frequency.

The electromagnetic spectrum ranges from cosmic rays at the shortest wavelengths to radiowaves at the longest wavelengths.

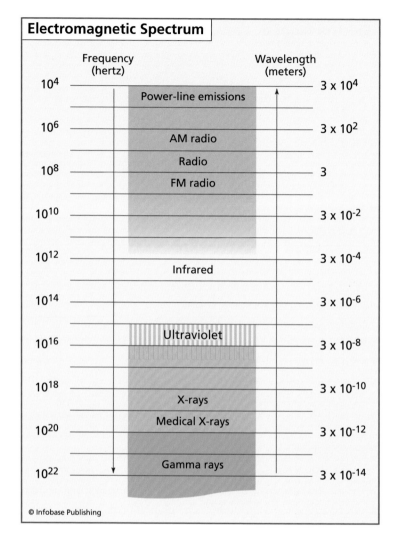

Electromagnetic Spectrum

Frequency (hertz)		Wavelength (meters)
10^4	Power-line emissions	3×10^4
10^6	AM radio	3×10^2
10^8	Radio / FM radio	3
10^{10}		3×10^{-2}
10^{12}	Infrared	3×10^{-4}
10^{14}		3×10^{-6}
10^{16}	Ultraviolet	3×10^{-8}
10^{18}	X-rays	3×10^{-10}
10^{20}	Medical X-rays	3×10^{-12}
10^{22}	Gamma rays	3×10^{-14}

© Infobase Publishing

polarization of the radio waves transmitted by that antenna: A vertical antenna emits vertically polarized waves, and a horizontal antenna emits horizontally polarized waves. Similarly, a horizontal antenna is best at receiving horizontally polarized waves and a vertical antenna at vertically polarized waves. The best communications are obtained when the source and receiver antennas have the same polarization. This is why, when trying to adjust television antennas to get a better signal, having the two antennae at right angles to each other can maximize the chances of receiving a signal.

The human eye stops being able to detect radiation at wavelengths between 3,000 and 4,000 angstroms, which is deep violet—also the rough limit on transmissions through the atmosphere (see the table "Wavelengths and Frequencies of Visible Light"). (Three thousand to 4,000 angstroms is the same as 300–400 nm because an angstrom is 10^{-9} m, while the prefix nano- or n means 10^{-10}; for more, see appendix 1, "Units and Measurements.") Of visible light, the colors red, orange, yellow, green, blue, indigo, and violet are listed in order from

Waves can be thought of as plane or circularly polarized.

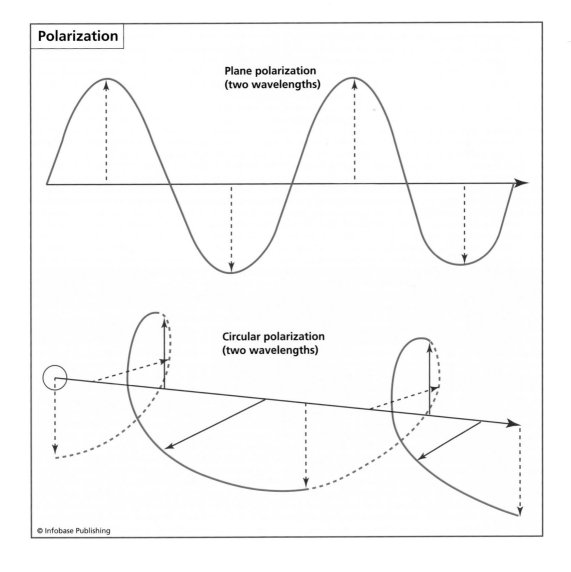

Polarization

Plane polarization
(two wavelengths)

Circular polarization
(two wavelengths)

longest wavelength and lowest energy to shortest wavelength and highest energy. Sir Isaac Newton, the spectacular English physicist and mathematician, first found that a glass prism split sunlight into a rainbow of colors. He named this a "spectrum," after the Latin word for ghost.

If visible light strikes molecules of gas as it passes through the atmosphere, it may get absorbed as energy by the molecule. After a short amount of time, the molecule releases the light, most probably in a different direction. The color that is radiated is the same color that was absorbed. All the colors of visible light can be absorbed by atmospheric molecules, but the higher energy blue light is absorbed more often than the lower energy red light. This process is called Rayleigh scattering (named after Lord John Rayleigh, an English physicist who first described it in the 1870s).

The blue color of the sky is due to Rayleigh scattering. As light moves through the atmosphere, most of the longer wavelengths pass straight through: The air affects little of the red, orange, and yellow light. The gas molecules absorb much of the shorter wavelength blue light. The absorbed blue light is then radiated in different directions and is scattered all around the sky. Whichever direction you look, some of

WAVELENGTHS AND FREQUENCIES OF VISIBLE LIGHT

Visible light color	Wavelength (in Å, angstroms)	Frequency (times 10^{14} Hz)
violet	4,000–4,600	7.5–6.5
indigo	4,600–4,750	6.5–6.3
blue	4,750–4,900	6.3–6.1
green	4,900–5,650	6.1–5.3
yellow	5,650–5,750	5.3–5.2
orange	5,750–6,000	5.2–5.0
red	6,000–8,000	5.0–3.7

WAVELENGTHS AND FREQUENCIES OF THE ELECTROMAGNETIC SPECTRUM

Energy	Frequency in hertz (Hz)	Wavelength in meters
cosmic rays	everything higher in energy than gamma rays	everything lower in wavelength than gamma rays
gamma rays	10^{20} to 10^{24}	less than 10^{-12} m
X-rays	10^{17} to 10^{20}	1 nm to 1 pm
ultraviolet	10^{15} to 10^{17}	400 nm to 1 nm
visible	4×10^{14} to 7.5×10^{14}	750 nm to 400 nm
near-infrared	1×10^{14} to 4×10^{14}	2.5 [μm to 750 nm
infrared	10^{13} to 10^{14}	25 [μm to 2.5 μm
microwaves	3×10^{11} to 10^{13}	1 mm to 25 μm
radiowaves	less than 3×10^{11}	more than 1 mm

this scattered blue light reaches you. Since you see the blue light from everywhere overhead, the sky looks blue. Note also that there is a very different kind of scattering, in which the light is simply bounced off larger objects like pieces of dust and water droplets, rather than being absorbed by a molecule of gas in the atmosphere and then reemitted. This bouncing kind of scattering is responsible for red sunrises and sunsets.

Until the end of the 18th century, people thought that visible light was the only kind of light. The amazing amateur astronomer Frederick William Herschel (the discoverer of Uranus) discovered the first non-visible light, the infrared. He thought that each color of visible light had a different temperature and devised an experiment to measure the temperature of each color of light. The temperatures went up as the colors progressed from violet through red, and then Herschel decided to measure past red, where he found the highest temperature yet. This was the first demonstration that there was a kind of radiation that could not be seen by the human eye. Herschel originally named this range of radiation "calorific rays," but the name was later changed to infrared, meaning "below red." Infrared radiation has become an important way of sensing solar system objects and is also used in night-vision goggles and various other practical purposes.

At lower energies and longer wavelengths than the visible and infrared, microwaves are commonly used to transmit energy to food in microwave ovens, as well as for some communications, though radio waves are more common in this use. There is a wide range of frequencies in the radio spec-

COMMON USES FOR RADIO WAVES

User	Approximate frequency
AM radio	0.535×10^6 to 1.7×10^6Hz
baby monitors	49×10^6Hz
cordless phones	49×10^6Hz 900×10^6Hz $2,400 \times 10^6$Hz
television channels 2 through 6	54×10^6 to 88×10^6Hz
radio-controlled planes	72×10^6Hz
radio-controlled cars	75×10^6Hz
FM radio	88×10^6 to 108×10^6Hz
television channels 7 through 13	174×10^6 to 220×10^6Hz
wildlife tracking collars	215×10^6Hz
cell phones	800×10^6Hz $2,400 \times 10^6$Hz
air traffic control radar	960×10^6Hz $1,215 \times 10^6$Hz
global positioning systems	$1,227 \times 10^6$Hz $1,575 \times 10^6$Hz
deeo space radio	$2,300 \times 10^6$Hz

trum, and they are used in many ways, as shown in the table "Common Uses for Radio Waves," including television, radio, and cell phone transmissions. Note that the frequency units are given in terms of 10^6 Hz, without correcting for each coefficient's additional factors of 10. This is because 10^6 Hz corresponds to the unit of megahertz (MHz), which is a commonly used unit of frequency.

Cosmic rays, gamma rays, and X-rays, the three highest-energy radiations, are known as ionizing radiation because they contain enough energy that, when they hit an atom, they may knock an electron off of it or otherwise change the atom's weight or structure. These ionizing radiations, then, are particularly dangerous to living things; for example, they can damage DNA molecules (though good use is made of them as well, to see into bodies with X-rays and to kill cancer cells with gamma rays). Luckily the atmosphere stops most ionizing radiation, but not all of it. Cosmic rays created by the Sun in solar flares, or sent off as a part of the solar wind, are relatively low energy. There are far more energetic cosmic rays, though, that come from distant stars through interstellar space. These are energetic enough to penetrate into an asteroid as deeply as a meter and can often make it through the atmosphere.

When an atom of a radioisotope decays, it gives off some of its excess energy as radiation in the form of X-rays, gamma rays, or fast-moving subatomic particles: alpha particles (two protons and two neutrons, bound together as an atomic *nucleus*), or beta particles (fast-moving electrons), or a combination of two or more of these products. If it decays with emission of an alpha or beta particle, it becomes a new element. These decay products can be described as gamma, beta, and alpha radiation. By decaying, the atom is progressing in one or more steps toward a stable state where it is no longer radioactive.

The X-rays and gamma rays from decaying atoms are identical to those from other natural sources. Like other ionizing radiation, they can damage living tissue but can be blocked by lead sheets or by thick concrete. Alpha particles are much larger and can be blocked more quickly by other material; a sheet of paper or the outer layer of skin on your hand will

RADIOACTIVITY OF SELECTED OBJECTS AND MATERIALS

Object or material	Radioactivity
1 adult human (100 Bq/kg)	7,000 Bq
1 kg coffee	1,000 Bq
1 kg high-phosphate fertilizer	5,000 Bq
1 household smoke detector (with the element americium)	30,000 Bq
radioisotope source for cancer therapy	100 million million Bq
1 kg 50-year-old vitrified high-level nuclear waste	10 million million Bq
1 kg uranium ore (Canadian ore, 15% uranium)	25 million Bq
1 kg uranium ore (Australian ore, 3% uranium)	500,000 Bq
1 kg granite	1,000 Bq

stop them. If the atom that produces them is taken inside the body, however, such as when a person breathes in radon gas, the alpha particle can do damage to the lungs. Beta particles are more energetic and smaller and can penetrate a couple of centimeters into a person's body.

But why can both radioactive decay that is formed of subatomic particles and heat that travels as a wave of energy be considered radiation? One of Albert Einstein's great discoveries is called the photoelectric effect: Subatomic particles can all behave as either a wave or a particle. The smaller the particle, the more wavelike it is. The best example of this is light itself, which behaves almost entirely as a wave, but there is the particle equivalent for light, the massless photon. Even alpha particles, the largest decay product discussed here, can act like a wave, though their wavelike properties are much harder to detect.

The amount of radioactive material is given in becquerel (Bq), a measure that enables us to compare the typical radioactivity of some natural and other materials. A becquerel is one atomic decay per second. Radioactivity is still sometimes measured using a unit called a Curie; a Becquerel is 27×10^{-12} Curies. There are materials made mainly of radioactive elements, like uranium, but most materials are made mainly of stable atoms. Even materials made mainly of stable atoms, however, almost always have trace amounts of radioactive elements in them, and so even common objects give off some level of radiation, as shown in the table on page 238.

Background radiation is all around us all the time. Naturally occurring radioactive elements are more common in some kinds of rocks than others; for example, *granite* carries more radioactive elements than does sandstone; therefore a person working in a bank built of granite will receive more radiation than someone who works in a wooden building. Similarly, the atmosphere absorbs cosmic rays, but the higher the elevation, the more cosmic-ray exposure there is. A person living in Denver or in the mountains of Tibet is exposed to more cosmic rays than someone living in Boston or in the Netherlands.

APPENDIX 3:

A List of All Known Moons

Though Mercury and Venus have no moons, the other planets in the solar system have at least one. Some moons, such as Earth's Moon and Jupiter's Galileans satellites, are thought to have formed at the same time as their accompanying planet. Many other moons appear simply to be captured asteroids; for at least half of Jupiter's moons, this seems to be the case. These small, irregular moons are difficult to detect from Earth, and so the lists given in the table below must be considered works in progress for the gas giant planets. More moons will certainly be discovered with longer observation and better instrumentation.

KNOWN MOONS OF ALL PLANETS						
Earth	Mars	Jupiter	Saturn	Uranus	Neptune	Pluto
1	2	63	62	27	13	3
1. Moon	1. Phobos	1. Metis	1. S/2009 S1	1. Cordelia	1. Naiad	1. Charon
	2. Diemos	2. Adrastea	2. Pan	2. Ophelia	2. Thalassa	2. Nix (P1)
		3. Amalthea	3. Dalphnis	3. Bianca	3. Despina	3. Hydra (P2)
		4. Thebe	4. Atlas	4. Cressida	4. Galatea	
		5. Io	5. Prometheus	5. Desdemona	5. Larissa	
		6. Europa	6. Pandora	6. Juliet	6. Proteus	
		7. Ganymede	7. Epimetheus	7. Portia	7. Triton	

Earth	Mars	Jupiter	Saturn	Uranus	Neptune	Pluto
		8. Callisto	8. Janus	8. Rosalind	8. Nereid	
		9. Themisto	9. Aegaeon	9. Cupid (2003 U2)	9. Halimede (S/2002 N1)	
		10. Leda	10. Mimas	10. Belinda	10. Sao (S/2002 N2)	
		11. Himalia	11. Methone	11. Perdita (1986 U10)	11. Laomedeia (S/2002 N3)	
		12. Lysithea	12. Anthe	12. Puck	12. Psamathe S/2003 N1	
		13. Elara	13. Pallene	13. Mab (2003 U1)	13. Neso (S/2002 N4)	
		14. S/2000 J11	14. Enceladus	14. Miranda		
		15. Carpo (S/2003 J20)	15. Telesto	15. Ariel		
		16. S/2003 J12	16. Tethys	16. Umbriel		
		17. Euporie	17. Calypso	17. Titania		
		18. S/2003 J3	18. Dione	18. Oberon		
		19. S/2003 J18	19. Helene	19. Francisco (2001 U3)		
		20. Orthosie	20. Polydeuces	20. Caliban		
		21. Euanthe	21. Rhea	21. Stephano		
		22. Harpalyke	22. Titan	22. Trinculo		
		23. Praxidike	23. Hyperion	23. Sycorax		

(continues)

KNOWN MOONS OF ALL PLANETS *(continued)*

Earth	Mars	Jupiter	Saturn	Uranus	Neptune	Pluto
		24. Thyone	24. Iapetus	24. Margaret (2003 U3)		
		25. S/2003 J16	25. Kiviuq	25. Prospero		
		26. Mneme (S/2003 J21)	26. Ijiraq	26. Setebos		
		27. Iocaste	27. Phoebe	27. Ferdinand (2001 U2)		
		28. Helike (S/2003 J6)	28. Paaliaq			
		29. Hermippe	29. Skathi			
		30. Thelxinoe (S/2003 J22)	30. Albiorix			
		31. Ananke	31. S/2007 S2			
		32. S/2003 J15	32. Bebhionn			
		33. Eurydome	33. Erriapo			
		34. S/2003 J17	34. Siarnaq			
		35. Pasithee	35. Skoll			
		36. S/2003 J10	36. Tarvos			
		37. Chaldene	37. Tarqeq			
		38. Isonoe	38. Greip			
		39. Erinome	39. Hyrrokkin			

Earth	Mars	Jupiter	Saturn	Uranus	Neptune	Pluto
		40. Kale	40. S/2004 S13			
		41. Aitne	41. S/2004 S17			
		42. Taygete	42. Mundilfari			
		43. Kallichore (S/2003 J11)	43. Jarnsaxa			
		44. Eukelade (S/2003 J1)	44. S/2006/ S1			
		45. Arche (S/2002 J1)	45. Narvi			
		46. S/2003 J9	46. Bergelmir			
		47. Carme	47. Suttungr			
		48. Kalyke	48. S/2004 S12			
		49. Sponde	49. S/2004 S7			
		50. Magaclite	50. Hati			
		51. S/2003 J5	51. Bestla			
		52. S/2003 J19	52. Farbauti			
		53. S/2003 J23	53. Thrymyr			
		54. Hege-mone (S/2003 J8)	54. S/2007 S3			
		55. Pasiphae	55. Aegir			

(continues)

KNOWN MOONS OF ALL PLANETS *(continued)*

Earth	Mars	Jupiter	Saturn	Uranus	Neptune	Pluto
		56. Cyllene (S/2003 J13)	56. S/2006 S3			
		57. S/2003 J4	57. Kari			
		58. Sinope	58. Fenrir			
		59. Aoede (S/2003 J17)	59. Surtur			
		60. Autonoe	60. Ymir			
		61. Calirrhoe	61. Loge			
		62. Kore (S/2003 J14)	62. Fornjot			
		63. S/2003 J2				

Glossary

accretion The accumulation of celestial gas, dust, or smaller bodies by gravitational attraction into a larger body, such as a planet or an asteroid

achondite A stony (silicate-based) meteorite that contains no chondrules; these originate in differentiated bodies and may be mantle material or lavas (see also CHONDRITE and IRON METEORITE)

albedo The light reflected by an object as a fraction of the light shining on an object; mirrors have high albedo, while charcoal has low albedo

anorthite A calcium-rich plagioclase mineral with compositional formula $CaAl_2Si_2O_8$, significant for making up the majority of the rock anorthosite in the crust of the Moon

anticyclone An area of increased atmospheric pressure relative to the surrounding pressure field in the atmosphere, resulting in circular flow in a clockwise direction north of the equator and in a counterclockwise direction to the south

aphelion A distance; the farthest from the Sun an object travels in its orbit

apogee As for aphelion but for any orbital system (not confined to the Sun)

apparent magnitude The brightness of a celestial object as it would appear from a given distance—the lower the number, the brighter the object

atom The smallest quantity of an element that can take part in a chemical reaction; consists of a nucleus of protons and neutrons, surrounded by a cloud of electrons; each atom is about 10^{-10} meters in diameter, or one angstrom

atomic number   The number of protons in an atom's nucleus

AU   An AU is an astronomical unit, defined as the distance from the Sun to the Earth; approximately 93 million miles, or 150 million kilometers. For more information, refer to the UNITS AND MEASUREMENTS appendix

basalt   A generally dark-colored extrusive igneous rock most commonly created by melting a planet's mantle; its low silica content indicates that it has not been significantly altered on its passage to the planet's surface

bolide   An object falling into a planet's atmosphere, when a specific identification as a comet or asteroid cannot be made

bow shock   The area of compression in a flowing fluid when it strikes an object or another fluid flowing at another rate; for example, the bow of a boat and the water, or the magnetic field of a planet and the flowing solar wind

breccia   Material that has been shattered from grinding, as in a fault, or from impact, as by meteorites or other solar system bodies

CAIs (calcium-aluminum inclusions)   Small spheres of mineral grains found in chondritic meteorites and thought to be the first solids that formed in the protoplanetary disk

calcium-aluminum inclusion   See CAIs.

chondrite   A class of meteorite thought to contain the most primitive material left from the solar nebula; named after their glassy, super-primitive inclusions called chondrules

chondrule   Rounded, glassy, and crystalline bodies incorporated into the more primitive of meteorites; thought to be the condensed droplets of the earliest solar system materials

CI chondrite   The class of chondrite meteorites with compositions most like the Sun and therefore thought to be the oldest and least altered material in the solar system

clinopyroxene   A common mineral in the mantle and igneous rocks, with compositional formula $((Ca,Mg,Fe,Al)_2(Si,Al)_2O_6)$

conjunction   When the Sun is between the Earth and the planet or another body in question

convection Material circulation upward and downward in a gravity field caused by horizontal gradients in density; an example is the hot, less dense bubbles that form at the bottom of a pot, rise, and are replaced by cooler, denser sinking material

core The innermost material within a differentiated body; in a rocky planet this consists of iron-nickel metal, and in a gas planet this consists of the rocky innermost solids

Coriolis force The effect of movement on a rotating sphere; movement in the Northern Hemisphere curves to the right, while movement in the Southern Hemisphere curves to the left

craton The ancient, stable interior cores of the Earth's continents

crust The outermost layer of most differentiated bodies, often consisting of the least dense products of volcanic events or other buoyant material

cryovolcanism Non-silicate materials erupted from icy and gassy bodies in the cold outer solar system; for example, as suspected or seen on the moons Enceladus, Europa, Titan, and Triton

cubewano Any large Kuiper belt object orbiting between about 41 AU and 48 AU but not controlled by orbital resonances with Neptune; the odd name is derived from 1992 QB_1, the first Kuiper belt object found

cyclone An area in the atmosphere in which the pressures are lower than those of the surrounding region at the same level, resulting in circular motion in a counterclockwise direction north of the equator and in a clockwise direction to the south

debris disk A flattened, spinning disk of dust and gas around a star formed from collisions among bodies already accreted in an aging solar system

differential rotation Rotation at different rates at different latitudes, requiring a liquid or gassy body, such as the Sun or Jupiter

differentiated body A spherical body that has a structure of concentric spherical layers, differing in terms of composition, heat, density, and/or motion; caused by gravitational separations and heating events such as planetary accretion

dipole Two associated magnetic poles, one positive and one negative, creating a magnetic field

direct (prograde) Rotation or orbit in the same direction as the Earth's, that is, counterclockwise when viewed from above its North Pole

disk wind Magnetic fields that either pull material into the protostar or push it into the outer disk; these are thought to form at the inner edge of the disk where the protostar's magnetic field crosses the disk's magnetic field (also called X-WIND)

distributary River channels that branch from the main river channel, carrying flow away from the central channel; usually form fans of channels at a river's delta

eccentricity The amount by which an ellipse differs from a circle

ecliptic The imaginary plane that contains the Earth's orbit and from which the planes of other planets' orbits deviate slightly; the ecliptic makes an angle of seven degrees with the plane of the Sun's equator

ejecta Material thrown out of the site of a crater by the force of the impactor

element A family of atoms that all have the same number of positively charged particles in their nuclei (the center of the atom)

ellipticity The amount by which a planet's shape deviates from a sphere

equinox One of two points in a planet's orbit when day and night have the same length; vernal equinox occurs in Earth's spring and autumnal equinox in the fall

exosphere The uppermost layer of a planet's atmosphere

extrasolar Outside this solar system

faint young Sun paradox The apparent contradiction between the observation that the Sun gave off far less heat in its early years and the likelihood that the Earth was still warm enough to host liquid water

garnet The red, green, or purple mineral that contains the majority of the aluminum in the Earth's upper mantle; its compositional formula is $((Ca,Mg,Fe\ Mn)_3(Al,Fe,Cr,Ti)_2(SiO_4)3)$

giant molecular cloud An interstellar cloud of dust and gas that is the birthplace of clusters of new stars as it collapses through its own gravity

graben A low area longer than it is wide and bounded from adjoining higher areas by faults; caused by extension in the crust

granite An intrusive igneous rock with high silica content and some minerals containing water; in this solar system thought to be found only on Earth

half-life The time it takes for half a population of an unstable isotope to decay

hydrogen burning The most basic process of nuclear fusion in the cores of stars that produces helium and radiation from hydrogen

igneous rock Rock that was once hot enough to be completely molten

impactor A generic term for an object striking and creating a crater in another body

inclination As commonly used in planetary science, the angle between the plane of a planet's orbit and the plane of the ecliptic

ionosphere The uppermost atmosphere of a planet where most gases exist as ionized particles and electrons; on Earth the ionosphere begins at about 50 miles (80 km) altitude

iron meteorite Meteorites that consist largely of iron-nickel metal; thought to be parts of the cores of smashed planetesimals from early solar system accretion

isotope Atoms with the same number of protons (therefore the same type of element) but different numbers of neutrons; may be stable or radioactive and occur in different relative abundances

lander A spacecraft designed to land on another solar system object rather than flying by, orbiting, or entering the atmosphere and then burning up or crashing

lithosphere The uppermost layer of a terrestrial planet consisting of stiff material that moves as one unit if there are plate tectonic forces and does not convect internally but transfers heat from the planet's interior through conduction

magnetic moment The torque (turning force) exerted on a magnet when it is placed in a magnetic field

magnetopause The surface between the magnetosheath and the magnetosphere of a planet

magnetosheath The compressed, heated portion of the solar wind where it piles up against a planetary magnetic field

magnetosphere The volume of a planet's magnetic field, shaped by the internal planetary source of the magnetism and by interactions with the solar wind

magnitude See APPARENT MAGNITUDE

mantle The spherical shell of a terrestrial planet between crust and core; thought to consist mainly of silicate minerals

mass number The number of protons plus neutrons in an atom's nucleus

mesosphere The atmospheric layer between the stratosphere and the thermosphere

metal 1) Material with high electrical conductivity in which the atomic nuclei are surrounded by a cloud of electrons, that is, metallic bonds, or 2) in astronomy, any element heavier than helium

metallicity The fraction of all elements heavier than hydrogen and helium in a star or protoplanetary disk; higher metallicity is thought to encourage the formation of planets

metamorphic rock Rock that has been changed from its original state by heat or pressure but was never liquid

mid-ocean ridge The line of active volcanism in oceanic basins from which two oceanic plates are produced, one moving away from each side of the ridge; only exist on Earth

mineral A naturally occurring inorganic substance having an orderly internal structure (usually crystalline) and characteristic chemical composition

nucleus The center of the atom, consisting of protons (positively charged) and neutrons (no electric charge); tiny in volume but makes up almost all the mass of the atom

nutation The slow wobble of a planet's rotation axis along a line of longitude, causing changes in the planet's obliquity

obliquity The angle between a planet's equatorial plane to its orbit plane

occultation The movement of one celestial body in front of another from a particular point of view; most commonly the movement of a planet in front of a star from the point of view of an Earth viewer

olivine Also known as the gem peridot, the green mineral that makes up the majority of the upper mantle; its compositional formula is $((Mg, Fe)_2SiO_4)$

one-plate planet A planet with lithosphere that forms a continuous spherical shell around the whole planet, not breaking into plates or moving with tectonics; Mercury, Venus, and Mars are examples

opposition When the Earth is between the Sun and the planet of interest

orbital period The time required for an object to make a complete circuit along its orbit

pallasite A type of iron meteorite that also contains the silicate mineral olivine, and is thought to be part of the region between the mantle and core in a differentiated planetesimal that was shattered in the early years of the solar system

parent body The larger body that has been broken to produce smaller pieces; large bodies in the asteroid belt are thought to be the parent bodies of meteorites that fall to Earth today

perigee   As for perihelion but for any orbital system (not confined to the Sun)

perihelion (pl. perihelia)   A distance; the closest approach to the Sun made in an object's orbit

planetesimal   The small, condensed bodies that formed early in the solar system and presumably accreted to make the planets; probably resembled comets or asteroids

planetary nebula   A shell of gas ejected from stars at the end of their lifetimes; unfortunately named in an era of primitive telescopes that could not discern the size and nature of these objects

plate tectonics   The movement of lithospheric plates relative to each other, only known on Earth

precession   The movement of a planet's axis of rotation that causes the axis to change its direction of tilt, much as the direction of the axis of a toy top rotates as it slows

primordial disk   Another name for a protoplanetary disk

prograde (direct)   Rotates or orbits in the same direction the Earth does, that is, counterclockwise when viewed from above its North Pole

proplyd   Abbreviation for a *protoplanetary disk*

protoplanetary disk   The flattened, spinning cloud of dust and gas surrounding a growing new star

protostar   The central mass of gas and dust in a newly forming solar system that will eventually begin thermonuclear fusion and become a star

radioactive   An atom prone to radiodecay

radio-decay   The conversion of an atom into a different atom or isotope through emission of energy or subatomic particles

red, reddened   A solar system body with a redder color in visible light, but more important, one that has increased albedo at low wavelengths (the "red" end of the spectrum)

reflectance spectra   The spectrum of radiation that bounces off a surface, for example, sunlight bouncing off the surface of an asteroid; the wavelengths with low intensities show the kinds of radiation absorbed rather than reflected by the surface and indicate the composition of the surface materials

refractory   An element that requires unusually high temperatures in order to melt or evaporate; compare to volatile

relief (topographic relief)   The shapes of the surface of land; most especially the high parts such as hills or mountains

resonance   When the ratio of the orbital periods of two bodies is an integer; for example, if one moon orbits its planet once for every two times another moon orbits, the two are said to be in resonance

retrograde   Rotates or orbits in the opposite direction to Earth, that is, clockwise when viewed from above its North Pole

Roche limit   The radius around a given planet that a given satellite must be outside of in order to remain intact; within the Roche limit, the satellite's self-gravity will be overcome by gravitational tidal forces from the planet, and the satellite will be torn apart

rock   Material consisting of the aggregate of minerals

sedimentary rock   Rock made of mineral grains that were transported by water or air

seismic waves   Waves of energy propagating through a planet, caused by earthquakes or other impulsive forces, such as meteorite impacts and human-made explosions

semimajor axis   Half the widest diameter of an orbit

semiminor axis   Half the narrowest diameter of an orbit

silicate   A molecule, crystal, or compound made from the basic building block silica (SiO_2); the Earth's mantle is made of silicates, while its core is made of metals

spectrometer   An instrument that separates electromagnetic radiation, such as light, into wavelengths, creating a spectrum

stratosphere   The layer of the atmosphere located between the troposphere and the mesosphere, characterized by a slight temperature increase and absence of clouds

subduction   Movement of one lithospheric plate beneath another

subduction zone   A compressive boundary between two lithospheric plates, where one plate (usually an oceanic plate) is sliding beneath the other and plunging at an angle into the mantle

synchronous orbit radius   The orbital radius at which the satellite's orbital period is equal to the rotational period of the planet; contrast with synchronous rotation

synchronous rotation   When the same face of a moon is always toward its planet, caused by the period of the moon's rotation about its axis being the same as the period of the moon's orbit around its planet; most moons rotate synchronously due to tidal locking

tacholine   The region in the Sun where differential rotation gives way to solid-body rotation, creating a shear zone and perhaps the body's magnetic field as well; is at the depth of about one-third of the Sun's radius

terrestrial planet   A planet similar to the Earth—rocky and metallic and in the inner solar system; includes Mercury, Venus, Earth, and Mars

thermosphere   The atmospheric layer between the mesosphere and the exosphere

tidal locking   The tidal (gravitational) pull between two closely orbiting bodies that causes the bodies to settle into stable orbits with the same faces toward each other at all times; this final stable state is called synchronous rotation

tomography   The technique of creating images of the interior of the Earth using the slightly different speeds of earthquake waves that have traveled along different paths through the Earth

tropopause   The point in the atmosphere of any planet where the temperature reaches a minimum; both above and below this height, temperatures rise

troposphere   The lower regions of a planetary atmosphere, where convection keeps the gas mixed, and there is a steady decrease in temperature with height above the surface

viscosity A liquid's resistance to flowing; honey has higher viscosity than water

visual magnitude The brightness of a celestial body as seen from Earth categorized on a numerical scale; the brightest star has magnitude −1.4 and the faintest visible star has magnitude 6; a decrease of one unit represents an increase in brightness by a factor of 2.512; system begun by Ptolemy in the second century B.C.E.; see also APPARENT MAGNITUDE

volatile An element that moves into a liquid or gas state at relatively low temperatures; compare with refractory

x-wind Magnetic fields that either pull material into the protostar or push it into the outer disk; these are thought to form at the inner edge of the disk where the protostar's magnetic field crosses the disk's magnetic field (also called DISK WIND)

Further Resources

Alvarez, L. W., W. Alvarez, F. Asaro, and H. V. Michel. "Extraterrestrial Cause for the Cretaceous-Tertiary Extinction." *Science* (2008): 1,095–1,108. The definitive first scientific paper on the topic.

Barringer, D. M. "Meteor Crater (Formerly Called Coon Mountain or Coon Butte) in Northern Central Arizona." Paper presented at the National Academy of Sciences, Princeton University, November 16, 1909. Barringer's first scientific publication on the famous crater now bearing his name.

Beatty, J. K., C. C. Petersen, and A. Chaikin. *The New Solar System*. Cambridge: Sky Publishing and Cambridge University Press, 1999. The best-known and best-regarded single reference volume on the solar system.

Binzel, R. P., T. Gehrels, and M. S. Matthews. *Asteroids II*. Tucson: University of Arizona Press, 1989. One of the series of volumes from the University of Arizona Press, containing the latest compilation of scientific results on meteorite research.

Bissell, Tom. "A Comet's Tale." *Harper's* (February 2003). Accessible article on comets.

Booth, N. *Exploring the Solar System*. Cambridge: Cambridge University Press, 1995. Well-written and accurate volume on solar system exploration.

Comins, Neil F., and William J. Kaufmann. *Discovering the Universe*. New York: W. H. Freeman, 2008. The best-selling text for astronomy courses that uses no mathematics. Presents concepts clearly and stresses the process of science.

Dodd, R. T. *Meteorites: A Petrologic-Chemical Synthesis*. Cambridge: Cambridge University Press, 1981. One of only a few good books assembling data on meteorite compositions and formation theories.

Fradin, Dennis Brindell. *The Planet Hunters: The Search for Other Worlds*. New York: Simon and Schuster, 1997.

Herschel, W. "Observations on the Two Lately Discovered Celestial Bodies." *Philos. Trans. R. Soc. London* 2 (1802). An original paper by the discoverer of Uranus and several moons and asteroids.

Kleine, T., C. Munker, K. Mezger, and H. Palme. "Rapid Accretion and Early Core Formation on Asteroids and the Terrestrial Planets from Hf-W Chronometry." *Nature* 418 (2002): 952–955. The science of dating the time of core formation, early in solar system history.

Norton, O. R. *The Cambridge Encyclopedia of Meteorites*. Cambridge: Cambridge University Press, 2002.

Papike, J. J. *Planetary Materials*. Vol. 36 of Reviews in Mineralogy. Washington D.C.: Mineralogical Society of America, 1998. Scientific compilation of the state of knowledge of meteorites, lunar and Martian material, and interstellar dust grains, including significant compositional tables.

Paul, N. *The Solar System*. Edison, N.J.: Chartwell Books, 2008. Begins with the origin of the universe and moves through the planets. Includes history of space flight and many color images.

Peebles, C. *Asteroids: A History*. Washington, D.C.: Smithsonian Institution Scholarly Press, 2001. This well-reviewed text covers the past and present scientific understanding of asteroids.

Rees, Martin, et al. *Universe*. London: DK Adult, 2008. A team of science writers and astronomers wrote this text for high school students and the general public.

Rivkin, A. *Asteroids, Comets, and Dwarf Planets*. Portsmouth, N.H.: Heinemann Educational Books, 2009. Up-to-date understanding of the small bodies of the solar system written by an active academic expert in the field.

Schmadel, L. D. *Dictionary of Minor Planet Names*. Berlin: Springer-Verlag, 1999. Complete list as of its publication date, including explanations for naming conventions.

Sparrow, Giles. *The Planets: A Journey Through the Solar System*. Waltham, Mass.: Quercus Press, 2009. Solar system discoveries told within the structure of the last 40 years of space missions.

Spence, P. *The Universe Revealed*. Cambridge: Cambridge University Press, 1998. Comprehensive textbook on the universe.

Stacey, Frank D., and Paul Davis. *Physics of the Earth*. Cambridge: Cambridge University Press, 2008. Fundamental geophysics text on an upper-level undergraduate college level.

Stevenson, D. J. "Planetary Magnetic Fields." *Earth and Planetary Science Letters* 208 (2003): 1–11. Comparisons and calculations about the planetary magnetic fields of many bodies in our solar system.

Wetherill, G. W. "Provenance of the Terrestrial Planets." *Geochimica et Cosmochimica Acta* 58 (1994): 4,513–4,520.

INTERNET RESOURCES

Blue, Jennifer, and the Working Group for Planetary System Nomenclature. "Gazetteer of Planetary Nomenclature." USGS, Astrogeology Research Program. Available online. URL: http://planetarynames.wr.usgs.gov/. Accessed January 22, 2008. Complete and official rules for naming planetary features, along with list of all named planetary features and downloadable images.

Brown, Mike. "Mike Brown, Professor of Planetary Astronomy." California Institute of Technology. Available online. URL: http://web.gps.caltech.edu/~mbrown/. Accessed January 22, 2008. Brown's weekly column on planets, details on the dwarf planets including Eris, Sedna, and Quaoar, and details of his research and lectures.

Hahn, Gerhard, Stefano Mottola, and the DLR—Institute of Planetary Research, Berlin. "The Near-Earth Asteroid Database," Available online. URL: http://earn.dlr.de/nea/. Accessed January 22, 2008. Discovery information, statistics, and listing of near-earth asteroids.

Jewitt, David. "Kuiper Belt," University of Hawaii, Institute for Astronomy. Available online. URL: http://www.ifa.hawaii.edu/faculty/jewitt/kb.html. Accessed January 22, 2008. Source of information on Kuiper belt bodies and comets compiled by one of the experts in the field.

LaVoie, Sue, Myche McAuley, Elizabeth Duxbury Rye, Karen Boggs, and Alice Stanboli. "Planetary Photojournal." Jet Propulsion Laboratory and NASA. Available online. URL: http://photojournal.jpl.nasa.gov/index.html. Accessed January 22, 2008. Large database of public-domain images from space missions.

Lunar and Planetary Institute. Universities Space Research Association and NASA. Available online. URL: http://www.lpi.usra. edu/. Accessed January 22, 2008. Wide variety of educational resources on planetary science.

Meteoritical Society. "Meteoritical Bulletin Database." The Meteoritical Society. Available online. URL: http://tin.er.usgs.gov/meteor/. Accessed February 12, 2008. The official list of meteorite names, classifications, find data, and compositions.

NASA Specialized Center in Research and Training in Exobiology. "Earth Impact Craters." University of California, San Diego. Available online. URL: http://exobio.ucsd.edu/Space_Sciences/ earth_impact_craters.htm. Accessed January 22, 2008. History of impact research and comprehensive list of terrestrial impact craters.

O'Connor, John J., and Edmund F. Robertson. "The MacTutor History of Mathematics Archive." University of St. Andrews, Scotland. Available online. URL: http://www-gap.dcs.st-and. ac.uk/~history/index.html. Accessed January 22, 2008. A scholarly, precise, and eminently accessible compilation of biographies and accomplishments of mathematicians and scientists through the ages.

Rowlett, Russ. "How Many? A Dictionary of Units of Measurement." University of North Carolina at Chapel Hill. Available online. URL: http://www.unc.edu/~rowlett/units. Accessed January 22, 2008. A comprehensive dictionary of units of measurement, from the metric and English systems to the most obscure usages.

Valsecchi, Giovanni. The Spaceguard Foundation. Available online. URL: http://spaceguard.esa.int/SGF/INDEX.html. Accessed January 22, 2008. Links to information about asteroid threats to Earth; see in particular the link titled "Spaceguard Central Node."

White, Maura, and Long Trinh. "JSC Digital Image Collection." Johnson Space Center. Available online. URL: images.jsc.nasa. gov/index.html. Accessed January 22, 2008. A catalog of over 9,000 NASA press release photos from the entirety of the manned space flight program.

Williams, David. "Planetary Fact Sheets," NASA. Available online. URL: http://nssdc.gsfc.nasa.gov/planetary/planetfact.html. Accessed January 22, 2008. Detailed measurements and data on the planets, asteroids, and comets in simple tables.

————, and Dr. Ed Grayzeck. "Planetary Sciences at the National Space Science Data Center." NASA. Available online. URL: http://nssdc.gsfc.nasa.gov/planetary/planetary_home.html. Accessed January 22, 2008. NASA's deep archive and general distribution center for lunar and planetary data and images.

Yeomans, Don, and Ron Baalke. "NASA's Near Earth Object Program." Available online. URL: http://neo.jpl.nasa.gov/index.html. Accessed January 22, 2008. The complete Near-Earth Asteroid program from NASA.

ORGANIZATIONS OF INTEREST

American Geophysical Union (AGU)
2000 Florida Avenue N.W.
Washington, DC 20009–1277
USA
www.agu.org
AGU is a worldwide scientific community that advances, through unselfish cooperation in research, the understanding of Earth and space for the benefit of humanity. AGU is an individual membership society open to those professionally engaged in or associated with the Earth and space sciences. Membership has increased steadily each year, doubling during the 1980s. Membership currently exceeds 41,000, of which about 20 percent are students. Membership in AGU entitles members and associates to receive Eos, *AGU's weekly newspaper, and* Physics Today, *a magazine produced by the American Institute of Physics. In addition they are entitled to special member rates for AGU publications and meetings.*

Association of Space Explorers
1150 Gemini Avenue
Houston, TX 77058
http://www.space-explorers.org/
This association is expressly for people who have flown in space. It includes 320 individuals from 34 nations, and its goal is to support space science and education. Outreach activities include a speakers program, astronaut school visits, and observer status with the United Nations.

European Space Agency (ESA)
8–10 rue Mario Nikis
75738 Paris
Cedex 15
France

http://www.esa.int/esaCP/index.html

The European Space Agency has 18 member states that together create a unified European space program and carry out missions in parallel and in cooperation with NASA, JAXA, and other space agencies. Its member countries are Austria, Belgium, Czech Republic, Denmark, Finland, France, Germany, Greece, Ireland, Italy, Luxembourg, the Netherlands, Norway, Portugal, Spain, Sweden, Switzerland, and the United Kingdom. Hungary, Romania, Poland, and Slovenia are cooperating partners.

International Astronomical Union (IAU)

98bis, bd Arago

75014 Paris, France

www.iau.org

The International Astronomical Union (IAU) was founded in 1919. Its mission is to promote and safeguard the science of astronomy in all its aspects through international cooperation. Its individual members are professional astronomers from all over the world, at the Ph.D. level or beyond and active in professional research and education in astronomy. However, the IAU maintains friendly relations with organizations that include amateur astronomers. National members are generally those with a significant level of professional astronomy. With now over 9,100 individual members and 65 national members worldwide, the IAU plays a pivotal role in promoting and coordinating worldwide cooperation in astronomy. The IAU also serves as the internationally recognized authority for assigning designations to celestial bodies and any surface features on them.

Jet Propulsion Laboratory (JPL)

4800 Oak Grove Drive

Pasadena ,California 91109

USA

www.jpl.nasa.gov

The Jet Propulsion Laboratory is managed by the California Institute of Technology for NASA. JPL manages many of NASA's space missions, including the Mars Rovers and Cassini and also conducts fundamental research in planetary and space science.

The Meteoritical Society

The International Society for Meteoritics and Planetary Science

3635 Concorde Parkway, Suite 500

Chantilly, VA

www.meteoriticalsociety.org

The Meteoritical Society is a nonprofit scholarly organization founded in 1933 to promote the study of extraterrestrial materials and their history. The membership includes 950 scientists and amateur enthusiasts from over 33 countries who are interested in a wide range of planetary science. Member's interests include meteorites, cosmic dust, asteroids and comets, natural satellites, planets, impacts, and the origins of the solar system.

National Aeronautics and Space Administration (NASA)

300 E Street S.W.

Washington DC 20002

USA

www.nasa.gov

NASA, an agency of the U.S. government, manages space flight centers, research centers, and other organizations including the National Aerospace Museum. NASA scientists and engineers conduct basic research on planetary and space topics, plan and execute space missions, oversee Earth satellites and data collection, and many other space- and flight-related projects.

The Planetary Society

65 North Catalina Avenue

Pasadena, CA 91106-2301

USA

http://www.planetary.org/home/

This is a society of lay individuals, scientists, organizations, and businesses dedicated to involving the world's public in space exploration through advocacy, projects, and exploration. The Planetary Society was founded in 1980 by Carl Sagan, Bruce Murray, and Louis Friedman They are particularly dedicated to searching for life outside of the Earth.

Index

Italic page numbers indicate illustrations. Page numbers followed by *t* indicate tables, charts, or graphs.